The Suicidal Patient

Principles of Assessment, Treatment, and Case Management

The Suicidal Patient

Principles of Assessment, Treatment, and Case Management

John A. Chiles, M.D.
Professor of Psychiatry
University of Texas
Health Science Center at San Antonio
Medical Director
Center for Health Care Services
San Antonio, Texas

Kirk Strosahl, Ph.D.
Adjunct Clinical Professor
Department of Psychiatry and Behavioral Sciences
University of Washington
Staff Psychologist and Research Evaluation Coordinator
Group Health Cooperative of Puget Sound
Mental Health Department
Seattle, Washington

American Psychiatric Press, Inc.

Washington, DC
London, England

Copyright © 1995 American Psychiatric Press, Inc.
ALL RIGHTS RESERVED
Manufactured in the United States of America on acid-free paper
98 97 96 95   4 3 2 1
First Edition

American Psychiatric Press, Inc.
1400 K Street, N.W., Washington, DC   20005

Library of Congress Cataloging-in-Publication Data
Chiles, John.
  The suicidal patient : principles of assessment, treatment, and
case management / John A. Chiles, Kirk Strosahl. — 2nd ed.
    p. cm.
  Includes bibliographical references and index.
  ISBN 0-88048-554-X (alk. paper)
  1. Suicidal behavior—Treatment.   2. Suicide—Prevention.
I. Strosahl, Kirk, 1950– . II. Title.
  [DNLM: 1. Suicide, Attempted—prevention & control.   2. Suicide,
Attempted—psychology.   3. Affective Symptoms—therapy.
4. Psychotherapy.   WM 171 C537s 1995]
RC569.C48   1995
616.85′8445—dc20
DNLM/DLC
for Library of Congress   94-41298
                                                                          CIP

British Library Cataloguing in Publication Data
A CIP record is available from the British Library.

Contents

Preface

This book is the result of more than a decade of spirited debate, friendly repartee, basic research, and clinical collaboration between a psychiatrist and clinical psychologist. Our greatest sense of pride in this work comes from our willingness to put training and disciplinary differences in proper perspective and join in developing a workable approach to dealing with the suicidal patient. We hope what has emerged is a valuable, practical approach for clinicians in the field. This book is not meant to be an academic text on suicidal behavior. There are other excellent sources, many of which are cited throughout the text. Our goal is to provide you with a sense of what to do with the suicidal patient. The best indicator of our success in this venture will be the use of this book in the field, where we hope it will provide clinicians with a strong sense of direction when working with suicidal patients.

When we first joined forces in 1981, we came from very different schools of thought, one the medical model underpinning general psychiatry, the other a "hard core" behavioral model. One thing we shared was a healthy skepticism about traditional approaches to the suicidal patient, approaches that overemphasized the role of mental disorder and seemed overfocused on the prevention of catastrophic outcomes. We also felt there were and continue to be gaps in the treatment literature, resulting in poor outcomes (i.e., continued suicidal behavior) for many of our patients. Our experiences in training residents and interns; presenting national, regional, and local workshops; and serving as expert witnesses in court suits have only strengthened this belief.

The most powerful result of our work is our decision to treat suicidal behavior as a method of solving problems and to focus on nonfatal forms of the behavior. Suicide attempts and debilitating suicidal ideation are major public health problems that are distinct from the problem of completed suicide. As is evident in Chapter 1, the introductory chapter, we as clinicians have significant difficulty with suicidal patients who do not die and continue to require some form of treatment and/or case management. These patients engender mixed feelings in us, principally related to our moral reactions to suicidal behavior, ethical problems coming from the general standard of care, and our fears about being sued if a patient commits suicide. Chapter 2 discusses the moral, ethical, and legal issues surrounding suicidal behavior by providing a context in which to understand these mixed reactions and how they influence treatment.

A corollary of these issues is whether suicide can actually be predicted and prevented, and, if so, what types of assessment approaches are the best. The discussion of suicide risk prediction in Chapter 3 illustrates why it is extremely difficult, if not impossible, to predict suicide. It is not our intent to be nihilistic about the value of suicidal behavior assessment. Rather, we will show how this type of information can be meaningfully integrated into a proactive treatment model. Chapter 4, the final chapter of the first section, presents a basic clinical treatment model. The objective is to present a concrete, practical framework for addressing suicidal behavior. We try to make judicious use of research on suicidal patients to highlight key factors in their psychological and environmental functioning that need to be targeted in treatment. The basic problem-solving model is introduced in this chapter, and this serves as a foundation for the many treatment strategies described in the remainder of the book.

The next section of the book is the "meat and potatoes" of the clinical treatment model. We attempt to provide "how to" information, using case vignettes as examples. Chapter 5 presents an outpatient psychotherapy model for the suicidal patient. The course of therapy is broken down into three distinct phases. Therapy objectives and strategies for obtaining those objectives are also presented.

Chapter 6 is very much an offshoot of the preceding chapter in that it addresses the therapist attitudes and behaviors that tend to work best with the suicidal patient. We emphasize a collaborative, accepting approach that validates the patient's sense of emotional pain while remaining consistent and clear about alternative methods for solving personal difficulties. We examine the many ways the therapist's anxiety and/or anger negatively affects the therapeutic relationship and describe ways to detect and correct these problems before they interfere with treatment.

Chapter 7 presents a learning-based model for both acute care and case management with the suicidal patient. Case managers are a new discipline in mental health, and we hope this chapter will be especially useful to them. A major difficulty in therapy with the suicidal patient is the recurrence of a suicidal crisis. How this crisis is planned for will have a lot to say about the end result of treatment. Often, the therapist's response inadvertently reinforces suicidal behavior or creates a confrontation in the therapy relationship. Our model provides a less reactive and more productive alternative. Chapter 8 examines inpatient treatment with the suicidal patient. The potential uses and abuses of this modality are looked at in detail. Appropriate treatment objectives are presented, along with suggestions for optimal length of stay. We believe that some of the most innovative developments in the field involve alternatives to traditional inpatient treatment, alternatives with the goals of weathering the suicidal crisis and returning the person to the natural environmental as soon as possible.

The last section of the book is devoted to those special clinical problems that can elicit anxiety in therapists. We get frequent requests for consultation in regard to chronically suicidal patients, and our approach to this difficult group is described in Chapter 9. This type of patient tends to bring out the best and worst in therapists, and creates all kinds of system interface problems. Our approach attempts to simplify what often becomes a confusing mess.

As far as we know, there has never been anything close to a "how to" approach for dealing with the suicidal patient in the primary health care setting, even though primary care is a major component of the mental health system in the United States. Chap-

ter 10 provides steps and recommendations for managing the suicidal patient in the general medical setting, where most of the treatment of this patient already occurs. We describe intervention
strategies that are adaptable to the 10- to 20-minute session that is
the backbone of the primary care work pace. Our goal in this
chapter is to enable the general physician to work more effectively
with the suicidal patient, both during the process of referring the
patient for specialty mental health care, and, when referral is not
possible, for the duration of the suicidality.

In Chapter 11, we examine special populations and address
techniques and assessments that can be used *in addition* to our
general approach. In this chapter we address the thorny issue of
using medications with suicidal patients. When more than one
provider is involved, there is potential for triangulation between the
psychiatrist, patient, and nonmedical psychotherapist. Chapter 11
also addresses the substance-abusing suicidal patient. Over 50% of
suicide attempts and completed suicides involve significant abuse of
alcohol or drugs. These patients often move between the mental
health and chemical dependency treatment systems without receiving comprehensive treatment in either one. We look at specific steps
to take in treating these types of patients, regardless of the treatment
system. In this chapter we also discuss treatment of the young and
the elderly suicidal patient. Chapter 11 deals with the suicidal
adolescent and his or her usually complicated family situation. The
difficulties with treating the suicidal adolescent come primarily from
the tremendous positive or negative influence that immediate support systems have on the teenager's behavior. This often brings up
ethical issues about patient identity (e.g., Is it the adolescent? The
family? Both?) as well as anxiety over treating so many people. We
also look at indications and contraindications for family therapy with
this type of patient. In this chapter we take note of the most
neglected "at risk" group, namely, the elderly. Although newspapers
tend to sensationalize adolescent suicide, the elderly are at much
greater risk. Moreover, the social and environmental conditions
surrounding the suicidal elderly patient are often at the heart of the
suicidal crisis, and different types of intervention are required.
Despite the formidable life events that are part of the aging process,

we see the elderly patient as a very good candidate for the interventions we describe.

There are some stylistic conventions we have adopted in this book that are designed to make it more user friendly. First, referencing in the text is done sparingly and in a newspaper style; pertinent suggested readings will be provided at the end of each chapter for the reader who wishes to expand on the points made in the chapter. A comprehensive bibliography is presented at the end of the book. Second, we have developed some hands-on exercises that are designed to bring critical issues in working with the suicidal patient into clearer focus. This book will mean more to the reader who takes the time to go through these exercises.

A number of mentors and colleagues have, over the years, been of inestimable value in shaping and polishing our ideas. These include, but are certainly not limited to, the following: Milton Miller, M.D., Carl Whitaker, M.D., Bob Freidel, M.D., David Dunner, M.D., Norman Kreitman, M.D., Keith Hawton, M.D., Marsha Linehan, Ph.D., Zheng Yanping, M.D., Michael Quirk, Ph.D., Steven Hayes, Ph.D., Neil Jacobson, Ph.D., Kris Solberg, Ed.D., Richard Pollard Ph.D., and Jim Ascough, Ph.D. Our wives, Judith K. Chiles, R.N., and Patricia Robinson, Ph.D., provided much needed support and gave helpful clinical suggestions during the preparation of this book. We thank Elizabeth Alcala and Betty Salvatierra for their good work and cheerfulness in preparing this manuscript. And, finally, we thank our patients. In the midst of troubles and in the worst of times they trusted us, stuck with us, and by their honesty and frankness helped us grow. We sincerely hope that the reader will find our work readable, sensible, and clinically valuable. If the end result is a newfound confidence and direction when working with the suicidal patient, then we have succeeded.

Section I
Understanding Suicidality

 Chapter 1

Introduction

The Dimensions of Suicidal Behavior

Charles D. came from a family in which alcoholism had been a multigenerational problem. His father, a chronically depressed man who had frequent drinking bouts, died by suicide when Mr. D. was 12 years old. In late adolescence, Mr. D. began drinking heavily and was chronically depressed. He had frequent thoughts of suicide, ideas which, for years, he shared with no one. At the age of 32, he married and had a child. At age 35, he entered psychiatric treatment and within 2 years had no further problem with depression, alcoholism, or suicidal ideation.

Andrea M. had been known for most of her life as an individual who quickly displayed a variety of emotions. Her relationships with others were usually intense and often conflictual. Since mid-adolescence, Ms. M. frequently talked about ending her multiple frustrations by killing herself. Intermittently, her acquaintances would become concerned and urge her to get into treatment. She never has. As of her 40th birthday, Ms. M. continues to communicate suicidal ideation. She has never made a suicide attempt.

Ralph H. grew up in a single parent family. His mother worked full-time and raised six children. At the age of 15, Mr. H. fell deeply in love with one of his classmates. They dated for a while and

3

when she ended the relationship, he became very despondent. His thoughts turned to suicide, and he decided to end his life. He shot himself in the chest with a 22-caliber rifle. His family rushed him to the hospital, and in time he recovered. Eighteen years later Mr. H. is leading a productive life and truly glad to be alive. He has had no further suicidal ideation.

Mariel G. is 34 years old and has been treated intermittently for depression for 12 years. In that time, she has made six suicide attempts, each involving an overdose of prescribed medication. Ms. G. leads a difficult life, with frequent and numerous problems. She has multiple worries about her husband's infidelity, her children's illnesses, her employer's behavior toward her, and her finances. Each suicide attempt has been precipitated by an escalation of one of these problems. Her physician is aware of this history, and will prescribe antidepressant medication for her only 1 week at a time.

Jose G. committed suicide at the age of 76. Prior to taking a lethal overdose of his heart medication, he spent 2 days making sure his will was in order and wrote a lengthy goodbye note to his children and grandchildren. Mr. G. had led a long and productive life and, up to the week of his death, had had no history of suicidal thoughts or attempts. His wife had died 3 months before, he was living alone, and he was experiencing increasing difficulties with the daily activities of life.

Each of these brief but real case vignettes demonstrates some aspect of suicidal behavior. Suicidal behavior covers a spectrum of thoughts, communications, and acts, ranging from the least common, completed suicide, to the more frequently occurring, attempted suicide and suicidal communications, to the most common, suicidal ideation and verbalizations.

A startling fact about suicidal behavior is how much of it there is. A good deal of the suicidality literature is focused on completed suicide, with the overall base rate for the United States relatively stable over the past 20 years at about 12.7 deaths by suicide per 100,000 population per year. Suicide is the eighth leading cause of death for the general population and the third leading cause of death for individuals 18–24. However, the suicide rate in the elderly is more than double that of the 18–24 group. These figures are based for the most part on coroners' reports and may understate the actual suicide rate. Death by accident confounds the issue. For example, an 18-year-old man dies in an automobile wreck. He was known to be upset over a romantic breakup. While driving alone on a straight road on a clear day, his car plows into a telephone pole and he is killed. Friends suspect suicide, the coroner reports the accident, and the truth will never be known.

Compared with completed suicide, suicide attempting (deliberate self-harm with some intent to die) is a vastly more common occurrence. Studies designed to establish its frequency provide variable results depending on the population being studied. Asking Emergency Trauma Centers how many attempters they see per year will produce one result, whereas asking a general population sample if they have ever deliberately harmed themselves with some intent to die will yield quite a different figure. Overall, lifetime prevalence studies of suicide attempting vary from 1% to 12%. Our own general population studies have revealed that 10%–12% of respondents admit having made at least one suicide attempt. Thinking about suicide (suicide ideation) is by far the most common form of suicidality. The significance of this ideation can range from a symptom of a severe psychiatric illness (e.g., depression or schizophrenia) to a comforting thought (e.g., if it gets any worse I can always kill myself). As a colleague once put it, "Thoughts of suicide have gotten me through many a bad night." In our work with general population surveys, we have found 20% of those asked report at least one episode of *moderate* severe suicidal ideation (defined as ideation lasting at least 2 weeks, forming a plan, and identifying the means) at some point in their lives. Another 20% report at least one episode of troublesome suicidal ideation that did not involve formation of a plan.

In this book, we focus our discussions of suicidality on three forms: ideation, attempt, and completion. There are many types of self-destructive behavior that may not involve a conscious wish to die. Self-mutilation for the purpose of relieving pain and/or provid ing a clear boundary between one's body and the environment occurs in a distinct population. The chronic use of drugs (e.g., alcohol, tobacco) or high-risk behaviors like race car driving or mountaineering have been described as a kind of subintentional suicide. These behaviors are not the focus of this book, but we encourage the reader to explore them further.

Although discussions of suicide behaviors often link ideation, attempt, and completion, suicidality is complex and there is little evidence that it exists on a continuum. Table 1–1 shows some of the distinctions between the forms. Most people who think of suicide do not go on to make an attempt. The vast majority of people who make a suicide attempt do not ultimately die by suicide. This lack of continuity of one form to another is a key observation from which much of the discussions, observations, and techniques in this book emanate.

Given the prevalence of suicidal behavior and the multitude of causal influences, our conclusion is that, at heart, the behavior often is designed to solve problems in a person's life rather than to end his or her life. It is our strong feeling that much of the therapy for suicidality should be based on a learning model, one that teaches new approaches to problems, rather than a prevention model. Either of these approaches can be used in tandem with treatment for a specific diagnosis. Prevention models, predicated in part on the

Table 1–1.   Common characteristics of suicidal behaviors

Suicidal behavior	Suicide ideation	Suicide attempt	Suicide completion
Sex	Unknown	More female	More male
Age	Unknown	Younger	Older
Psychiatric diagnosis	Unknown	50% have no diagnosis	Depression Schizophrenia Alcoholism Panic disorder Comorbidity
Method	Not applicable	Cutting, overdose more common	Shooting, hanging more common

assumption that suicide can be predicted on an individual basis, rely on three principal strategies. The first strategy is to *emphasize pathology;* that is, to work on the assumption that the suicidal person is experiencing some pathological process, often thought to be depression. The second strategy is to deliver a *maximum response to negative behaviors.* An increase in suicidal behavior prompts a heightened response from professionals that is often centered on the person's weaknesses or deficits. The third strategy is to attempt to decrease suicidal risk by techniques that *lower individual autonomy.* At its most restrictive, this strategy calls for involuntary hospitalization.

A learning model approach, with less dependence on the assumption that suicidal behavior can be predicted and controlled, reverses these strategies. Intervention focuses on both problems that the suicidal behavior seeks to solve and clinical diagnosis. Efforts are made to focus on the reinforcement of personal strengths in addition to delineation, diagnosis, and treatment of pathology. Maximum response is placed on positive behaviors—the person's unique resources for addressing and modifying the suicidal behavior—as new approaches are found for life circumstance problems. Efforts to reduce suicidal risk are accomplished by techniques that maximize individual autonomy. A person exhibiting suicidality is assumed to be doing the best he or she can do at that moment to deal with life's difficulties. Our initial task is not to judge or criticize but to acknowledge the struggle and pain the patient has, and to begin exploring other ways of dealing with this sea of troubles. Much of this book focuses on developing and finding practical ways to use learning and problem-solving strategies with suicidal patients as they present in a variety of clinical settings.

Can You Predict Suicide?

A therapist can claim to have prevented a behavior only if it can be shown that the behavior would have occurred without the intervention. The assumption that suicide can be predicted is a myth in search of some facts. It is so important that you understand the ins and outs of attempts to predict suicide that we dedicate a chapter to this topic (see Chapter 3). However, we will tip our hand early. We do not feel the tools are there to make predictions. Although many mental health professionals presume that an important clinical skill is the ability to assess the imminent risk of suicide, this capacity has never been empirically demonstrated. The algebra for such predictive abilities is just not there. Partly, this a base rate problem because, fortunately, suicide is a rare event. Suicide risk factors are useful in identifying high-risk *groups,* but they are much less useful in identifying high risk *individuals.* Additionally, clinically relevant risk prediction is more concerned with the short term (hours to weeks), whereas much of the prediction literature is concerned with the long term (years to lifetime). Further, some long-term risk factors may not be stable. For example, marital status, employment, and current psychiatric diagnoses can all change. In short, on a case-by-case basis, our ability to predict either short-term or long-term suicidal risk is significantly flawed. Unless and until significant new risk predictors are developed and evaluated, it is unjustified to assume a suicide can be predicted. More importantly, this mistake can lead us to use less meaningful interventions.

The Role of Psychiatric Diagnosis

Clinicians know, and the psychiatric literature confirms, that suicidality is *not* the province of any one mental disorder. Studies of suicide in different diagnostic categories show suicide death rates consistently ranging from 5% to 15%. Comorbid disorders, especially combinations involving antisocial personality, borderline personality, substance abuse, schizophrenia, panic disorder, and depression may be particularly lethal. Psychiatric diagnosis has been most emphasized in reports of completed suicide. Suicide attempters are less likely to have a psychiatric condition, and very little is known about the psychiatric state of the multitude of people who have had thoughts of suicide.

Several major studies (see Black and Winokur 1990), based in part on retrospective diagnoses and coroners' reports, have stated that approximately 50%–90% of adults who commit suicide have an associated psychiatric disorder. These studies suffer an intrinsic flaw. The dead individual cannot be interviewed, and the recall of others can easily be influenced by the aftermath of a suicide. If you assume that suicide is an indication of a psychiatric illness, you may be more likely to recall events and statements that confirm that assumption. Depression, probably because of its high rate in the general population, is the most frequent diagnosis for completed suicides, but the percentage of suicides among the depressed population is about the same as in several other mental disorders (e.g., schizophrenia, personality disorders).

Depression poses a particular problem in evaluating the suicidal person in that it is both overdiagnosed and underdiagnosed. DSM-IV (American Psychiatric Association 1994) lists suicidal behavior as a diagnostic criteria in only one Axis I category: depression in its various presentations. Perhaps because of this, the two are sometimes equated (i.e., you are suicidal; therefore, you must be depressed) and treatment, particularly pharmacotherapy, is started. Obviously, the diagnosis is based on a series of criteria, not just one. Antidepressant therapy may not be helpful if the depression is not there. Even more, some antidepressants (the tricyclics) are quite lethal in overdose and should not be prescribed unless an indication is well established. The rule is simple: Do not *assume* a suicidal person has a depressive illness, but *always* evaluate for a depressive illness in a suicidal person.

In addition, it is now obvious that, on a national level, depression is underdiagnosed. Information from the Epidemiologic Catchment Area (Sussman et al. 1987) studies tells us that over 50% of people meeting criteria for depression are *not* diagnosed and *not* treated. Effective treatments exist, and the effects of treatment on personal productivity and well-being are potentially enormous. Accordingly, all of us need to screen for depression in our evaluations. The best way to do this is to ask if your patient has ever had a period of 2 weeks or more when he or she felt sad, blue, or depressed; lost interest in things; lost energy; or felt hopeless, helpless, worthless, or guilty? If you get a "yes" in this brief inquiry, go on to review the criteria for depression and, if established, treat or refer for treatment.

Recognizing and treating psychiatric diagnoses is important and needs strong emphasis. However, as we present in many ways in this book, treating the mental disorder is essential but not sufficient for many of our patients, and many suicidal patients (perhaps as many as 50%) do not meet criteria for *any* mental disorder. We recommend that suicidality be treated *in addition* to other treatments administered, and we base this recommendation on two observations: First, many accounts of suicidality have occurred in adequately treated individuals or populations (i.e., suicidal behavior occurred *in spite of* treatment). Second, effective therapies, particularly pharmacotherapies, have been available for years for major illnesses such as depression, schizophrenia, and anxiety disorders. There is scant evidence that these treatments, per se, have reduced suicidality in these populations over time.

Demographic Factors

Suicide is more common in the elderly, rates are higher for men, and, at least in the 1980s, suicidality was most rapidly on the rise among those age 16–24. Suicide attempting seems much more common in the young, with few reports of attempting, especially first time attempting, after the age of 45. Women attempt more than men. In the United States, many who attempt do so again. The repetition rate for those hospitalized for attempting is close to 50%. In addition to age and sex, other important demographic factors are race, marital status, religion, employment, and seasonal variation. In the United States, suicide is more common among whites. It is more common among the single, separated, divorced, or widowed. Loss of a spouse increases suicidal risk for at least 4 years following the spousal death. Suicide rates are higher among Protestants than Catholics or Jews, and suicide rates and unemployment correlate positively in many countries. Other factors include the presence of a physical illness, bereavement (both recent or based on an ongoing reaction to a childhood loss), and physical abuse.

Personality and Environmental Characteristics

Many studies have attempted to understand both personality and environmental characteristics of suicidal patients. Understanding these characteristics is crucial to the treatment model we present, and our chapter on the origins of suicidal behavior (see Chapter 4) delineates the many issues involved. Personality studies, in the main, have been conducted with attempters and ideators, and focus on four areas of functioning: cognition, emotional distress, interpersonal functioning, and environmental stress. Each of these factors seems important, and they probably interact in an interdependent fashion. Many cognitive function studies have focused on problem-solving abilities. Generally, suicidal individuals have been found to be poor problem solvers. They think in a dichotomous fashion, seeing things in terms of black or white, good or bad, right or wrong. A major goal of our treatment approach is to help our patients see the gray areas that define most of human interactions. Suicidal individuals are both less flexible in their thinking and more passive in the way they solve problems. Much of what they do seems predicated on fate, luck, or the efforts of others. In addition, suicidal individuals often pay scant attention to how often or how well their problem-solving efforts work. They either lack the skills to assess or do not think about assessment. Without assessment, they are at risk for both choosing and sticking with solutions to problems that probably will not work either very well or at all. As this book develops our treatment schema, we will return again to those aspects of personality that affect clinical approaches.

Suicidal patients, the cognitive literature tells us, seem very impatient. They set unrealistically short time lines for success and are apt to jettison a problem-solving solution if it does not produce immediate results. The focus is on short-term gain, and there is often little or no appreciation for long-term consequences. Our own work has shown us that many suicide attempters have favorable evaluations of suicide as an effective problem-solving behavior. Moreover, the strength by which they rate suicidal behavior as a problem-solving device correlates quite highly with the seriousness with which they intend to kill themselves. Another important cognitive factor in suicidality is hopelessness, which is predictive of eventual (but not immediate) suicide. The essence of hopelessness is a general sense of pessimism and a feeling of futility about the possibility of life changing for the better. For some individuals, hopelessness may be the link between feeling depressed and then becoming suicidal.

Many suicidal patients are caught in a difficult bind: They have a lot of pain and have a faulty ability to tolerate it. Their troubled emotional lives are often characterized by anxiety, depression, anger, boredom, and guilt. They dislike the way they feel and have trouble accepting and working with their emotions. They are frustrated, and suicidal ideation and attempting can become a vehicle to discharge pent up emotion that has no other outlet. Many suicidal patients live in a world of limited social networks and frequent conflict with friends and family. Personal loss and threat of rejection are common, and both are a frequent precipitant of suicidal behavior. Suicidal patients often lack *competent* social support, that is, people who can provide sympathetic and effective help. Incompetent social support tends to cajole and lecture rather than listen effectively, support, and teach. Many suicidal patients must deal frequently with the "all you need to do is" form of advice. It is like having a group of religious zealots at your door, each wanting 30 seconds to "change your life." It is difficult for many suicidal individuals to reach out, to form meaningful supportive relationships. New interpersonal situations bother them, and they often suffer social anxiety and withdrawal.

Life stress, both negative and positive, is a major precipitant of suicidal behavior. Suicidal patients have a high rate of stress, particularly on the negative side. Life for them is a sea of troubles, and daily hassles describe the world of many of these individuals. In addition to long-term stressors such as physical illness, financial uncertainty, and life phase changes, suicidal individuals are often beset by a day-in, day-out variety of annoyances. The 24 hours before a suicide attempt is fraught with both minor stress and a high likelihood of interpersonal conflict or loss. Attempts at marshaling support and reassurance from others usually fails, increasing the sense of discomfort and emotional distress.

The Role of Genetics

Genetics plays some role in understanding suicidality. Family history is pertinent to suicidal behavior, but we have more information about completed suicides than about attempts or ideation. Suicide does cluster in families, suggesting a genetic role. Recent data with both monozygotic and diazygotic twins indicate this clustering may represent a genetic disposition to the psychiatric disorders associated with suicide, rather than suicide itself. The question remains open whether there is an independent genetic component for suicide. Genetic influence on other forms of suicidal behaviors is much less certain. A family history of suicide does increase the risk of a suicide attempt, thus pointing to a possible clustering of this behavior within families. We found in our own research that suicide attempters are less likely to know other attempters, whether in their family or not, than other psychiatric patients or nonpsychiatric control groups. This raises the possibility that attempters do not have models that demonstrate longer term negative consequences of suicidality and are accordingly more likely to see only the short-term, more positive outcomes of their actions. This area is in much need of further investigation.

The Role of Biochemistry

Laboratory work over the past 20 years has focused on serotonin as it relates to suicidal behavior. Serotonin is a major neurotransmitter, and low levels of this chemical, as measured by its spinal fluid metabolite, predict for suicidal behavior in depressed patients. This "low serotonin" observation has been made in other diagnostic groups, including schizophrenia, personality disorders, and alcoholism. Because these findings are noted across diagnostic lines, work in the upcoming decade may shift the focus of pharmacotherapy of suicidality from depression to a more suicide-specific strategy. Whether medications that target serotonergic function will be helpful in treating suicidal behaviors is a question for further research. At this point, the selective serotonin reuptake inhibitor (SSRI) class of antidepressants are attracting considerable interest, but as yet have not shown a superior impact on suicidality compared with other antidepressants.

Conclusion

In the 1940s, chlorpromazine (Thorazine) was developed as an antihistamine. In the early 1950s, its antipsychotic properties were reported.

Within a few years, it was being used worldwide for treating psychotic illness. Almost every study of this medication showed it to be significantly better than placebo. The hunt began, using chlorpromazine as the pharmacological model, for new and better antipsychotic agents. Contemporaneous with chlorpromazine, streptomycin was developed and soon used in treating tuberculosis. The results were as dramatic as the effect of chlorpromazine on schizophrenia—bed rest and streptomycin worked, bed rest and placebo did not. Eventually, the developers of streptomycin were awarded the Nobel Prize. Tuberculosis, at least until recently, waned markedly in much of the world. In the United States, TB sanatoriums disappeared.

No one has received the Nobel Prize for chlorpromazine. Newer and better agents, at least until recently, have not been forthcoming. Schizophrenia is as prevalent now as it was 40 years ago, and, unlike the sanatorium, the mental hospital is still very much with us.

Like chlorpromazine, the psychotherapies developed in the '40s, '50s, and '60s for dealing with suicidality have been at best partially successful. To date, preventive treatment strategies for suicidality have not succeeded. Little that has emanated from any of the mental health disciplines has had much effect on rates of any form of suicidal behavior. Individuals have been helped, but the problem has persisted. In this book, we do not pretend that we have the answers. We struggle daily with troublesome patients and, like everyone else, we look, in each case, for what works best. We are optimistic. The 1990s has been declared the decade of the brain, and a national goal for the reduction of suicidality has been set. We hope our clinical approaches will help achieve this goal. We hope individuals can use our book to make their own practices more efficient and productive. Lastly, our fondest hope is that we might push somebody past a frontier. To use the schizophrenia analogy, perhaps there is someone out there who can find the suicidality therapy equivalent of something better than chlorpromazine.

Helpful Hints

♦ Suicidality comes in several forms, and one form does not necessarily lead to another.

- Nonfatal suicidal behavior is extremely common. The rarest form is completed suicide.
- It is useful to think of suicidality as a method of problem solving.
- Although suicidality is often associated with psychiatric illnesses, it is not necessarily treated by treatments targeting those illnesses.

Selected Readings

Blumenthal SJ, Kupfer DJ: Suicide Over the Life Cycle: Risk Factors, Assessment, and Treatment of Suicidal Patients. Washington, DC, American Psychiatric Press, 1990

Chiles JA, Strosahl K, Cowden L, et al: The 24 hours before hospitalization: factors related to suicide attempting. Suicide Life Threat Behav 16:335–342, 1986

Ettlinger R: Evaluation of suicide prevention after attempted suicide. Arch Gen Psychiatry 39:701–703, 1982

Hawton K, Catalan J: Attempted Suicide: A Practical Guide to its Nature and Management, 2nd Edition. New York, Oxford University Press, 1987

Mann JJ, McBride PA, Brown RP, et al: Relationship between central and peripheral serotonin indexes in depressed and suicidal psychiatric inpatients. Arch Gen Psychiatry 49:442–446, 1992

Montgomery SA, Montgomery D: Pharmacological prevention of suicidal behaviour. J Affect Disord 4:291–298, 1992

 Chapter 2

Examine Your Attitudes

Affective, Ethical, and Legal Issues in the Treatment of the Suicidal Patient

In this chapter, we review the most difficult aspect of working with the suicidal patient: the reactions elicited within you. These reactions generally center on emotional, moral/ethical, and legal matters, and are sometimes outside of the therapist's consciousness. Unless these reactions are understood, evaluated, and dealt with, they can and often do sabotage the course of treatment. Our approach is to discuss these issues and to have you perform exercises that will enable you to get more in touch with areas that might pose problems for you. The first section of this chapter addresses the types of emotions that are stirred up by suicidality. The next section discusses moral philosophies of suicide. This important because your moral stance on suicide and nonfatal suicidal behavior may well influence your actions. We then examine the ethical dilemmas that arise around providing good care when system constraints and nontreatment management issues are on the table. Finally, we look at legal issues, a hot topic and one that influences the behavior of many therapists.

Understanding Your Affect

Understanding your emotional responses is the first and most important step in becoming a skilled treater of the suicidal person. We will start with an imaginary exercise. Think first of someone you know who is difficult to understand and somewhat unpredictable. This person is often moody and is intensely involved with other people. Her involvement is often supportive and even flattering, but you've seen it take a dark turn. She can suddenly, and sometimes for very little reason, become quite angry. The anger is usually transient, but on one or two occasions you have seen it become permanent. This person can turn on a friend, and may never speak to that person again. Your own relationship with this person is that of an acquaintance. Your interactions have been social and cordial. Imagine first your feelings about this person as we have just described her. Pause a second, and then imagine that you have just heard that this person has just made a suicide attempt. Following the breakup of a stormy relationship, she has cut her wrist, was rushed by friends to the hospital, and was admitted to a psychiatric unit. Imagine now what your emotional reaction is. To finish out this sequence, you find out that she has a history of at least three other suicide attempts, one by wrist cutting and two by overdosing. These have taken place over 10 years, and all have involved a breakup in an interpersonal relationship. Now think about your emotional reactions to this person. Write each of these emotional responses down.

Now imagine a different person, a friend from your childhood. This person is now in his mid-40s and has had a rough time of it for the past 3 or 4 years. His two teenage children have been troublesome, and one, a daughter who was failing in school, has recently been arrested for drunk driving. This person's spouse has become increasingly withdrawn from the marriage and has made many trips to various doctors because of physical ailments, none of which has been identified with any particular illness. Six weeks ago, your friend was laid off from his job. Imagine your emotional response to this person, pause, and then imagine your response on learning that he has made a suicide attempt. This past weekend he was drinking heavily, something that he hardly ever did. Late Saturday night this person shot himself in the chest with a handgun. This person's family rushed him to the hospital, and he is now in serious but stable condition. Imagine your emotional response on hearing of this person's suicide attempt. Write these responses down.

As the last part of this exercise, think about the persons just described but make one change. Rather than hearing that they have made a suicide attempt, you have learned that each has committed suicide. Think of your emotional responses at this point and write them down.

The majority of us have strong reactions to acts of nonfatal self-destructive behavior, suicidal ideation, and/or suicidal verbalization to others. We tend, however, to feel and behave differently when dealing with a completed suicide. Passivity and philosophical resignation are often present with suicide. In contrast, suicide attempting, ideating, and verbalizing have powerful and often negative emotional pull. In describing patients that manifest these behaviors, clinicians unfortunately tend to use a variety of highly charged phrases such as "he is a manipulator," "that was only a suicide gesture," or "that is typical behavior for a borderline personality." These statements can cause difficulties in working with an acutely suicidal patient. If you have not dealt with your capacity to have these responses, their negative impact will most likely arise in the midst of a suicide crisis—in other words, the worst possible time. The clear thinking required could become muddled at precisely the moment when it is most needed.

Recall now your emotional responses to the cases described above. In Case 1, a typical response on hearing about the suicide attempt is that it made some sense; it fit the way that person was leading her life. You may have felt some concern but also some relief that you were not the person involved in the chaotic relationship that set it off. You may have felt some anger at that person for using suicidality in a "manipulative" way. Learning that there had been multiple suicidal attempts, a typical reaction would be to find your rejection of the patient increasing, along with an increasing relief at not being involved and a certain wariness about having much to do with this person in the future. What did you feel when the situation was changed, and the person completed suicide? For many, passivity, resignation, and some sadness would be present, often accompanied by the feeling that there was a lot more happening than you knew about.

For many, it is easier to relate to Case 2. So many rotten things were going on that the emergence of suicidality is understandable. Adding the weekend bout of alcoholism makes it even easier to both have a sense of the situation and begin to think of some solutions. In this man's case, we might be less likely to become angry or irritated, and more likely to have a sense of both "yes I understand that" and even "there but for the grace of God go I." Imagine (one more time) that 3 years have passed and you have lost contact with this person for some time. He recovered from the gunshot wound, and left the hospital. Now you learn that not only did the drinking continue, but it has come to light that he had been quietly drinking too much for years and had frequently been verbally abusive to both his wife and children. Since the gunshot wound, he has made three other suicide attempts, all by overdosing. The overdosing has been done with antidepressants, for he has been in some form of treatment for some time. He has divorced, lives alone, is still out of work, and is still drinking. He has just contacted you and asked for a loan, stating, "If you can't help me, I don't know what I will do." What is your emotional response at this point?

There is even a more difficult side to our reactions. It involves our ability to heal and the reduction of that ability in the midst of a suicidal crisis. Most health and mental health providers got into the profession because they like to help people. Their tandem assumption is that the patient seeks these services to be helped. However, the suicidal patient may be ambivalent about being helped, and this ambivalence can seriously impair treatment. In this situation, these clinicians are reminded that both their healing authority and their powers of persuasion are limited. When persuasion fails, clinicians get in touch with their powerlessness and have to deal with it. In this situation, many of us experience frustration and anger that, if we are not careful, we will blame on the patient's behavior. We can feel off balance and begin to react to, rather than treat, our patient. Interactions can begin to center on the patient's ambivalence and negative attitudes rather than on the work that needs to get done. What often surfaces is a showdown over conformity, with the patient's potential for suicidal behavior in the center of the struggle. In these moments, we can, unfortunately, challenge the patient to "put up or shut up," to either play by our rules or seek help elsewhere. Whatever the outcome, the working relationship is over, as much because of our issues as the patient's problems.

Moral Stances on Suicide

An exercise that we have found very helpful in workshops is to discuss philosophies about suicide—philosophies that have evolved over several thousand years—and express almost every possible point of view. Philosophies are certainly an important part of our attitudes, and from these attitudes come our affective responses. Please read the following review of this topic, and then pick a few colleagues and have an honest discussion. You also might use our case examples or make up a few of your own. For many of us, our philosophies are not stable, but tend to change depending on the circumstances with which we are dealing. We urge you to do this, because when all is said and done, you must decide if you can comfortably work with suicidal individuals. Some of us have a temperament and a point of view that makes such work very difficult, if not impossible. There is nothing right or wrong about this. It is a matter of inclination and type of talent. If working with suicidality is not for you, then don't do it! It is far better to deal with this now then when you have an acutely suicidal person on your hands, a person to whom you have made some sort of treatment commitment.

Let us now take a look at philosophies about suicide. We all have them, and we probably think about suicide in different ways at different times. It is very important for you to thoroughly understand your attitudes about suicide. Do you see it as a wise choice some times? Does it make you angry? Is it a difficult and troubling topic for you to talk or think about? If, after reviewing these various philosophies you feel some trouble or concern, talk it over with your colleagues. Seek counseling for yourself if you feel that would help. Before you see your next patient, get a good handle on how you feel. The worse time to have to deal with this is when your patient is in a crisis.

In many societies throughout history, suicide has been the focus of philosophy. The stances range from statements about suicide being unequivocally wrong to statements that suicide is an intrinsically positive act. What follows is a summary of this spectrum of approaches. Each approach has its adherents, and arguments about validity (or lack thereof) can be made about each point. Read through these, and think about your own philosophy. At the end, we will tell you ours.

Suicide has been described as an unequivocally wrong and harmful act. It can be viewed as doing violence to the dignity of human life, as something against basic human nature. A philosophy that reveres every human life, that feels that life should be preserved at all cost, is at its foundation opposed to suicide. In a religious context, suicide can be seen as a wrongful consequence of pride, usurping God's prerogative to give and take away human life. Suicide can be seen as homicide and thus forbidden. A more socialistic philosophy might indicate that suicide is wrong because it represents a crime against the state. Here, a person would be described primarily as a social being, the property of the state. No person has the right to deprive the state of its property. Suicide has been described as unnatural. When a person commits suicide, violence has been done to the natural order. From a more psychological perspective, suicide can be seen as wrong because it presents an oversimplified response to a complex and necessarily ambivalent situation. It is an irrevocable act that denies future opportunity for learning or for growth. From the viewpoint of systems psychology, suicide can be seen as wrong because it adversely affects the survivors, both the immediate family and the general community. Bending a little from the unequivocal wrongness of suicide, one could think of suicide as permissible under certain conditions. This philosophy would support the suicide of a person who has no opportunity for quality of life. A person dealing with a painful, incurable, and lethal illness, for example, could justifiably commit suicide.

Suicide may be viewed as an issue without moral or ethical overtones. Suicide has occurred across cultures and across time, and is a phenomenon of life that is subject to scientific study much as any other phenomenon might be. Suicide can be seen as an act that takes place beyond the realm of reason. Suicide can occur by motivations that are unintelligible to the rational mind but justifiable based on mystical experience. Suicide may be a morally neutral act. Every person, through the right of free will, can make or take his or her life.

Just as a number of philosophies have evolved that describe suicide in a negative way, so a number have evolved that describe it in a positive way. For example, the purpose of life has been described as enjoyment. When pleasure ceases, death becomes a comfortable and available alternative. In some cultures, suicide is viewed as a reasonable choice. Death can be considered a lesser evil than dishonor, and suicide can be encouraged: a preference for self-destruction rather than defeat. Some cultures use suicide as a way of dispensing justice. For example, tribal law that prohibits incest might be enforced by requiring anyone breaking this law to leave the tribe and kill himself. Justice would thus be restored. Suicide might be a permissible act when it is performed for some great purpose, for example, self-immolation in the cause of peace. Suicide may save face when a person is perceived to have lost honor. Suicide might be a positive way in which one can immediately reunite with valued ancestors and with loved ones. At times, suicide has been presented in a personified and eroticized manner, a poetic expression of both beauty and the seductiveness of death.

Now that you have reviewed some philosophies regarding suicide, please have a discussion with a couple of friends or colleagues. Talk about philosophies, feelings, and cases. To aid in this discussion, please refer to Appendix 1, which is an annotated outline of philosophies about suicide. Make a couple of copies and pass them around to get the discussion going.

More Self-Examination

Two instruments we use to evaluate the suicidal patient are found in Appendix 2, the Consequences of Suicidal Behavior Questionnaire, and Appendix 3, the Reasons for Living Inventory. These are included because we would like you to take them as part of this process of self-examination.

The Consequences of Suicidal Behavior Questionnaire

Appendix 2, the Consequences of Suicidal Behavior Questionnaire, is another exercise of the imagination. Before starting the questionnaire, put yourself in a suicidal frame of mind and then list some consequences of your suicide attempt and your completed suicide. We cannot give you much information about how to imagine that you are suicidal. For some of us the affect would be hopelessness, for others anger, and for others anxiety. Likewise, the problems that precipitate suicidality vary. For some it would be a massive and overwhelming difficulty. For others a series of long-term, daily hassles. You have to create this frame of mind for yourself. If we knew, in some universal sense, what caused suicidality, then the field would have made a major advance.

Now that you have completed the Consequences for Suicidal Behavior Questionnaire, go back through your results. How closely do these correlate with the feelings and philosophies that you just reviewed? Did you see any good in the consequences of your attempted suicide? For example, would other people become more focused in helping you? Would your problems become more apparent, both to you and others, making help that much easier to obtain? What about bad results? Does embarrassment or loss of face play a role in your reactions? Did the results of your suicide attempt tend to be all bad or all good? Go back to the exercise and try to produce some more results, this time in some different direction from your original consequences. By doing this, you will get a sense of both the complexity and ambivalence of the suicidal crisis. Another factor to look at in your attempted suicide results is the nature of the problems you listed. First, did you list any problems? It is our contention that suicidal behavior is problem-solving behavior, and if most of your answers relate to how you or other people feel, revisit them. Look beyond that statement of feeling to a statement of problem. Feelings must be dealt with and can be a definitive block of successful treatment. *Always* look past the feeling for the problem being addressed.

A second part of the Consequences for Suicidal Behavior Questionnaire involves the completion of suicide. Are there religious or philosophical overtones to your sense of what happens to you after death? Is it easy to come up with two different results, or is it hard? For many of our patients, even those who have thought long and hard about suicide, we have found that the spectrum of potential consequences has not been examined. The suicidal patient de facto sees things as being better after death whether an afterlife concept is present or not. Many magazines have stories about "near death" experiences that are positive and peaceful in overtone. This tends to be the sole consequence with which the patient is in touch. If the patient generates results that are bad, this might have an antisuicidal effect. Another dimension of the exercise is the importance or unimportance of individual consequences of your suicide. Some consequences of suicide that seem to be universally important (i.e., effects on children left behind) may in fact be rated as unimportant by a patient. Check the consequences of suicide that you feel are important and unimportant and compare them with your friends or colleagues. What are the similarities and differences? Return to this exercise now and try to come up with two more results that have a degree of goodness and importance that are different from your first ones. Again, this will help you think through the ambivalence and complexity of suicidality.

The questions concerning those left behind are in this questionnaire to force an issue. When a person is expressing suicidality, these aspects are seldom thought about. You probably found this fairly easy to do. In imagining suicide, it is not hard to come up with effects on the survivors. Generally, doing this exercise will dampen your ardor for your imagined suicide. Look back at the two case examples we gave earlier in the chapter. A good part of your emotional response to the suicidal patient could come from your concern about the consequences on the survivors. You are on the outside looking in and can see the effect on those left behind. When you are on the inside, when you are the suicidal person, this is much harder to do.

The last part of this exercise involves comparing your reasons for committing suicide with the reasons others give. What reasons did you conjure up for yourself, and do they differ from the reasons you attribute to other people? Most importantly, do your reasons for committing suicide differ from those you attribute to other people who attempt suicide but do not die? Many of us do this, assigning different sorts of reasons for those out there who attempt suicide. Often these reasons suggest that the attempt was manipulative and based on a certain weakness of character. They seem less important than those that we would attribute to our own imagined circumstance. If this is so, it can again color your emotional reaction to suicidality. If you find the reasons varying in these three sections, come up with some additional ones. Most successful therapists have the ability to put themselves in their patients' shoes, to see the world, as sympathetically as possible, as their patients see it. Use this exercise to test your limits for that ability.

The Reasons for Living Inventory

The Reasons for Living Inventory, the other exercise in this section, has to do with the positive side of suicidal ambivalence, the reasons for "Why I want to stay alive." In Appendix 3, the Reasons for Living Inventory has been rearranged to show the six dimensions that it examines. Ask yourself the following question: "If I were thinking of suicide, what are the reasons I would have for *not* killing myself?" Now read through this inventory with that question in mind. Is your sense of being able to survive and cope important? What about your responsibility to your family or to your children? Does the act of suicide scare you, such that this fear becomes a reason for avoiding suicidal behavior? What about social disapproval, the fear of "losing face?" Lastly, what about moral objections? After taking inventory of yourself, go back to the two case examples that we gave or to other examples that you may have generated from your own experience. Think about those two suicidal persons answering this scale. More than that, go ahead and answer this scale for them, make them as real as possible and get a sense of how much they would agree or disagree with each question. Having done that, has your affective response to this person changed? It probably has because you have just expanded your view of the patient. You may have come up with a way of assigning the patient some positive attributes. Further, you have some new tools for a therapeutic discussion and probably feel more comfortable about your ability to engage with a suicidal person.

The lesson here is of universal importance in dealing with suicidality, and reflects a practical philosophy about suicide. As a clinician, always try to understand the totality of the patients' view of suicide, then reinforce the positive side of suicidal ambivalence. Make the following assumption: This person is talking to me because of ambivalence about suicide. If there was an unequivocal desire to commit suicide, this person would probably already be dead. My job is to find that spark of life that brought the person here and reinforce it. My philosophy is this: Suicide is one way of solving problems, but there are usually better ways.

Ethical Issues

All therapists are required to adhere to ethical standards within their discipline. Almost always, the first rule is to administer no harmful treatment. *"Primum non nocere"* was pronounced by Hippocrates millennia ago: "First, do no harm." A second standard most of us strive for is to use only effective treatment approaches. Both these general ethical statements can cause problems with a suicidal patient. A terribly misguided concern is present in some therapists because of their desire to first do no harm. The concern is, if you ask about suicidal behavior you might be planting a suggestion in a vulnerable person and he or she will go on to engage in such behavior. There is no clinical experience or research that supports this assumption. Asking about suicidality is the first step toward treating suicidality. This fear has been particularly expressed about children and adolescents, who are seen as more vulnerable to the power of suggestion. Again, there is no data that in any way supports this assumption. In fact, the harm comes from *not* asking about suicidality. At best, you will miss important information. At worst, you will leave your patient with a sense that this is a taboo topic and is a problem for which they can expect no help.

A dedication to using only effective treatment approaches is an ever-present but all too often ignored ethical standard. The problem comes when the documentation for the effective treatment is still lacking. Parenthetically, this is a problem for a variety of human ailments. To date, there is little in the treatment literature about suicidality that substantiates the clinical utility of existing inpatient or outpatient treatments. Often, the therapist is aware that the treatment is not working but has no good alternatives. Sometimes, the therapist is convinced that a particular treatment strategy would work, only to find that agency policy and procedure does not allow that strategy. We have seen several examples in which systems dictate procedures regarding suicidal risk management that providers believe to be at best ineffective and at worst bad for the patient. An example of this is an insistence on hospitalization for everyone voicing suicidal ideation. This discomfort over the feeling that current interventions are not working and needed interventions are not available is a major ethical dilemma. The frustration arising from this dilemma, if not dealt with directly and appropriately, can lead to bad outcomes. Sessions can deteriorate into lecturing, pleading, or confrontation about suicidal behavior. None of these techniques work very well; in fact, they may harm the patient by fracturing the working alliance. The therapist may start secretly hoping that the patient will not show up for the next appointment and begin behaving in a variety of ways that will give that message. The patient can feel equally frustrated. Once again, things are being talked over, and not much is happening. For some patients, this is an unfortunate repetition of an experience they have had many times before. There are several ways to minimize ethical dilemmas. First and foremost is to remember that the intervention is designed to help the patient. At regular and agreed upon intervals, ask whether the treatment is helping. If not, ask the patient what needs to be done to make the sessions more helpful. Put aside your defensiveness; you are not omnipotent and you may not be on the right track with this particular patient. Refer the patient on if both of you agree that would be more helpful. A second way to avoid ethical binds is to stay abreast of developments in the field. This maximizes your chances of being effective, even within system constraints. It is also important to use what you learn to build up an internally consistent approach that you can hang your hat on. The more you believe in your approach, the more effective you will be with it.

Finally, it is becoming increasingly clear that systems as well as providers are going to be held accountable for policy-based interventions. If you work in a system that has policies that guarantee ineffective or harmful treatment, you need to gather peer support and attempt to change these policies. Remember, if a policy is rubbing you the wrong way, the great likelihood is that it is doing the same to others. The "quality of care" protest, especially when formalized in writing and signed by several staff, is a very effective change device.

Legal Concerns: A Powerful Determinant of Therapist Behavior

Consider the following case example from one of the author's recent expert witness testimony:

A 42-year-old man is referred by family members to a psychiatrist for counseling because of increasingly frequent talk about killing himself. He has recently completed a messy divorce and reports that he has been drinking two to four beers per night to help calm himself down. He reports that he has little social interest and mainly spends his time at home ruminating about his divorce. He indicates that his thoughts frequently turn to vivid and specific images of loading his handgun, putting it in his mouth, and pulling the trigger. He reports feeling a greater sense of peace when thinking about suicide. He reports that he does have a handgun at home, and it is loaded. He reports that 5 years ago, after a particularly bad marital dispute, he took an overdose of 30 aspirin but took himself to an emergency room before any physical damage occurred. It occurred to him at that time that he did not want to die; now, he is not so sure. He reports that he has tried everything he can think of to feel better but believes that most of his subsequent efforts to correct his life will fail.

After diagnosing the patient as severely depressed, the psychiatrist initiates a phased-in prescription of trazodone 300 mg/day. A no suicide contract is secured from the patient and the patient agrees to give his guns and ammunition to a neighbor. This action is confirmed by the patient at the next visit 3 days later. The psychiatrist feels at this time the patient could not be involuntarily committed; the patient does not want to be hospitalized and reports feeling somewhat better. Vegetative signs of depression are improving. A third appointment is scheduled 3 days later. The patient calls and cancels the appointment, stating he is going back to work. He accepts a new appointment 5 days later. On the phone, he reports feeling much better; vegetative signs are much improved. That night, he does not return home and his wife calls the psychiatrist, who recommends that she contact the police. The next morning the patient is found in his pickup dead from a gunshot wound, the gun having been purchased the day before. The widow sues the psychiatrist and the associated physicians' group, claiming that the patient should have been involuntarily hospitalized, that the psychiatrist should not have accepted a no suicide contract from a patient with a mental disorder and that the psychiatrist should have made contact with the patient's friends and family about the treatment plan. Each of these actions or omissions failed to safeguard the patient, causing the suicide.

This case was settled by the defendant's insurance company for several hundred thousand dollars, without going to trial. This occurred despite a deposition process in which the plaintiff's expert witnesses admitted that the community standard of care had been followed. One expert even testified that he did not work with suicidal patients and had not for several years! Debriefing with the defendant's attorneys revealed that the insurance company had calculated the costs of putting on a trial, compared that to the cost of settlement, and decided the difference did not favor going to trial.

Legal concerns come from a variety of directions, but two predominate. The first concern arises from the dictates of state statues that almost invariably require involuntary hospitalization of a patient who is assessed as an imminent threat to commit suicide. If commitment steps are not followed in such situations, the therapist is potentially liable for damages that could accrue from the patient's future actions. To make matters worse, this can be a legal double bind. A lawsuit is possible if there is failure to hospitalize given the presence of generally accepted suicide risk indicators. On the other hand, there is the growing potential of civil rights lawsuits from patients who are detained and later claim they never met commitment criteria. These suits are potentially more troublesome because they correctly take suicide risk prediction and assessments of dangerousness to task.

Once involuntary treatment is initiated, another dilemma arises. Performing legally required treatment is certainly not the same as performing good treatment. There is often a discrepancy between what is stated in the law for social control and what seems the best and most appropriate clinical way to approach the problem. Hospitalization is usually addressed in the state laws as a prescribed treatment, yet it is clearly of equivocal value for the suicidal patient. In some patients, it may elevate suicide risk, especially for the longer term, by decreasing their sense of autonomy and efficacy.

Most hospitals and associated systems have risk management departments whose chief concern is to reduce the threat of successful lawsuits. These departments have not been overly successful, but the risk management business continues to thrive. For example, many hospitals via policy will not discharge or give a pass to a patient who *admits* to being suicidal. This can create a pretext of good risk management in which the patient is encouraged to lie about his or her real state of mind. Ironically, negligent death suits are raised regardless of whether the inpatient site did or did not assess prepass or predischarge suicidality. Staff can be sued for either not assessing or incorrectly assessing. The message is this: Do not mistake good risk management for good treatment.

The second predominant legal concern comes from the fear of potentially disastrous legal consequences arising from the suicide of a patient. Many clinicians fear that no matter what they do, they will be blamed and legally pursued in such a circumstance. They may be right. Many lawsuits have been launched with a scant basis for negligence. The tactic in these suits seems to be to cast a very broad net, looking for the proverbial "deep pocket," and hoping that the entity (usually an insurance company) will settle out of court. Most negligence suits cite one or more of the following causes: 1) failure to properly assess suicidal potential, 2) failure to take adequate measures to safeguard the patient, and 3) failure to perform appropriately aggressive treatment of the patient's condition.

Often, these cases are settled out of court for economic reasons. The settlement relates to the cost of putting on a trial versus the amount sought (i.e., if the costs of trial are deemed greater than the cost of agreement). If negotiations reduce the gap to an acceptable level, the insurance company will settle rather than risk, even if unlikely, a large jury settlement. Many clinicians still do not understand this settlement mentality; they see the court action as an opportunity to be vindicated. A settlement can therefore leave the clinician with mixed feelings: relief that the suit is over and a simultaneous belief of being found guilty. The message is this: In malpractice matters, the American legal system is no longer a pure justice system. Economic concerns can become paramount. Our best advice is to remember that in the litigious climate in the United States, lawsuits can happen anytime and for any reason. You may not be able to keep from being sued, but you can increase your chances of a successful defense. Think clearly and document your thinking. If you do not write it down, it did not happen. Have a reasonable treatment plan and stick with it. If you are worried about malpractice suits, increase your malpractice insurance. The following five steps are all indicative of good practice and therefore proactively address legal concerns.

1. **Document suicidality.** This is discussed elsewhere in our book. Make sure you ask the right questions and document the answers. Ask about diagnosis, ask about substance abuse, and ask about suicidality. In the majority of cases in which we have been asked to give expert testimony, the major problem has been failure to document assessment, not the assessment activity itself.

2. **Do ongoing assessment.** Once the problem has been identified, explicitly assess the condition and its response to treatment in each progress note. Again, failure to document can be a major problem.

3. **Prepare to be assertive.** In your notes, state what you did and why you did it. Document your thinking. In addition to writing this down, make sure the patient understands what you are doing and why you are doing it. If other family members are involved, take the same approach with them. This is a proactive measure. Individuals who have been informed of your course of actions and have had a chance to agree or disagree are much less likely to drag you into court.

4. **Document your concerns about the totality of treatment and the actions you have taken to build a system of care for your patient.** Stress the involvement of other appropriate disciplines and members of a social support system. Document your actions in putting together a competent social support system. Suicidality, if it occurs, is probably not going to happen in your office. It is going to happen out in the world. If you recognize this and are working with your patient and the social support system to take positive measures, you are demonstrating that you are conducting good systemic treatment.

5. **Explicitly cover your decision to hospitalize or not.** This is covered in Chapter 8 of this book. It is most important that you document your thinking in this regard.

Although it is inherently absurd to assume that a self-inflicted act such as suicide can be *caused* by the actions of another, this is "reality" as defined by the American legal system. In the final analysis, the legal system is based on the interpretation of broad statutes. One way to begin reducing the volume of litigation is to sponsor laws that better define what types of psychiatric outcomes can by definition be related to negligence. Moving suicide into the realm of nonculpability would much more accurately represent the nature of the act itself and specifically honor the fact that the mental health profession does not currently possess the technology for accurate prediction or prevention of the act.

Helpful Hints

♦ If you do not have a handle on your attitudes about suicidality, you will not treat your patients in a logical and consistent fashion.

♦ Use our exercises and appendixes, discussions with your colleagues, and supervision if available to understand your attitudes.

♦ Advocate for your profession, and for our society, to develop rational expectations regarding suicidality.

Selected Readings

Gutheil TG: Paranoia and progress note: a guide to forensically informed psychiatric recordkeeping. Hosp Community Psychiatry 31:479–482, 1980

Linehan M, Goodstein J, Nielson S, et al: Reasons for staying alive when you're thinking of killing yourself: the Reasons for Living Inventory. J Consult Clin Psychol 51:276–286, 1983

Litman RE: Psycholegal aspects of suicide, in Modern Legal Medicine, Psychiatry, and Forensic Science. Edited by Curran W, McGarry AL, Petty CS. Philadelphia, PA, FA Davis, 1980, pp 841–853

Murphy GE: Problems in studying suicide. Psychiatr Dev 1:339–350, 1983

Nolan JL (ed): The Suicide Case: Investigation and Trial of Insurance Claims. Chicago, IL, American Bar Association, 1988

Perr IN: Suicide litigation and risk management: a review of 32 cases. Bull Am Acad Psychiatry Law 13:209–219, 1985

 Chapter 3

Assessing Suicidal Potential

Myths and Realities

B asic to the clinician's dilemma in working with a suicidal patient is the possibility that suicidal behavior will occur after the initial contact. This can happen in a variety of contexts. The patient may present for help either because of intense suicidal ideation or following a suicide attempt. Alternatively, a patient may initially not be suicidal but becomes so during the course of treatment. However this situation unfolds, you will experience pressure from a variety of sources (some internal, some external) both to predict whether suicidal behavior is likely to occur and, if so, to prevent it.

There are two implicit and widely accepted assumptions that create this pressure: 1) there are specific factors that foretell suicidal behavior in a given individual (i.e., risk factors), and 2) there is a correct intervention (either medication or crisis intervention) that will prevent the behavior from occurring. Unfortunately, there is very little research that supports either of these ideas. For the most part, they are an unsubstantiated part of clinical lore. Nevertheless, the notion that clinicians have the capacity to predict and prevent suicidal behavior has worked its way deep into the community standard of care for all the mental health disciplines. As was discussed in the previous chapter, most malpractice or negligence lawsuits hinge on the implicit truth of these assumptions. Without them, civil litigation secondary to a suicide would probably become a less frequent occurrence.

Our goal in this chapter is to highlight the many difficulties with accurate suicide risk prediction and to introduce an alternative approach that uses assessment to reframe suicidal behavior in a way that contributes to the success of treatment.

The Basic Problem

Clinicians are almost always under pressure to figure out whether a patient is going to attempt suicide in a very short time frame, usually no more than 24–48 hours. Few patients can sustain a bona fide suicidal crisis longer than that. The prediction question is short term—that is, whether something is going to happen in the next couple of days. Most states require you to take preventive action if you determine there is an imminent risk of suicide, usually defined as the immediate and likely threat of a suicide attempt. The question then becomes how to separate patients who are thinking of suicide from those who will actually make an attempt. As was discussed in Chapter 2, thinking about suicide is extremely common in the general population, whereas completed suicide is extremely rare. This is sometimes referred to as a *base rate problem*. The statistical power is insufficient to make a useful determination. Practically speaking, it means that thinking or talking about suicide is not really an accurate predictor of attempting suicide in the next 24–48 hours. Why? Because there will be a thousand or more such patients for every one completed suicide. If you like playing the lottery, you will have a good understanding of these odds!

Many clinicians counter this problem by hospitalizing patients who fit a *high-risk profile*. If these factors were evenly applied throughout the United States at any given point in time, in all probability there would not be enough hospital beds in all medical and psychiatric facilities to hold the high-risk patients. Unfortunately, many clinicians ignore the *false-positive dilemma,* specifically, the possible invasive, destructive side effects of hospitalization on a presumably high-risk patient who never would have gone on to attempt or complete suicide in the first place. Here, the potential benefits must be weighed against the prime directive of mental health ethics: Do not harm the patient with the treatment. This issue is discussed further in Chapter 8.

Risk Prediction Systems

For nearly three decades, suicidologists have tried to overcome the prediction problem by developing statistically derived risk prediction systems. The strategy is to compare key environmental, personality, historical and/or biological characteristics of suicides with normal control subjects (e.g., nonsuicidal psychiatric patients). Variables that emerge as significant in these comparisons are then combined into prediction equations. The goal is to find the best set of factors that correctly identify the suicides. There have been many investigations of this sort, and the result has been a number of suicide risk prediction instruments. Generally, these instruments provide clinical information useful in its own right, but they are fundamentally unable to do anything more than identify that a patient is in an elevated risk group for suicide. This is *not* the same as defining imminent risk.

The true test of a suicide risk prediction system is whether it can correctly identify suicides and suicide attempters before the fact. This requires prospective studies of patients at risk to see which factors actually predict suicidal behavior. These studies are very expensive to conduct because they require large sample sizes (remember the base rate problem) and the development of sophisticated tracking procedures. Four major studies like this have been conducted in the last decade. Two of these studies (Goldstein et al. 1991; Pokorny 1983) examine the panoply of suicide risk factors derived from the many previous studies in this area. The results of the two studies are amazingly consistent: There is virtually no predictive power even when high-risk patients are followed for years. Remember, you, the clinician, are not being asked about years, but about hours or days! Two studies of the Beck Hopelessness Scale (Beck et al. 1985, 1989) have produced slightly more promising results. In both the studies, approximately 80% of eventual suicides were correctly predicted over a multiyear follow-up period on the basis of hopelessness scores obtained at the start of inpatient or outpatient treatment. However, the time frame needed to develop this result was years from the initial contact. In a short time frame study (Strosahl et al. 1984) of the same instrument, we found that the Beck Hopelessness Scale misclassified 100% of high-lethality suicide attempters admitted to an inpatient psychiatric service.

What conclusions can be drawn about the suicide prediction issue? First, it is difficult if not impossible to clinically intervene and prevent a behavior that cannot be accurately predicted. Second, previous research has not been conducted using a clinically relevant time frame; we have no way of knowing if acute risk factors are the same as postevent factors. Third, a community standard of care is needed that does not misstate what the clinician's capabilities are in terms of suicide prediction and prevention. It is hard enough to work with a suicidal patient without the added pressure of making an impossible prediction.

Assessing Suicidal Behavior

The systematic interview of a suicidal patient is most important in that it will yield useful clinical information and produce for you a thorough and relevant clinic record. In doing this interview, it is most important to remember some basic principles. First, recall that there are many forms of suicidal behavior and each may vary according to its frequency, intensity, and duration. *Frequency* means how often specific episodes of suicidal behavior ideation or verbalization occur. *Intensity* is a measure of how concentrated the suicidal behavior is at any given point in time. *Duration* is how long an episode of suicidal behavior lasts. These dimensions vary independently; measuring one cannot be taken as a measure of the others. In general, we look at increases in frequency, intensity, and duration as an indicator of severity. Patients tend to respond with the most alarm to increased intensity, followed by duration.

Second, asking a patient about suicidal behavior will not cause the patient to commit suicide. Rather than being distressed, the patient is often relieved that the question is asked; it puts an end to what often has been a carefully kept secret and a source of personal shame and humiliation.

Third, a willingness to disclose suicidal ideation does not make the patient less of a risk. Clinical reports suggest that some truly lethal patients deny any suicidal intent, but systematic research has not substantiated this notion. All communication about suicidal intent is equally valid. Remember, suicidal communication and ideation is a feature of suffering in its own right.

Fourth, suicidal ideation is not primarily an emotional feeling. It is more accurately described as a thought about how to solve a particular set of problems. Often, the problem is that the patient is feeling depressed, anxious, angry, or some other dysphoric emotion. When suicidal thinking is assessed as if it were a feeling, there is a danger that more basic negative feelings get pushed down the priority list. Ask the patient to describe the problem that would be solved if the he or she were dead. This is a better, more direct way of accessing basic negative emotional states.

Finally, be sure to collect the information that is in support of your specific clinical purpose. Going through textbook suicide risk factors for their own sake can be a futile exercise and can be antitherapeutic if it leaves your patient with a sense of not being understood. Be sure to collect information that can be used in a positive set of interventions. As presented in Tables 3–1 and 3–2, it is important to differentiate background and foreground data. Background data is typically historical information that defines the patient as at risk, whereas foreground material deals with the patient's current suicidality. As a general rule of thumb, place less emphasis on background factors with the exception of prior suicide attempts. Instead, focus on the current suicidal behavior and positive forces that would serve to deter the patient from attempting/completing suicide. Pay close attention to the patient's suicide-specific beliefs and expectancies. For example, patients who believe strongly that

Table 3–1.   Key factors in assigning risk for suicidal behavior

Risk factor	Question format
1. Positive evaluation of suicidal behavior	1. How effective would suicide be in solving your problems? On a 1–5 scale, 1 = not effective, 5 = completely effective (+ = 3 or above)
2. Low ability to tolerate emotional pain (intolerable)	2. If your current situation didn't change, could you tolerate the way you feel? On a 1–5 scale, 1 = could not tolerate at all, 5 = could tolerate it well (+ = 3 or below)
3. Hopelessness (interminable)	3A. As you look into the future, do you see things getting better in your life, either as a result of your own efforts or natural change? On a 1–5 scale, 1 = nothing will change, things will stay bad; 5 = sure that the future will be better (+ = 3 or below)
	or
	3B. Beck Hopelessness Scale = 8 or above.
4. Inescapability	4. In your current situation, does it seem that no matter what you do, things just seem to stay bad or get worse? On a 1–5 scale, 1 = what I do has made a lot of difference, 5 = what I do has had no effect at all (+ = 3 or above)
5. Low survival and coping beliefs	5A. When you think about reasons for not killing yourself, how important are the the ideas that life is intrinsically worth living, curiosity about your future or your desire to see this situation through to the end? On a 1–5 scale, 1 = these reasons are not important at all, 5 = these reasons are extremely important in my wanting to stay alive (+ = 3 or below)
	or
	5B. Reasons for Living, survival, and coping beliefs scale average score is 3.00 or below (see Appendix 3)

Table 3–2. Foreground and background assessment points with the suicidal patient

Background	Finding	Foreground	Finding
1. Prior suicide attempt	Present	1A. Current suicidal ideation	Present
		a. Frequency of episodes	Daily increasing
		b. Intensity of thoughts	Detailed images, trouble "fighting them off"
		c. Duration of episodes	At least 30 minutes, increasing in length
		and/or	
		1B. BeckScale for Suicide IdeatorsSSI score ≥18	
2. Suicide intent in prior acts	Present	2. Preparatory behavior	Present
a. Expectation about lethality	Believed death was likely	a. Security means	Means are available
b. Attempts to avoid detection	Strong, discovery was a fluke	b. Honor code	Suicide attempts made, others promised
c. Final arrangements	Made	c. Attempts to elude detection	Others have been misled about whereabouts, behavior is planned in a social vacuum
		d. Final arrangements	A new will written belongings given away, a suicide note written
		e. Time frame is established	Date is set, "anniversary of another suicide"

(continued)

Table 3–2. Foreground and background assessment points with the suicidal patient *(continued)*

Background	Finding	Foreground	Finding

3. Medical lethality of prior acts
  a. Type of method
  b. Condition upon discovery
  c. Medical condition
	Very lethal
	Un-/semiconscious
	Required "real" ER/ICU services
		3. Current drug/alcohol abuse	Present; increasing consumption

4. Family history of suicide	Present in first-degree family member	4. Current psychiatric condition	Depression, schizo-affective disorder, substance abuse disorder
		5. Current physical health	Poor; chronic disease or pain
		6. Current negative life stress	High; major financial, job, or relationship problems or loss
		7. Current social support	Low; social alienation or only negative supports available

suicide would solve their problems with only minimal negative drawbacks are more likely to have engaged in high-intent suicide attempts. A simple scaling question, done after problems leading to suicidality have been described (On a 1–5 scale, with 1 meaning not effective at all and 5 meaning extremely effective, how effective would suicide be as a way to solve your problems?), will give you this information (Chiles et al. 1989). The other side of the equation is just as important. A recent study (Strosahl et al. 1992) found that in a sample of hospitalized suicide attempters, the importance attached to survival and coping beliefs as reasons for going on with life despite current problems was a more important predictor of suicide intent than hopelessness. When the suicide-as-problem-solving question and ratings of survival and coping attitudes are compared, the problem-solving question can be evaluated in a clinically richer context. This is discussed further in Chapters 5 through 8 of this book. Although clinicians are often told to focus on the plan-availability-lethality triangle (i.e., Do you have a plan? Do you have a method? Is the means to enact your method readily available? How lethal is the plan?), experience suggests that shifting the focus to suicide-specific beliefs and positive life-sustaining beliefs allows for a much more upbeat problem-solving intervention.

Using Assessment to Reframe Suicidal Behavior

For many clinicians, there is the assessment phase of treatment and then there is the treatment phase of treatment. When the clinician is in the suicide assessment mode, there can often be little room for positive movement to occur because the focus is on preventing something negative. Conversely, clinicians can have great difficulty when they are in the treatment mode and are interrupted by a distraught patient who develops a suicidal crisis requiring some assessment activity. This distinction comes from the traditional medical model, which requires that a formal operating diagnosis be made before appropriate treatment can begin. But is this really the case in working with the suicidal patient? Certainly this approach is necessary when major mental illness is present and appropriate medication selection is needed. However, most suicidal patients require both a diagnostic assessment and an intervention that starts at first contact. For this reason, you should use the assessment process as part of, rather than distinct from, treatment proper.

Take, for example, the initial interview with a suicidal patient. In the two vignettes below, we demonstrate an assessment-focused assessment and a treatment-focused assessment. While reading them, think carefully about the feeling tone created in each sequence.

Assessment-Focused Assessment

Therapist: I understand from what you're telling me that you're under a lot of stress on the job and your marriage isn't going well either. You're obviously pretty depressed . . . have you been thinking about suicide?

Patient: Well, I've had some thoughts like that.

Therapist: Can you tell me how seriously you're thinking about it . . . by that I mean do you have a specific way that you would do it . . . do you think about it pretty much daily?

Patient: I've been thinking about it quite a bit lately but I'm not sure I'd actually do it.

Therapist: Do you have a method or plan about what you would do?

Patient: I usually imagine driving my car through a curve up in the mountains.

Therapist: Have you actually driven your car around that curve and imagined that you went straight?

Patient: Yes, I drive that road quite a bit as part of my job and, sometimes, I imagine that I just end it all. That way, my wife and kids would get my life insurance. At least that way, they'd have something positive to remember me by.

Therapist: So you've been having these thoughts more often lately, is that right?

Patient: Yes, but it's not something I think about all the time; just when I'm having a lousy day. I have had quite a few lousy days lately.

Therapist: Well, I'm hearing some things that make me concerned that you might actually try to kill yourself if you had a real bad day. I'm wondering . . . would you be willing to make an agreement with me that you will not try anything like that without first calling me to talk about it? I'd like us to agree that you won't try anything like this for the time being while we work on your problems.

Patient: I suppose I can agree to that.

Treatment-Focused Assessment

Therapist: You've told me that you've got some pretty big problems in your life right now, including problems with your job and your marriage. Sometimes when people feel like there are no solutions to problems like these, they begin to think about suicide as one way to take care of the problem. Have you thought about suicide as one way of solving these problems?

Patient: Well, I've had some thoughts like that recently.

Therapist: When you think about suicide as an option here, what specific aspects of the problem do you think would be solved if you killed yourself?

Patient: Well, I wouldn't have to go work and deal with my crummy supervisor; if I were dead, then my wife and I certainly couldn't argue as much as we have.

Therapist: So, the thing that you imagine being better if you committed suicide is that you wouldn't have to participate in these conflicts, for example, with your boss or with your wife. Another way of saying this is that suicide might help you with the problem of feeling bad as a result of these interactions. Does that make sense?

Patient: Yeah, I suppose I've just about had it with feeling frustrated and angry all the time. As many times as I've tried to approach the situation more positively, I'm just getting to believe that nothing is really going to make a difference.

Therapist: So, in addition to feeling bad, frustrated, and angry about what these interactions do to you, you're also getting pessimistic that anything you do to solve the problems is going to work, is that right?

Patient: Yeah, I guess it is my last resort, and I feel like I'm getting to that point now.

Therapist: Before you get to that point, would it make sense for us to work together to explore what you've actually done to try to solve these problems and to see if we can't come up with something that might work better and doesn't involve you having to be dead?

Patient: I suppose I can agree to that.

These two vignettes show a contrasting style of approaching the patient's suicidality. Table 3–3 summarizes some pivotal contrasting strategies generated by the assessment-only versus the assessment-/treatment-oriented models. In the more assessment-focused vignette, the therapist is most interested in collecting data about the suicidal behavior per se and trying to determine risk. The implicit focus of the interview is to prevent the occurrence of suicide by examining the patient's intent. Notice that in this approach, very few concepts that are integral to problem-solving treatment have been used. In a sense, the issue of suicide is now on center stage and is the *problem* that the therapist is going to focus on.

Conversely, the treatment-focused approach is more likely to validate and understand the patient's suicidal ideation and increasing suicidal intent. Moreover, the issue is reframed in the context of problem-solving behavior. The effect is to legitimize the occurrence of suicidal ideation as a response to developing pessimism, frustration, and anger, while keeping the door open that other solutions might be available. Although the therapist is asking the patient to defer the decision to commit suicide until other problem-solving options have been examined, this certainly is not the primary clinical intervention. The therapist has also gleaned much information about the patient's affective state and general problem-solving style by *not focusing* on the issue of suicidal behavior. When a patient is acutely suicidal, approaching the problem from this angle immediately reassures the patient. It not only validates what the patient believes is an abnormal, stigmatized event (i.e., thinking seriously about

Table 3–3. Comparison of assessment-/risk-oriented vs. assessment-/treatment-oriented approach to the suicidal patient

Clinical issue	Assessment/risk oriented	Assessment/treatment oriented
1. Focus of session	Assess and manage suicide risk	Reframe suicidality as problem solving
2. Importance of knowing suicide risk factors	Very important, central part of interaction	Less important, collected in problem-solving context
3. Importance of assigning "reliable risk"	Central to type and frequency of treatment	Less important, suicide potential is not predictable
4. Risk management concerns	Very high, focus on risk factors, be prepared to take strong steps to protect patient	Low, suicidal behavior per se cannot be prevented, focus on patient's underlying problems
5. Stance regarding ongoing suicidal behavior	Prohibitive, requires ongoing detection and prevention	Anticipated, forms a basis for collecting data about problem solving
6. Legitimacy of suicidal behavior	It is the problem; the goal is to get rid of it	It is a legitimate but costly form of problem solving
7. Time allotment for discussing suicidality	Much more session time	Much less session time
8. Prevention orientation	Most strategies built around preventing suicidal behavior	Fewer prevention strategies

suicide), but it also begins to create some perspective on how people come to consider suicide as an option. Although the therapist is still able to gather relevant information about the patient's suicidal intent, the general flow of the session is much calmer and more accepting of the patient's suffering and frustration.

Whenever possible, you should attempt to use the problem-solving reframe when discussing suicidal ideation or suicide intent. As described earlier in this chapter, *ideation* refers to the act of thinking about suicide, whereas *intent* represents the patient's developing commitment to engage in some sort of overt behavior. It is important to understand that the movement from ideation to intent is probably based on certain types of cognitive appraisals of suicide as a problem-solving device. Thus problem-solving language is enormously powerful in that it links the patient's prior experience of low-intent ideation with current higher intent as a form of problem solving. The shift from mild ideation to serious intent is scary for the patient and is experienced as a sign of being out of control. When you are able to explain this type of experience in a simple yet credible model, basic features of an acute suicidal crisis are being addressed even while the assessment is being conducted. If you can at the same time validate and normalize intense suicidal ideation while shifting the focus to problem solving and tolerance of emotional pain, there will often be an immediate reduction in suicidal intent and/or ideation.

Using Self-Monitoring to Study Suicidal Behavior

In keeping with the principle that assessment and treatment should be used interchangeably with the suicidal patient, it is important to find ways to incorporate assessment strategies into ongoing treatment. One of the most effective strategies is to use self-monitoring assignments between treatment sessions. Self-monitoring is an incredibly flexible and powerful therapeutic tool, and its reactive treatment effects have been well documented with a variety of clinical problems. Reactive treatment effects occur when the act of collecting the information has an impact on the behavior that is being studied. When a suicidal patient collects information about episodes of suicidal ideation, there is a corresponding shift from a participant mentality to an observer mentality. This cognitive shift is fundamental to many behavior change processes; it is much easier to see what needs to be done from the viewpoint of an observer than it is from the viewpoint of the participant. Suicidal ideation always looks and feels different when it is being studied as opposed to when it is simply being experienced.

This strategy also tends to bring ongoing (and often undisclosed) suicidal ideation or behavior into the mainstream of therapy. For example, if a patient continues to experience suicidal ideation as treatment continues, a self-monitoring assignment can be agreed to that will attempt to identify environmental triggers for suicidal thinking. Along with these triggers, ask the patient to list the associated thoughts and feelings. The patient may keep a daily log of intensity, frequency, and duration of suicidal episodes, or may carefully track the time of day when suicidal ideation tends to occur. These are examples of using what the patient brings into therapy to promote an *aboveboard approach* to suicidality while remaining committed to finding solutions for the patient's real life dilemmas.

Prescribing Self-Monitoring Tasks

Often, the patient feels that resisting thinking about suicide using sheer willpower is the only way to get better. Paradoxically, for many, the more suicidal ideation is resisted, the worse it tends to get. This is truly the epitome of being out of control to most patients. The patient decides to stop thinking about suicide, yet ironically finds the suicidal ideation getting bigger and stronger each day. Prescriptive self-monitoring tasks can reverse this misguided notion about therapeutic change by providing a scientific paradigm in which to study the suicidal behavior rather than resist it. There are times when the patient is so locked in on the willpower strategy that self-monitoring can be used almost in a paradoxical way. You can provide an eloquent rationale for the need to study suicidal impulses so the patient can learn more about their topography. You can predict that it will be very hard for the patient to make the kinds of changes that would be required to problem solve events in a nonsuicidal way without allowing suicidal options to exist. Using a self-monitoring framework, you can distract the patient from the futile task of resisting repetitive and self-reinforcing cognitive processes, knowing that the patient's negative attention in fact acts as a reinforcer for the recurrence of suicidal ideation. Instead, your patient has permission to have the suicidal ideation and record it for further analysis. This communicates your confidence in the patient's capacity to have, and at the same time think about, suicidal impulses. This type of intervention is usually effective with patients who use excessive willpower to get rid of suicidal ideation. It is intended to reduce your patient's level of discomfort about the out-of-control experience of failing at the willpower game.

Collaboration in Data Collection

It is important to develop assignments in collaboration with your patient. This makes the activity relevant to your patient's problems and leads to a greater likelihood that the patient will actually follow through with the assignment. It is important to include your patient in the design of self-monitoring strategies as well as any written forms that are used to keep daily data. The therapist's eye is always on making the process user friendly and focusing on issues that are important to the patient. When a self-monitoring assignment has been generated, you should make sure the patient feels the assignment is possible, given all of the emotional twists and turns in the patient's environment. Your patient should feel ownership for the self-monitoring assignment and how the data is eventually used. This increases the patient's commitment to developing the observer/scientist perspective on the problem as well as yielding much greater compliance rates. The therapist who hands the patient a piece of paper and says, "Here, keep this information for me. It is important," is inviting failure.

It is also important to see such homework activities as an integral part of the intervention structure. These activities are not something that should be tacked on in the last 2 minutes of an interaction with a patient but should be the focus of 15–20 minutes of good, solid collaborative work. When your patient agrees to put in the time and effort to collect information, you cannot ignore or forget about this assignment in the next session. Distressingly, this is what commonly happens when homework assignments are simply tacked on. If a patient goes to the time and effort to produce this information and then is ignored by the therapist in the next session, this type of between-session activity will quickly disappear. The patient has just learned to do less work between sessions.

You should devote the first part of each session to thoroughly reviewing any homework assignments that have been developed with the patient in prior sessions. You should use the information in a way that tells the patient it is linked to the eventual success of therapy. Your patient should be actively involved in the process of looking for trends or for important comparison points. It is useful to start the review process by asking the patient to discuss any possible trends in the information that has been collected since the last session. When a dialogue develops around the patient's perspective on the data, the process is much more likely to lead to important discoveries by the patient.

Using Self-Report Inventories

As mentioned in a prior section, currently marketed suicide risk instruments are of limited predictive value to the clinician. There are, however, occasions when self-report inventories or scaling questions are useful in the process of assessment/treatment. For example, when there is a mental condition such as depression or anxiety disorder present that is related to the patient's suicidal preoccupations, it makes sense to periodically administer depression or anxiety inventories to monitor mood levels. If the therapist is interested specifically in suicide-specific thoughts, then the Beck Hopelessness Scale (Beck and Steer 1988), the Reasons for Living Inventory (Appendix 3), or the scaling questions about problem solving and tolerance for emotional distress can be given. Generally, self-report assessment processes inform the clinician of the patient's current emotional state and can suggest useful therapeutic targets. These assessments also can be used to classify a patient according to a comparison population who are at risk for suicidal behavior. If a patient reports high levels of hopelessness with low importance attached to reasons for living and a positive evaluation of suicide as a problem-solving option, that patient likely has a strong commitment to suicidal behavior. If the patient has been slow to divulge this information, a self-report assessment process can be a lead-in for you to ask the patient directly about the presence of suicidal thinking. Occasionally, you will also want to look at various characteristics of the patient's suicidal behavior repertoire. To this end, the Suicidal Thinking and Behaviors Questionnaire (Appendix 4) is a very useful summary measure. Also recommended for the assessment of contemporary suicidal ideation is Beck's Scale for Suicidal Ideation (Beck et al. 1979), an interview-based measure of the intensity of suicidal thinking. The most important principle is to use assessment devices when they fit a particular purpose relevant to treatment. An example may be to provide a profile of the patient at the outset of therapy or use it for some other specific purpose after therapy has begun. For instance, you may be interested in the amount of change a patient has undergone over the course of several sessions. In this case, it is wise to administer and re-administer these questionnaires.

The principal benefit of using self-report inventories is that they provide a quantifiable way of comparing the patient to various clinical populations and clinical syndromes. Interestingly, patients often feel more positive about the therapist when inventories are used at the outset of therapy. Using inventories often creates the impression that the therapy is credible and that the practitioner is very knowledgeable. For the patient who is scared and out of control, it is reassuring to encounter an interviewer who seems to have special knowledge.

Helpful Hints

♦ It is virtually impossible in the short term to predict who will commit suicide and who will not.

♦ Suicide risk prediction scales may provide useful clinical information but are not able to predict who will commit suicide.

♦ There are different forms of suicidal behavior and each can vary with respect to its frequency of occurrence, duration, or intensity.

♦ The patient's evaluation of suicide as a problem-solving method is strongly related to ongoing suicidal behavior.

♦ Reframe suicidal behavior as problem-solving behavior in the assessment sequence.

♦ Do not differentiate between assessment and treatment with the suicidal patient; use the two strategies interchangeably.

♦ Use self-monitoring (diary keeping) homework assignments to help the patient objectify suicidal behavior.

♦ Be sure to involve (collaborate with) the patient in developing relevant assessment strategies.

♦ Self-report inventories can provide useful clinical information and can be integrated with self-monitoring and interviewing forms assessment.

Selected Readings

Beck A, Schuyler D, Herman I: Development of suicidal intent scales, in The Prediction of Suicide. Edited by Beck AT, Resnik HL, Lettieri DJ. Bowie, MD, Charles Press, 1974, pp 45–56

Beck A, Weissman A, Lester D, et al: The measurement of pessimism: The Hopelessness Scale. J Consult Clin Psychol 42:861–865, 1974

Beck A, Rush J, Shaw D, et al: Cognitive Therapy for Depression: A Treatment Manual. New York, Guilford, 1979

Beck A, Steer RA, Kovacs M, et al: Hopelessness and eventual suicide: a 10 year prospective study of patients hospitalized with suicidal ideation. Am J Psychiatry 142:559–563, 1985

Beck A, Brown G, Steer R: Prediction of eventual suicide in psychiatric inpatients by clinical ratings of hopelessness. J Consult Clin Psychol 57:309–310, 1989

Chiles JA, Strosahl K, Zheng YP, et al: Depression, hopelessness, and suicidal behavior in Chinese and American psychiatric patients. Am J Psychiatry 146:339–344, 1989

Goldstein RB, Black DW, Nasrallah A, et al: The prediction of suicide. Arch Gen Psychiatry 48:418–422, 1991

Linehan M, Goodstein J, Nielson S, et al: Reasons for staying alive when you're thinking of killing yourself: the Reasons for Living Inventory. J Consult Clin Psychol 51:276–286, 1983

Litman R: Predicting and preventing hospital and clinic suicides. Suicide Life Threat Behav 21:56–73, 1991

Pokorny AD: Prediction of suicide in psychiatric patients: report of a prospective study. Arch Gen Psychiatry 40:249–257, 1983

Strosahl K, Chiles J, Linehan M: Prediction of suicide intent in hospitalized parasuicides: reasons for living, hopelessness and depression. Compr Psychiatry 33:366–373, 1992

Strosahl K, Linehan M, Chiles J: Will the real social desirability please stand up? Hopelessness, depression, social desirability and the prediction of suicidal behavior. J Consult Clin Psychol 52:449–457, 1984

Chapter 4

The Origin of
Suicidal Behavior
A Basic Clinical Framework

I n this chapter we provide you with a simple, effective, and clinically useful way of thinking about suicidal behavior. Our focus is on suicidal behavior as a learned method of problem solving. As discussed earlier, the near universality of suicidal experience suggests that this behavior cannot be tied to the presence or absence of a mental disorder, although it certainly is increased in a variety of mental disorders. If the presence of a mental disorder does not fully explain why a patient gets suicidal, then what additional information do you need to have a comprehensive framework from which to build a complete treatment program for your patient? Serious psychopathology must be recognized and treated, and examples of this will be given elsewhere in the book. However, even in the presence of such psychopathology, we have found the model of suicidality presented in this chapter not only helpful but sometimes essential in treating a psychiatrically disordered and suicidal individual. Dealing with suicidal behavior as a distinct and important issue with this type of patient is often a necessary part of a comprehensive treatment package. For example, antidepressants undoubtedly help many depressed and suicidal individuals, but certainly not all, as most painfully evidenced by the number of antidepressant overdoses each year. Conversely, many suicidal individuals do not have a mental disorder and may not benefit from treatments, including pharmacotherapy, targeting that illness. For them, the approach we advocate may well be your most important intervention.

Figure 4–1 shows a learning model of suicidal behavior, derived from a review of the research literature. It is also confirmed by our clinical experience with a wide range of suicidal patients over the last decade. This model emphasizes that suicidal behavior is a form of learned *problem-solving behavior.*

The Role of Problems

Suicidal behavior is viewed by the patient as a legitimate way of solving internal states and/or external problems. *Internal states* are negative feelings, such as depression, anxiety, loss, unremitting boredom, anger, or any number of other unpleasant affective experiences. Emotional pain is a basic ingredient of all suicidal crises. Often there are *external problems* in the patient's life as well. For example, severe feelings of loss or guilt may be triggered by a marital separation or impending divorce. Anger may be precipitated when the patient has been betrayed or undermined by someone who was counted on as a friend or support. A newer concept of stress involves *daily hassles,* or the day-to-day problems that can drive one to distraction. These often accumulate, and one particular daily hassle may function as the proverbial straw that broke the camel's back.

The Role of Learning

The notion that suicidal behavior is *learned* means that it is *shaped* and *maintained* by *reinforcements.* A reinforcement is an event that occurs before or after the suicidal behavior that either rewards it or punishes it. A *reward* is something that encourages more of the behavior. A *punishment* is something that promotes less of a behav-

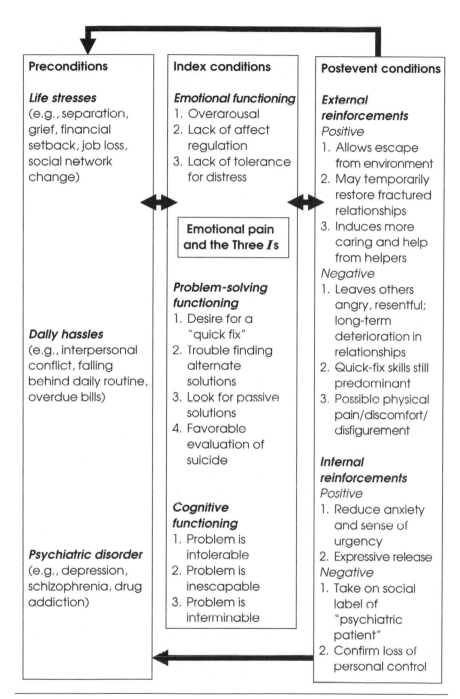

Figure 4–1. A problem solving model of suicidal behavior.

ior. Suicidal behavior is *shaped* by rewards and punishments. Shaping means changing a behavior so it receives maximum rewards and minimum punishments. Continued suicidal behavior is produced by maximizing reinforcements and minimizing punishments. Suicidal behavior, once it is shaped, is *maintained*. The concept of maintenance means that suicidal behavior will remain so long as it continues to receive reinforcement. When *all* reinforcements are removed from the behavior, it will *extinguish* (i.e., it will disappear).

The Role of Reinforcement

Just as suicidal behavior is a response to internal or external problems, the reinforcements are also *internal* or *external*. Internal reinforcements involve changes in one's physical, mood, or mental state. For example, anxiety or fear reduction is an extremely potent internal reinforcer. Many suicidal patients report a sense of relief after making a suicide attempt. The anxiety over whether self-destructive urges can be controlled is gone, even though suicidal behavior has occurred. From then on, a suicide attempt is looked at as a way to relieve the terrible sense of anxiety and internal pressure that is at the heart of an emotional crisis.

External reinforcements are those events that occur in the world as a response to an individual's suicidal behavior, and there are lots of them. Several external reinforcers are shown in Figure 4–1. Of these, the most important positive consequences are *increased attention and caring* and *escape from environmental stresses*. Negative consequences also occur and tend to take longer to develop.

The Role of Short-Term Versus
Long-Term Consequences

To truly understand how suicidal behavior is learned and persists, one must appreciate the difference between short- and long-term consequences. A *short-term consequence* is an immediate effect of suicidal behavior. The time frame can be from minutes to several days. Anxiety relief is a very short-term consequence; it occurs within minutes or seconds of the suicidal act. A *long-term conse-quence* may take weeks, months, or even years to develop. The building anger/resentment of a family member over a suicidal act may take a long time to surface, and it may in fact be overridden by an immediate desire to care for and help the suicidal patient. In general, the short-term consequences of suicidal behavior are pow-erful and positive. Morality aside, it does solve some very difficult problems in the short run.

It is important to emphasize suicidal behavior as a *legitimate* form of problem solving. In the patient's mind, suicide is viewed as a way to successfully solve complex or simple problems. The surrounding culture's fixation with the unacceptability of suicidal behaviors should not mislead the clinician into believing that the patient shares this view. As a class, suicidal patients generally have favorable evaluations of suicide as a way of solving problems. This tension between cultural mores and the often anguished world of an individual who is trying to solve difficult problems is a major dynamic of the helping relationship.

Instrumental Versus Expressive Functions

Another way to think about the problem-solving capacity of suicidal behavior is to see it as having both instrumental and expressive functions. The term *instrumental* function means using suicidal behavior with the intent of solving a problem. For example, killing oneself is an instrumental solution to the problem of suffering unbearable emotional pain. When someone is dead, there is no feeling. Being dead is an instrumental solution for the problem of feeling bad.

Expressive function means that there is a communication value to the act of attempting suicide or of talking to others about suicide. Expressive functions usually have a problem-solving overtone (i.e., an attempt to elicit help or understanding from others, to activate a social network). However these functions can be expres-sions of emotional desperation in their own right. One of the major difficulties you will encounter in working with suicidal communication is making a distinction between instrumental and expressive functions. A misunderstanding can lead to negative labeling of the suicidal patient, especially one who is verbalizing intent. Terms such as *manipulative suicidal communication* often refer to the clinician's sense that suicidal communication is deliberately confusing, irrational, and hostile. In fact, the patient may be expressing a sense of desperation, albeit unclearly. A sound clinical framework involves attention to both the instrumental and expressive components of suicidal behavior. Without this kind of appreciation, it is very likely that you and your patient may proceed on different tracks.

The Suicidal Crisis: A Basic Formula

How is it possible that so many people in the United States can experience a significant suicidal crisis at some point in their lives? It is in fact a potential experience for all of us, given a specific set of conditions referred to in brief as the Three *I*s. Any person has the potential to become suicidal when confronted with a situation that produces emotional pain *and* is believed to be *inescapable, interminable,* and *intolerable* (i.e., the Three *I*s). When the person believes that no effort will be sufficient to solve the problem, it becomes inescapable. When there is no expectation that the situation will change of its own accord if it is not somehow solved, the problem becomes interminable. When the individual cannot tolerate the amount of emotional pain that the situation is producing, the problem is intolerable.

What does it take for a person to find him- or herself in a situation that meets these criteria? There are two prototype situations. The first is an external situation, which by its very nature presents the person with an overwhelming personal challenge. Examples are the sudden loss of job due to bankruptcy of a company, the death of a spouse or child, or contracting a chronic, painful disease. By most objective standards, the person is faced with overwhelmingly negative problems. The second and more pervasive type of situation occurs when the person lacks specific skills to address the demands of a situation that by itself is not overwhelming, but when combined with the person's skill deficits, becomes a major challenge. Examples of these types of situations might be an impending marital separation, disciplinary action on the job, chronic underemployment, or family conflict. For one reason or another, the person is not solving these particular problems well. This leads to more and more negative and action-oriented problem-solving options, among which is the prospect of suicide.

The person seldom looks at suicidal behavior as an option in a problem-solving vacuum. In other words, the suicidal person truly *believes* that all other reasonable attempts to solve the problem have been tried and have failed. As these problem-solving options are removed from the list of possibilities, the new options become more and more extreme, particularly if there is a great deal of emotional pain associated with the problem. Clinical experience suggests that there is an evolution in this regard. Few patients with whom we have worked start out with the assumption that suicide is an effective solution until they have experimented with and failed at less extreme forms of problem solving. Individuals who are repetitiously suicidal have come to believe that suicidal behavior is a solution for almost any problem, be it a major life stress or daily hassle. However, the typical suicidal person is someone who has become convinced over time that there really are no other available problem-solving options. This, in fact, is a key leverage point in intervening with the suicidal patient. Rather than attempting to convince the patient that the act of suicide is intrinsically bad, the focus is on getting the patient to discover that viable problem-solving options have been overlooked or improperly implemented. Every suicidal patient would like to find a less extreme way to solve problems but must have a direct experience that the effort and patience required is worth it. This in a nutshell is what is often referred to as the *ambivalence* of the suicidal patient.

Relationship to Suffering

A pivotal aspect of the suicidal crisis is the patient's relationship to his or her suffering. Our culture places a heavy emphasis on feeling good, and a great variety of technology has been developed to give the appearance that people do not have to suffer. This creates an interesting paradox for the person who is in emotional pain that is not likely to go away. The person struggles with the *willingness to suffer*. Acceptance of suffering is very, very low. When suffering occurs, the person believes that life is being unfair, a tendency that is even more pronounced with the repetitiously suicidal person. Even with the person who has never been suicidal before, there usually is an inner dialogue about pain being bad, abnormal, or a sign of personal weakness. In essence, the pain has to go away because the person will not accept it. This causes tremendous difficulties in regulating emotional arousal, which is often experienced as being out of control. The perception of loss of control is a central feature of all suicidal crises. Notice that the person's self-evaluation processes create the conditions of low pain tolerance. As more and more provocative self-cvaluations occur, acceptance is driven down and the sense of crisis increases. Chronic suicidal behavior occurs when a wider and wider range of situations tap limited problem-solving abilities in a person with an extremely low tolerance for and acceptance of any kind of suffering. Paradoxically, this type of person suffers night and day—life *is not* fair, it is what it is. Although mental disorders may impair pain tolerance, it is likely that low acceptance and pain tolerance skills are distributed normally and are just as likely to *cause* mental conditions such as depression or anxiety. This may explain why many patients with depression are not suicidal and many patients without depression are suicidal.

Some Characteristics of Individuals Prone to Suicide Crisis

With the clinical model in mind, it is easier to make sense of the vast literature on personality and environmental characteristics of suicidal patients. Some of the major characteristics of suicidal patients are listed in Table 4–1. The purpose of this section is to describe how certain of these characteristics will manifest themselves in your office.

Table 4–1. Personality and environmental characteristics of suicidal patients

Cognitive style
1. Black-or-white thinking
2. Rigid, inflexible cognitive style (things just are the way they are)
3. Generalized feelings of hopelessness

Problem-solving style
1. Preference for focusing on short- rather than long-term effects of actions
2. Positive expectancies regarding suicide as a problem-solving strategy
3. Lack of confidence in insight; actions speak louder than words
4. Poor problem-solving abilities
   - Generates less possible solutions
   - Prematurely rejects potentially viable alternatives
   - Exhibits passive problem-solving behaviors
   - Poorly executes problem-solving strategies

Affect regulation
1. Tendency toward chronic feelings of anger, guilt, depression, anxiety, and boredom
2. Inability to regulate emotional arousal in stressful situation (can't turn off feelings)
3. Intense, unstable affect with rapid changes in nature of feelings

Affect tolerance
1. Difficulty tolerating negative affect
2. Restrictive and negative beliefs about the place of negative feelings in the world; bad feelings are wrong
3. Tendency toward impulsive attempts to get rid of affect (e.g., cutting, drinking, drug taking, binge eating)

Interpersonal style
1. Lowered assertiveness, especially when alcohol problems are not present
2. Confusion of assertion and aggression, when alcohol problems are present
3. Frequent severe social anxiety, often accompanied by a feeling of being "evaluated"
4. Tendency toward social isolation, dependency conflicts, or severe mistrust
5. Relationships characterized by excessive conflict and frequent "ups and downs"

Table 4–1. Personality and environmental characteristics of suicidal
patients *(continued)*

Self-control style
1. Use of self-punishment as primary means for modifying behavior
2. Frequent "tandem" addictions (e.g., bulimia and polydrug use)
3. Limited skill repertoire for self-directed change

Environmental variables
1. More severe "single-shot" life stresses (e.g., job loss, separation/
    divorce)
2. Ongoing level of daily stress tends to be elevated
3. Very few competent social supports to buffer stress
    ♦ Significant others may be antagonistic to patient
    ♦ Significant others may be poor role models
    ♦ Significant others may lecture, moralize, or cajole the patient
    ♦ Significant others may offer poor advice (e.g., willpower cure)

Thinking Style

The most widely cited personality feature of the suicidal patient is
cognitive rigidity. The suicidal patient has trouble being flexible. He
or she gets stuck on one and only one version of the problem.
Perspective taking is extremely difficult. In a sense, the patient
cannot back away from life problems long enough to get any fresh
ideas. There is an overreliance on passive problem-solving strategies, which rely on luck, spontaneous change, or the actions of
others. This overreliance leads to the well-known phenomenon of
tunnel vision, which refers to the marked narrowing of the person's
problem-solving field. Problems get defined in rigid, value-laden
terms. This tends to fertilize black-and-white value judgments about
what the person ought to do.

Effective problem solving requires a specific set of skills. Suicidal
people have less of these abilities. It is not clear whether this is a state
or trait phenomenon. Suicidal crises may induce these characteristics,
or they may already exist in individuals who are prone to suicidal
behavior. In any event, the suicidal person generates few alternative
solutions to a particular situation, prematurely rejects effective solutions
as having been tried and failed, and looks for solutions with positive

short-term consequences without much consideration of long-term effects. There is a preference for passive or avoidance-based solutions (e.g., quit a job rather than confront a supervisor).

This problem-solving style leads the suicidal person to regard suicidal behavior as an effective problem-solving device. It precludes having to rely on and influence people in the external world and instead brings control over the solution entirely within the individual. Although it may be argued that suicide is an active form of problem solving, we regard this as the quintessence of passive responding. A common feature of the clinical dialogue with a suicidal patient is the issue of short-term versus long-term consequences. The suicidal patient is interested in short-term fixes and is less than receptive to discussions about the long-term implications of his or her behavior. For example, trying to convince the patient that a failed suicide attempt will probably result in more problems in the long term is generally a futile therapeutic exercise.

Managing Feelings

There are two characteristics of emotional functioning that tend to exacerbate suicidal crises. The first is the lack of effective techniques for regulating emotional arousal. The suicidal person simply has no way of turning off emotional arousal. A common clinical complaint is emotional exhaustion or numbness, related to prolonged exposure to excessive negative emotional arousal. Developing affect-regulating behaviors or cognitions is very important in working through a suicidal crisis. The suicidal patient experiences intense and variable mood states that can change very rapidly, with or without some apparent cause. Often, the patient will complain that feeling bad is hard but not as difficult as intense mood swings. Anxiety, depression, and anger are by far the most common mood states.

The second feature of emotional functioning is low tolerance for and acceptance of emotional pain. As a consequence, impulsive problem solving emerges as a more and more favored type of solution. Intense and prolonged negative affect leads the person to make desperation-driven decisions. This relates to the tendency for addictive behaviors such as drinking, bulimia, or drug use to accompanying suicidal behavior. In the attempt to avoid feeling bad, the person can and will select any number of poisons, including deadly ones.

Social Behavior

Generally, the suicidal person is not interpersonally effective, although it is not clear whether this is a cause or result of suicidal crisis. The suicidal person experiences social anxiety, fear of rejection, or chronic feelings of inferiority. He or she is socially isolated and may have few people who could offer social support. Relationships are often marked by excessive dependency, submissiveness, and avoidance of interpersonal conflict. The suicidal person generally places a premium on maintaining the appearance of normalcy around others. This false togetherness can be misleading to the therapist, who may in fact overestimate the patient's social or behavioral competence. Usually, this superficial competence deteriorates when confronted with the daily flow of life challenges.

Social supports are usually limited both in terms of numbers of potentially helpful persons and in the usefulness of the support that is provided. Principal figures in the support system may be equivocal in their support of the patient. This is particularly true with family members who may at one and the same time be hopeful that the patient will solve problems and be angry that the difficulties existed in the first place. The term *competent social support* acknowledges that some individuals in the patient's social support network are actually the opposite of supportive. In activating the patient's social support network, it is important to identify the real versus the imagined social support structure. Many a therapeutic plan has failed when the patient accesses a social support, only to be barraged with criticism, moralizing, and useless directives.

Behavior Change Skills

Suicidal individuals are poor at applying self-control skills or personal behavior modification strategies. The suicidal person is often perfectionistic and may liberally use punishment and withdrawal of rewards as a means of coercing "better" behavior. Because of the anxiety generated by this self-reinforcement style, the suicidal patient often reports a long history of failed attempts at behavior change. Because the internal self-reward system is dysfunctional, the patient will drift to external reinforcers such as alcohol or drugs because of their rewarding properties. Therapeutic interventions that rely exclusively on self-reinforcement strategies (such as willpower) often do not work. Admonitions to immediately change behavior (just do it) are meaningless because the person usually has negative experiences with willpower cures. The *all you need to do* admonitions, whether from you, a family member, or friend, can be quite disheartening. Advice such as, "Just be nicer to your spouse," or, "Quit worrying about your health," is rarely useful.

Life Stress

Life stress has long been associated with suicidal behavior and is an important way of gauging the degree of disturbance in the patient's environment. Frequently, stresses are chronic (e.g., sustained unemployment, inadequate social network); there also is a much higher than normal rate of acute stresses (e.g., separation/divorce, recent death of loved one). Daily hassles to which the person is continually exposed wear down emotional resistance and probably create a basic predisposition to suicidal crisis when a truly negative life event occurs. A commonly reported problem in working with the suicidal patient, especially the repetitious patient, is the *crisis of the week* syndrome. In essence, the patient presents with some new life stress at each therapy session, making it difficult if not impossible for the therapist to implement a basic treatment plan. This problem suggests there are strong benefits to developing a focus on handling routine matters in one's daily life rather than simply solving big problems. Indeed, the learning model emphasizes that small solutions eventually culminate in generalized change.

Final Comments

A learning-based problem-solving model is a flexible tool for reframing suicidal behavior, both for clinician and patient. It objectifies the process of suicidal behavior, and it tends to reduce the negative self-evaluations within the patient and pejorative labeling by the therapist. This reframe also has a strong normalizing quality to it; it implicitly decreases the patient's sense of social stigma and isolation. The emphasis on finding solutions to problems is far more upbeat than focusing on what is wrong with the patient. The patient spends less time obsessing about whether he or she is crazy and more time focused on solving problems. The interventions that fall out of this approach tend to be bite-sized, concrete, and possible rather than global and personality-change oriented. In turn, there is a greater likelihood that the patient experiences immediate success in destabilizing the Three *I*s. You should always be alert for clinical situations in which the problem-solving model is less applicable, for example, the actively psychotic patient who is hearing command hallucinations to commit suicide. However, even the severely disturbed patient at some point needs to begin solving real-life problems, which no doubt have had a bearing on the development of symptoms in the first place. As soon as the cognitive abilities of your patient are capable of dealing with the rudiments of a problem-solving approach, it is time to use this technique.

Helpful Hints

♦ Suicidal behavior is a learned, reinforced problem-solving behavior that is used when all other options seem to have failed.

♦ The essence of suicidal crisis is a situation that is viewed by the patient as both painful *and* interminable, inescapable, and intolerable (the Three *I*s).

♦ The suicidal patient views suicide as a legitimate problem-solving device, despite any social stigma attached to the behavior.

♦ The suicidal patient has poor problem skills and uses passive strategies in situations that require active strategies.

♦ The thinking style of the suicidal patient is rigid, black or white, and full of "shoulds."

♦ The suicidal patient lacks tolerance for and acceptance of emotional pain.

◆ The suicidal patient has trouble regulating feelings and tends to go "up and down."
◆ The suicidal patient prefers short-term over long-term solutions.
◆ The suicidal patient is poor at developing new behaviors or changing old ones.
◆ The suicidal patient is socially avoidant and has limited social supports.
◆ The environment of the suicidal patient has a larger than expected rate of chronic and acute life stress.

Selected Readings

Blumenthal SJ, Kupfer DJ: Suicide Over the Life Cycle: Risk Factors, Assessment, and Treatment of Suicidal Patients. Washington, DC, American Psychiatric Press, 1990

Linehan M: A social-behavioral analysis of suicide and parasuicide: implications for clinical assessment and treatment, in Depression: Behavioral and Directive Intervention Strategies. Edited by Glazer H, Clarkin JF. New York, Garland, 1981, pp 229–294

Maris R: Pathways to Suicide: A Survey of Self-Destructive Behaviors. Baltimore, MD, Johns Hopkins University Press, 1981

Patsiokas A, Clum G, Luscomb R: Cognitive characteristics of suicide attempters. J Consult Clin Psychol 47:478–484, 1979

Schotte DE, Clum GA: Problem-solving skills in suicidal psychiatric patients. J Consult Clin Psychol 55:49–54, 1987

Section II
The Clinical Treatment Model

 Chapter 5

Outpatient Interventions With the Suicidal Patient

In this chapter, we discuss interventions that you can use with the suicidal outpatient in a range of clinical encounters. These encounters vary from the one-time crisis session where the goal is to stabilize the crisis and refer the patient on for further treatment, to techniques for establishing a longer term treatment relationship. Regardless of the length of your involvement, the chief clinical goal and associated strategies to meet that goal strive for the same result: to establish a consistent, caring, and credible therapeutic framework that will reassure the patient and normalize the suicidal crisis. It is critical that you understand any of your own issues, your "hot buttons," that might confound or undermine this objective. If you skipped over Chapter 2 on moral, ethical, and legal issues in relation to suicidal behavior, we encourage you to go back and examine that chapter closely before proceeding with interventions. The attitude and behavior of the provider are often the most important determinants of successful treatment. The issue of suicidal behavior is so volatile for some therapists that it is better for them to stabilize the immediate situation and refer a patient on to another provider. Know what your tolerances are and what you can and cannot deal with in this area. Knowing your limits is an important part of your competence, not a sign of personal weakness.

An Overview of Treatment Philosophies

A suicidal crisis is a method your patient uses to confront a painful situation that he or she believes to be inescapable, intolerable, and interminable—the Three *I*s—and the goal of your treatment is to change one or more of these *I*s. This is accomplished through experimental, experience-based learning rather than lecturing. You have to show the patient that problems that are viewed as inescapable can in fact be dealt with effectively and sometimes resolved. You have to show that negative feelings vary constantly and are responsive to change in the patient's behavior. You have to show that negative feelings can be tolerated *and* behavior can still be adaptive. When these three goals are even partially obtained, your patient's own competencies and resources have the opportunity to take over and complete the work.

A variety of clinical interventions, focused on learning problem-solving and emotional-acceptance skills, will achieve these objectives (Table 5–1 lists the basic principles of treatment). Your patient must be taught either to use existing *problem-solving abilities* more effectively or learn new problem-solving techniques. This addresses the notion of inescapability by enabling your patient to solve "unsolvable" problems. The patient must develop *self-awareness/self-observation strategies* to observe natural and spontaneous fluctuations in pain levels and to make associations between doing things a little differently and feeling better. Once made, these associations will undermine the belief that emotional pain will stay intense, unwavering, and will last forever. Your patient needs to learn to tolerate *negative feelings* when they do arise through the acquisition of distancing or distraction skills. This will help your patient understand that, although emotional pain is part of life, it does not have to be experienced as acute and overwhelming.

These *three interventions* need to be integrated in a manner that allows your patient to use them to address all sorts of difficulties. Although one objective of therapy is to reduce suicidal behavior, the process for doing this involves helping an individual see how self-observation, problem solving, and emotional pain tolerance are a part of building a quality life. The success of treatment is measured by the capacity to weave these three abilities into the fabric of the patient's life. In other words, do not make a distinction between the patient's journey through life and the patient's particular problem; the two are intertwined and solutions for one are very likely solutions for the other.

Table 5–1. Basic principles of outpatient treatment with the suicidal patient

General approach to suicidal behavior

1. Suicidal behavior is an attempt to solve problems that are viewed as . . .
   - ♦ *Inescapable: You have to show that the problems can be solved.*
   - ♦ *Interminable: You have to show that the negative feelings will end.*
   - ♦ *Intolerable: You have to show the person that he or she can* stand *negative feelings.*
2. Suicidal behavior is usually not effective at solving problems. It generally increases them or brings about new ones.
   - ♦ *Stress that suicide is a permanent solution to what is most often a temporary problem.*
3. Feeling suicidal is a valid, understandable response to emotional pain.
   - ♦ *Focus heavily on understanding statements about this person's pain.*
4. Establish the fact that it is acceptable to talk openly and honestly about suicide.
   - ♦ *Be matter of fact.*
   - ♦ *Consistently assess for suicidal ideation and self-injurious behavior.*
   - ♦ *Avoid value judgments about the act of suicide as cowardly, sinful, or vengeful.*
5. Take a collaborative, rather than confrontive approach, to the issue of suicidal behavior.
   - ♦ *Beware of power struggles over the occurrence of suicidal behavior.*
   - ♦ *Offer assistance on how to solve the problem(s) but beware of willpower type advice.*
6. Offer attention and caring that is not contingent on suicidal behavior.
   - ♦ *Make random support phone calls.*
   - ♦ *Positive behavior assignments.*
7. Where possible, identify specific skill deficits that could be corrected in structured behavioral training
   - ♦ *Interpersonal skills*
   - ♦ *Stress management skills*
   - ♦ *Problem-solving skills*
   - ♦ *Self-control skills*

Reconciling and Suicidal Behavior

The concept of *reconciling opposites* is critical for an effective understanding of and working with the suicidal patient. At heart, the suicidal patient is a black-and-white thinker who often struggles with conflicting beliefs about the same issue. For example, happiness and sadness are opposites; the patient views one as good, the other bad. However, neither can exist in a meaningful way without the other. Reconciling the necessity of having both happiness and sadness in one's life lends full meaning to the actual experiences of happiness and sadness. Although this is not a new concept, most modern-day therapies do not work specifically at reconciling opposites and could be better characterized as *linear*. Specifically, heavy emphasis is placed on the role of logic and deductive reasoning as a way to run one's life. Thus, if the therapist can show that the advantages of suicide do not outweigh the disadvantages, the patient is expected to be rational and drop the suicidal behavior. When the patient does not go along with this, the therapist might express frustration with the failing treatment process by attaching such labels as "resistant," "oppositional," or "manipulative" to the patient. When the patient perceives that this labeling is occurring, a natural defensiveness can emerge that can create polarization and an adversarial relationship.

In contrast, the process of reconciliation involves learning to honor and value polarities rather than feel that one of them must vanquish the other. This creates a gray zone of understanding that is necessary for psychological health. Unreconciled contrasts are at the heart of the suicidal patient's world. Some of these contrasts are over whether to live or die; about being good or bad, normal versus abnormal, in control versus out of control; whether to approach or avoid emotional pain; whether to confront or hide from interpersonal conflict/rejection; and whether to be passive or active in a general approach to the world. In fact, tunnel vision in suicidal crisis occurs when the patient literally is unable to see more than one pole at a time.

To use reconciling processes therapeutically, it is important to understand that the tendency to search for the *right meaning* is equally seductive for both the patient and the therapist. People in distress experience an ever-present temptation to unilaterally decide on a particular kind of meaning to the exclusion of potentially opposite kinds of meanings. For example, a suicidal crisis is actually about living *and* dying, not the triumph of dying over living. To develop an affirmation of life, one must also understand that life can and will produce desperately low moments. These two poles must simultaneously be *in focus* for effective behavioral and emotional functioning. This is hard work for the therapist who is feeling pressure to do something constructive and optimistic in the heart of a suicidal crisis. Sometimes the most effective moments of therapy occur when the therapist models an acceptance of these competing forces.

When a suicidal patient indicates that the current level of suffering is unacceptable, he or she is in effect rejecting the reality and validity of pain and pleasure. Any individual who consistently fails to accept these opposites runs a grave risk of engendering tremendous amounts of suffering. This is because there is no *balance* that the individual can attain when suffering is present. Both you and your patient need to understand that the dilemma is in how to be both in control and out of control. By letting go of control, suicidal patients can attain balance. In fact, control is the problem, not the solution (see Hayes 1987).

The goal of establishing *balance* through reconciliation is essential not only for the immediate suicidal crisis, but also for developing a more robust adaptation to subsequent periods of pain and suffering. As an example, when you teach your patient to look at all sides of the issue when describing an experience, you are teaching an acceptance of opposites. When you join experiences that look mutually contradictory and help your patient make room for it, your patient learns that both can coexist within the same human being; one does not have to vanquish the other. In the linear mode, this is referred to as the *ambivalence* of the patient about dying; in the reconciling mode, these are concepts of life and death resonating against one another. We leave it to you to figure out which explanation sounds like a problem and which sounds like a resolution.

The Role of Suicidal Behavior in Therapy

The therapist is inviting failure if the sole goal of therapy is to prevent suicidal behavior in the patient. If suicidal behavior occurs again after therapy has started, and it sometimes does, the therapist may feel both defeated by and angry at the patient. An alternative view is that there is a continuity between real life and therapy that will not change because the patient enters treatment. There is little reason to believe that most individuals will stop being suicidal simply because they come in to your presence. It is helpful to remember the old saying: "It is much better to ride in the same direction as the horse." Avoid defining the context as one in which success is measured by whether the patient thinks about suicide or makes an attempt. Make it crystal clear that the recurrence of suicidal behavior is regrettable, but do not assume that the very problem the patient is seeking help for will disappear solely as a consequence of entering treatment. If that were true, the act of entering treatment would *be* the treatment. We could discharge every patient after (or perhaps before) the first contact. Beware of the dilemma your rescue fantasies can produce. As a profession, we do not take kindly to people who are reluctant to be rescued. Working with a suicidal person rarely involves an instant save. Your first task is to get down to the hard work of developing a consistent, honest, and caring approach.

The Initial Contact

Table 5–2 presents the most important objectives of the initial meeting with a suicidal patient. These objectives are valid whether the contact is the first in a series of repeated therapeutic contacts, a one-time session to generate referral, or a crisis management session.

The main goal of the treatment session is to reframe suicidal behavior as a problem-solving behavior and to provide the assurance and emotional support the patient needs. There is usually a sense of urgency and difficulty present. The goal is to form a working relationship with your patient and to respond to the many concerns that go along with a potentially explosive situation. At this initial meeting, you need to attend to simple realities. Documentation of various aspects of suicidality is important (see the Suicidal Thinking and Behaviors Questionnaire in Chapter 10). However, there is little likelihood that a brilliant maneuver or bad gaffe will prevent or precipitate a suicide, respectively. The odds against the patient dying by suicide are quite high, and, as noted earlier, risk factors are of little use to you in making a prediction. Accordingly, the definition of a quality contact is not simply keeping your patient alive but rather the degree to which you begin to collaborate on building better solutions in the patient's life.

There is a *checking out* process that can be the most dominant characteristic of the initial encounter with the suicidal patient. Your patient is ascertaining your attitudes about suicide. Do you label it as

Table 5–2. Goals and strategies of the initial session with the suicidal patient

Goal	Strategies
1. Reduce the patient's fear over suicidality.	1A. "Normalize" suicidal behavior.
	1B. Legitimize feeling suicidal in the current context.
	1C. Talk about different forms of suicidal behavior calmly and openly.
2. Reduce the patient's sense of emotional isolation.	2A. Validate the patient's sense of pain.
	2B. Form collaborative set with patient.
	2C. Validate the presence of the Three *I*s.
	2D. Look for competent social supports.
3. Activate problem solving in the patient.	3A. Reframe suicidal behavior as problem-solving behavior.
	3B. Isolate any spontaneous positive problem solving and praise it.
	3C. Develop idea of studying suicidal behavior in the context of problem solving.
	3D. Form short-term positive action plan (3–5 days).
4. Provide emotional and problem-solving support until follow-up care is engaged.	4A. Form crisis card with patient (discussed in Chapter 7).
	4B. Schedule support call.
	4C. Initiate medication regime where appropriate.
	4D. Set follow-up appointment or refer patient on.

abnormal, do you become anxious or upset, or do you seem to accept it and move on? Your patient is checking to see what you do about suicidal behavior per se. Are you going to take an invasive, directive approach or a less-invasive, more-tolerant approach? Most importantly, your patient is checking to see whether you seem comfortable talking about and dealing with the patient's own sense of desperation.

Some clinicians experience a form of desperation in this initial session: a sense of needing to do something definitive or risk losing the patient. This in itself creates a sense of anxiety within this initial session. The suicidal patient can be extremely sensitive to signs of discomfort on the part of the clinician. In other words, a nervous, pressured therapist creates a nervous, pressured client. Your composure and confidence are at least as important as the content of the interventions agreed to in the first meeting. Although there is an impact associated with using specific techniques, it is better to have a relaxed, matter-of-fact, calm clinician using a few techniques than a nervous, jittery, anxious clinician using many techniques.

The key outcome of the initial encounter is to validate your patient's emotional pain while creating a problem-solving set. Initially, the suicidal patient is preoccupied with negative feelings and has a limited sense of problem-solving options. You must help your patient begin to understand and become more comfortable with emotional distress. This is best done by having your patient talk about the life circumstances involved in the crisis. Even if your patient is chronically suicidal, there are usually precipitating events, however trivial, that have increased emotional pain and desperation. You repeatedly can take the opportunity to produce empathetic statements about the patient's sense of desperation without necessarily agreeing that the situation is indeed unsolvable, as in the following example: "The problems you have told me of are difficult ones. Almost anyone in your position would feel depressed and angry."

Validating emotional pain is made more difficult if you are eager to rescue. There is a tendency to jump over the patient's pain and get to the business of finding solutions and saving people. This is a frequent reason for a negative outcome in the first encounter. Remember, the patient must understand that you believe feeling suicidal is a valid, understandable response to emotional pain. When a patient's pain is not being heard, the patient may elevate the pain message to the point that it drowns out all subsequent activities in the session. In the worst case, the patient's suicidal potential may increase because the expressive component of the suicidal crisis has been downplayed or ignored. Tactics such as suggesting that the patient's level of emotional pain is not justified by the actual facts or that the patient has a lot to be thankful for (i.e., life is better than you think it is) almost are guaranteed to produce losing results.

The second major goal of this first encounter is to establish a problem-solving framework. Your use of language is critical. The way in which problems are reframed will help establish a clear connection between failed problem solving and suicidal behavior. Avoid making judgments as to whether your patient has truly tried to solve problems or not. Accept that the patient's prior attempts to solve problems may have met with limited success. At the same time, acknowledge that your patient views suicidal behavior as a *legitimate* problem-solving option. In a way this is obvious, for otherwise suicidality would not be part of the crisis. Even if your patient is ambivalent about following through with suicidal behavior, that ambivalence is no different than the ambivalence associated with pursuing any other solution. All solutions have positive and negative consequences associated with them and, to a degree, all solutions produce some level of ambivalence. The following clinical encounter illustrates how to use information to reframe a patient's difficulties within a problem-solving context.

Therapist: What brings you in here today?
Patient: I've really been having a hard time lately. I've lost my job and I'm not getting along well with my wife, and we've been talking about separating. I don't know where I'd live if we did separate and I'm not sure that I could stand losing her.
Therapist: How does that make you feel?
Patient: Well, I go from feeling really anxious about what's going to happen to figuring that there's no hope and it's all going to end up bad. The reason I came here is because I've been thinking more and more about just ending it all. This is really

starting to get scary. I've never felt this way before and I'm beginning to wonder if I have control over what I'm going to do.

Therapist: It sounds like the situation is really difficult for you; there are lots of big losses and big question marks in your life. You're experiencing a lot of painful feelings, I can tell. I'm curious, would you say that suicide would be one way of solving these problems?

Patient: Well, I'm just tired of feeling bad, that's all I know.

Therapist: What is it about your attempts to solve these problems up to now that has led you to feel so bad?

Patient: Well, everything I've tried with my wife hasn't really changed the situation and I don't see any prospect of getting work. I've put in several job applications and all I keep getting is *Nos*.

Therapist: So you're feeling really desperate because nothing you've tried with your partner seems to be working and there's no prospect in sight for getting a new job. That must bring up a lot of fears about being alone and not having money.

Patient: Yeah, it sure does, and I'm not going to live my life that way.

Therapist: So, what you're saying is that if you can't solve these problems, you'd rather be dead than to live the life you imagine unfolding in front of you.

Patient: Yeah, that's pretty much it.

In the dialogue above, the therapist both instituted a problem-solving set and strongly validated the patient's sense of emotional desperation. Notice that there is less emphasis on suicidal ideation as the *problem* and more emphasis on the patient's view of suicide in the problem-solving context. This strategy allows the intervener to avoid a showdown over the validity of suicidal problem-solving options while at the same time joining with the patient's desperation around feeling bad and seeing no way out. Giving the patient permission to feel desperate and to see suicide as a potential option (even if it is not the best option) has an ameliorative impact on the patient's sense of crisis. The patient is scared by the occurrence of suicidal ideation in the first place. Creating a larger frame of reference tends to defuse the self-control issue that is inherent in suicidal crisis. The problem-solving frame provides a different way of looking at the occurrence of suicidal behavior that lets the patient take some distance from it. This is a fundamental aspect of working with the suicidal patient during crisis.

Another way to establish a problem-solving set is to use humor. Although you should avoid humor that condescends to the patient or belittles emotional pain, it is often very effective to use a play on words or a pun in relation to suicide. Your sense of humor in such circumstances has a way of defusing the seriousness attached to the crisis. For example, you might end a session by saying, "I was just reading a study yesterday that conclusively showed that all treatment is ineffective with dead clients. Thought you might like to know." Use humor in a manner that implies your confidence in your patient's ability to exercise self-control and get through the problem. This strategy can destabilize the patient's rigid cognitive framework and is one of the chief ways of challenging any one of the Three Is.

The most desired outcome in this first contact is to establish that it is okay to talk matter-of-factly, directly, and openly about suicide and that there is a credible framework that explains how suicidal behavior can occur. This framework will provide an alternative to the patient's operating concepts, which usually involve mental illness, laziness, personal inadequacy, and/or loss of self-control.

The initial encounter should end with a plan of attack formulated and agreed to by you and your patient. This plan may involve an arrangement for the patient to contact another provider or to have a follow-up session. In this formulation, it is essential that you focus on small tasks rather than develop elaborate assignments. It is far more important for the patient to experience a small success than it is to strive for rarely obtained miracles. Often, it is helpful to ask, "If we could select a small task that, if you accomplished it, would tell you that things were just a little better, what would that be?" Together, you may form an activities plan that will change your patient's unrewarding daily routine or accomplish a specific task that is viewed as a positive step forward. If you plan a follow-up appointment, consider the use of a self-monitoring activity to increase the patient's observation and mental awareness of natural fluctuations in both negative states such as hopelessness, intolerance of emotional pain, or suicidal ideation and positive states such as humor, appreciation of beauty in the surroundings, and kindly thoughts.

In the event your patient will return for follow-up counseling, please read Chapter 7, which discusses case management and crisis intervention techniques. Many of the strategies in that chapter would normally be part of the concluding moments of this initial contact. This will include such things as setting up a crisis protocol with the patient, agreeing to an after-hours emergency protocol, and regular self-monitoring activities. Encourage your patient to focus on any moments when the situation seems to spontaneously be just a little bit better between now and the next session. Encourage the patient to be sensitive to spontaneous positive occurrences while sympathizing with the likely continuation of negative emotions. If the patient is going to see another provider, summarize together the key ingredients of the initial contact, with special emphasis on what your patient thought was helpful. This should be carefully relayed to the next provider so as to increase continuity of care.

The Early Stage of Treatment

The main goals and strategies for the continuation of treatment with the suicidal patient are listed in Table 5–3. The principal points to be achieved in the early phase of treatment are to install and reinforce a problem-solving set in the patient, to develop the patient's sense of competency to deal with emotional pain, and to begin solving problems in the real world. Remember, the essence of the suicidal patient's dilemma is, on the one hand, being exposed to severe life obstacles that tax coping resources while at the same time using assumptions about the role of suffering that paralyzes an adaptive response.

Learning to Find Solutions

The immediate suicidal crisis may dissipate as a consequence of the first session or it may continue on into the next several sessions. In

Table 5–3. Goals and strategies in continuing treatment with the suicidal patient

Goal	Strategies
1. Destigmatize suicidal behavior.	1A. Develop personal scientist climate. 1B. Use self-monitoring assignments. 1C. Teach situational approach.
2. Objectify the patient's suicidal behavior.	2A. Use problem-solving reframe. 2B. Provide ongoing validation of emotional pain—suicidal behavior relationship. 2C. Move suicidal behavior "off center." 2D. Calmly and directly discuss past, present, and likely future of suicidal behavior.
3. Address likelihood of recurrent suicidal behavior.	3A. Develop agreements with patient about after-hours and other unplanned contacts, behavioral crisis protocol. 3B. Reaffirm that crisis card is "workable" (see Chapter 7). 3C. Formulate a crisis management plan with likely contact points.
4. Activate problem-solving behavior in the patient.	4A. Teach personal problem-solving skills. 4B. Develop better understanding of short-term vs. long-term consequences. 4C. Look for spontaneously occurring problem-solving behavior and praise it. 4D. Set up small, positive problem-solving plans. 4E. Teach specific skills necessary for better personal or interpersonal functioning.
5. Develop emotional pain tolerance in the patient.	5A. Approach suicide as an emotional avoidance behavior. 5B. Teach distinction between just having vs. getting rid of feeling. 5C. Instill contextual approach to negative thoughts and emotions. 5D. Use acceptance exercises to teach distancing skills. 5E. Emphasize experiential contact with emotional willingness vs. suffering.
6. Develop specific interpersonal and problem-solving skills.	6A. Interpersonal skills. 6B. Problem-solving skills.

(continued)

Table 5–3. Goals and strategies in continuing treatment with the
suicidal patient *(continued)*

7. Develop intermediate-term life direction.	7A. Use "What do you want your life to stand for?" exercise.
	7B. Commitment to live life with negative thoughts and feelings.
	7C. Emphasize the process of striving for goals over the importance of reaching goals.
	7D. Set up intermediate-term goals and concrete, positive initial steps.
8. Terminate treatment with appropriate follow-up support.	8A. Develop relapse prevention plan.
	8B. Agree to a session-tapering schedule.
	8C. Reframe longer between-session intervals as "field trials."
	8D. Set up regular "booster" sessions.

general, better functioning patients, patients who are dealing with
significant problems but have reasonable interpersonal skills, tend to
resolve faster than patients who have underlying character disorders.
Regardless of the speed of resolution, the work in this phase of
treatment is to develop an acceptance of the crisis per se and a
commitment to find and act upon solutions. Your specific strategy is
twofold: to teach your patient how to *make room* for emotional pain
and suffering as a way of minimizing the impact of pain and
suffering, and to get your patient to look at solutions other than
suicide. Always, your treatment philosophy is that there may well be
better solutions; at the same time, you continue to make room for
suicide as an option your patient may continue to consider. *Never*
create a situation in which your patient is uneasy discussing suicide
with you.

From the initial session to the end of treatment, you must
continue to assault the stigma associated with suicidal behavior.
Your patient will often continue to harbor secret thoughts that
suicidal ideation or behavior is abnormal and cannot be "accepted."
Constantly take your patient's weekly hassles that lead to increased
suicidal ideation and integrate them more objectively into the problem-solving model. The idea is to help your patient see the flow of

events starting from the situation, building from a sense of frustration or blockage, and ending with the development of suicidal ideation. Therapy shifts attention from suicidal behavior per se to problem-solving behaviors that did or did not work, or were not tried, prior to the emergence of suicidality. Your patient learns over time that suicidal behavior is a natural offshoot of ineffective problem solving, especially when intense emotional duress is present.

Your patient should learn the concept of *situational specificity,* a hallmark of cognitive-behavioral interventions. Specific situations tend to elicit particular and unique cognitive, emotional, and behavioral responses; many of these are conditioned responses that may have outlived their usefulness. This concept assumes that suicidality is never experienced at a steady-state level. Instead, upswings in suicidal behavior are related to specific situations. These situations may appear trivial to the outside observer, but the interpretive weight, the sense of meaning attached to them by the patient, make them critical determinants of daily functioning. Just as the clinically depressed patient can see a piece of burnt toast as a symbol of all that is wrong with his or her life, a suicidal patient can envision similarly trivial events in the same way. This is not just the province of depression; it is the province of individuals who are not adapting well, who are frustrated and in pain.

Self-monitoring refers to the act of collecting information about one's thoughts, feelings, and behavior. These assignments are an elegant way of making a connection between the therapy process and the patient's real-life suicidal behavior without inadvertently overfocusing on suicidal behavior. You may have your patient keep a log of daily suicidal ideation with an intensity rating attached to it, an exercise that allows the patient to see firsthand that suicidal ideation may fluctuate dramatically from hour to hour. Another instrument of considerable utility is the daily positive events diary, compiled at the end of each day. The patient lists things that seemed to work reasonably well for that day. This type of self-monitoring helps your patient refocus attention on things that work well as opposed to things that are problematic. These strategies are designed to destabilize the patient's notions about what is wrong and to develop a new outlook on suicidal behavior.

Through this therapeutic process, your patient learns to identify situations that tend to trigger more emotional distress or lead to reduced tolerance for distress. Usually patterns begin to appear that reveal both the patient's underlying vulnerabilities and positive coping resources. Table 5–4 presents a typical self-monitoring form targeting episodes of increased *suicidal ideation*.

The example in Table 5–4 highlights *trigger* situations. It seems to involve the patient's spouse but does not generalize to similar situations with co-workers. This may suggest that the person has assumptions about the unacceptability of being criticized or abandoned by someone close. To teach effective problem solving, the patient must learn to break these situations down into bite-sized pieces. Trying to cope with feeling rotten all the time is an overwhelming task. Redressing a specific situation that produces emotional pain is within the realm of possibility. You and your patient can role-play the situation and experiment with alternative strategies for managing negative feelings.

With self-monitoring assignments, set the situation so that it is hard for your patient to fail. Beware of edicts such as, "You should make entries in your log *at least* two or three times a day." Accept the patient's reports and use them in a positive way. When your patient sees that more systematic reporting would be useful, he or she likely will do so. Many clinicians stumble badly around the issue of homework with suicidal patients and take compliance to be a measure of the patient's willingness to get better (i.e., resistance). Your general rule of thumb is to make sure that homework is seen as relevant by the patient and is packaged in bite-sized bits so that your patient cannot fail. For example, if the patient indicates some reluctance to keep a written record, you might say, "You know, there are two types of people in the world: people who make lists and people who don't. You figure out which type you are and collect this information in a way that works for you." If necessary, let the patient keep mental notes. Even if your patient brings in a seemingly trivial mental note, heap praise on the patient and use the material.

An important and empowering goal in this phase is to help your patient recognize which coping responses are working and which

Table 5–4. A sample weekly suicidal behaviors diary

Instructions: Each time you have a significant increase in suicidal ideation, please complete each of the columns below. Try to answer each column as this will help us understand your suicidal behavior.

Date	Situation	Negative thoughts	Negative feelings (rate standability 1–100)	Suicidal thoughts/behavior (rate intensity and episode length 1–100)	Other problem-solving attempts (rate workability 1–100)
5-4	Received a letter from wife's attorney requesting property accounting.	1. She's going to clean me out—I won't be able to go through this.	Afraid (20)	◆ I don't want to go on with this. (60)	◆ Took a long walk. (45 minutes) (30)
		2. She lied to me about trying to work it out. I was a sucker to ever believe it.	Anger (30)	◆ I just keep feeling worse and worse. (70)	◆ Talked to my lawyer. (70)
			Guilt (50)	◆ At least my children would get insurance if I did it right. (30)	◆ Tried to reach my brother but failed. (0)
		3. I will be alone again; maybe it's for the better.	Lonely (70)	◆ There's no reason for waiting. (10) (80) Length: 2 hours	◆ Tried to look at the bright side. (5)

are not. It is easier to get a patient to enlarge on existing skills than to teach new problem-solving skills. Even the actively suicidal patient is solving some problems in daily life. Unfortunately, the patient's perceptual set and associated self-talk is focused on what is not working and, accordingly, effective problem-solving efforts are overlooked. Your job is to help balance the picture by also focusing on and reinforcing efforts that are succeeding. Using the problem-solving model, you can avoid making value judgments simply by asking the patient to rate whether a particular coping strategy seemed to work.

For example, you can ask in a direct, somewhat curious way whether thinking about suicide in a specific situation worked as well as the patient might have hoped. The patient might reply immediately that it seemed to work better than just feeling bad; then on reflection, the patient might indicate that it did not really work for more than a few minutes. Mention that there seem to be both short-term and longer term consequences that attend to any problem-solving behavior. This technique may help your patient to increase coping behaviors that are working reasonably well and at the same time begin an evaluation of behaviors that are frustrating and not solving anything. Praise spontaneous occurrences of effective problem solving and build on the patient's strengths. As your patient feels more competent, effective, and *response-able,* stressful situations are inherently less intolerable, interminable, and inescapable.

This process is enhanced when you use the *personal scientist* approach, an approach basic to the cognitive behavioral model of treatment (see Beck et al. 1979). Ask your patient to try out the mind-set of being a scientist investigating his or her own behaviors. This approach can help your patient objectify problems, collect critical pieces of information for the evaluation process, and then modify responses according to the input. The patient can collect data in between sessions to test certain ideas. The emphasis is on developing responses that *really* work as opposed to responses that *ought to* work. When a new response is tried out, it is viewed as an experiment. That means, you explain, that the response may not work. All problem-solving activities are viewed as needing revision and change; there is no emphasis on success versus failure. Even the recurrence of suicidal behavior is labeled as an opportunity to investigate what worked and what did not with a specific problem. At a deeper level, the balance inherent in this approach (i.e., focusing on both strengths and weaknesses) makes it an important component of the treatment process.

Clinical Pitfalls of the Early Stage of Treatment

A common error in the early part of treatment is to inadvertently focus the process of therapy around the presence versus absence of suicidal behavior. Often, this initial suicidality is quite intense even though it may be very short-lived. You may respond to this intensity by loading up on interventions designed to prevent suicidal behavior, with the unintended impact of narrowing the focus of therapy. In your efforts, you need to maintain an effective balance between intervening with the suicidal behavior while setting the stage for a broader range of interventions that will occur down the road.

A second pitfall is the tendency to move faster than your patient's condition will allow. You need to remember that a principal motivation of the patient may be to please others and be accepted. With all the urgency surrounding the suicidal crisis, the patient may mislead you about his or her actual level of functioning. To avoid this, you must constantly check out interventions with the patient and then help trim the interventions down to bite-sized bits. This gives your patient permission to go slow and makes it clear that you are quite happy with a pace that allows for a thorough understanding of what is transpiring. It is not the speed of change per se in which you are interested. It is the capacity of your patient to understand how change occurs and to build on that capacity.

A final pitfall is what is known as the *halo effect,* a phenomenon whereby your patient automatically reports doing better partly because of the halo or positive context of seeking therapy. This effect can produce a brief period of improvement, but this improvement is often followed by a strong rebound into suicidal crisis. This can catch you by surprise and can lead to conflict, confrontation, and premature termination. The key intervention is to be positive about positive change while acknowledging that learning is an irregular process. A train never leaves the station smoothly. It always starts with bumps and jerks. This is a handy analogy for this process. (Maybe your patient can think of a better one!) It is important to accept that functioning may be worse this week than it was the last week and to do so in a way that does not abandon optimism about progress over time. Remind your patient that even though things are going better right now, do not be surprised if some of the same problems resurface in the near future. Emphasize the importance of working with both positive and less-positive outcomes in the overall learning process.

Session Logistics and Course of Treatment

It is common practice to see a suicidal patient more often early in therapy and then to have regular, less-frequent sessions as the situation stabilizes. This approach may inadvertently reinforce your patient for being in crisis because more of your attention is forth-coming if the patient remains in crisis. The decision about session frequency must be geared to the patient's longer term functioning and the degree to which the suicidal crisis is likely to respond to more intensive treatment. This may involve addressing the patient's fear about going a whole week without any contact with you. In addressing (problem solving) these fears, you may schedule an additional session or set up a telephone contact at a specific time midway through the week. Generally, the more chronic the suicidal behavior, the less one should use additional session scheduling. An important goal with the chronic patient is to teach emotional tolerance. This is achieved when your patient realizes that regular sessions are helpful *and* that the distress experienced between sessions can be tolerated and somewhat mastered. With better-functioning patients, use one to two sessions a week in the acute phase if clinical benefits accrue. The usual session frequency is once weekly; you can go to once every other week as the situation stabilizes and your patient is able to conduct more and more *fieldwork* and personal scientist activities between sessions. There is actually a benefit in scheduling biweekly sessions. It takes time to collect data about situational triggers; many of the important situations do not occur weekly.

There is no preset length of time or number of sessions associated with this initial phase of treatment. Broadly speaking, look for indications of your patient's acceptance and spontaneous use of the problem-solving mind-set in session. Another important indication that initial-phase work has been completed is your patient's belief that you understand the patient's sense of desperation and pain. Some patients will move through this phase in one or two sessions, whereas other patients may take months. Finally, look for indications of experimentation with problem-solving strategies in the field. This may involve even rudimentary attempts to use alternative strategies for dealing with stress and emotional pain.

The Intermediate Phase: Developing the Acceptance of Feelings and a Commitment to Act

We all know that every crisis provides an opportunity, and the depth of a suicidal crisis is an opportunity for your patient to develop a better understanding of suffering and its role in the experience of the world. Many people who have worked through suicidal behavior describe what they have learned in these terms. The primary goal during this phase of treatment is to help your patient develop a tolerance for emotionally distressing events. The focus is on learning that emotional pain can be tolerated and brought to a resolution. Your patient must understand that the meaning of events and associated suffering is produced in the private realm of his or her own thoughts, feelings, and thoughts about feelings. Emotional distress is a direct result of accepting one way of thinking about things instead of another. Think of this as your patient *attaching* to certain *hot* cognitions. Low tolerance arises when these hot cognitions refer to the unacceptability of feeling bad. For example, many hopelessness cognitions are hot because they raise provocative implications about suffering (i.e., there is no purpose in staying alive if one has to suffer). It is only logical to assume that the patient will experience depression, anxiety, despair, sadness, and, eventually, suicidal ideation, in relation to these thoughts.

Two major therapeutic models can be followed during this phase of therapy. The more conventional route is to use cognitive therapy to help the patient develop more realistic self-talk about either the life events or the negative feelings that occur in relation to life events. This is a more traditional and cultural supported approach because it relies on logic as a way to change the patient's thinking, feeling, and behaving. The suicidal patient is always a victim of taking a particular stand with regard to a difficult life situation. For example, the phenomenon of tunnel vision is not limited to the suicidal depressive patient, but is a characteristic or feature of the suicidal patient in general. You and your patient should work collaboratively to uncover critical cognitive errors and construct field tests of their validity. In cases in which the patient clearly agrees there is a distorted interpretation, he or she can experiment with a more reasonable interpretation and see if it works better the next time the situation occurs. Many of the deeper assumptions that indirectly or directly lead to suicide as a viable option can be examined by the patient and clinician. (The interested reader is urged to study the work of Beck et al. [1979].)

A second approach, and one we often favor, is to develop an acceptance of emotional pain through the use of distancing and nonevaluative self-observation strategies. The key goal in this approach is to learn to *make room* for distressing thoughts and feelings while doing what needs to be done to respond to the demands of the outside world. There are two key strategies for increasing acceptance of uncomfortable emotions and thoughts: First, *recontextualization* is the process of teaching your patient to look at the relationship of thoughts, feelings, and behaviors in a way that provides more options for handling problems. Second, the act of *comprehensive distancing* involves stepping back from one's thoughts and feelings and looking at them as an observer rather than a participant.

Recontextualization

Each day brings all of us an incredible array of thoughts and feelings. Humans literally process thousands of cognitive and emotional experiences daily, usually with only minimal awareness. These processes are not unconscious because they can be accessed directly through voluntary shifts of attention. They are better thought of as automatic conditioned responses. Many of us tend to treat thoughts and feelings as if they were literal substitutes for experience; that is, cognitions and emotions are put in a position of being at least as real as the reality they represent.

For people in acute or chronic crisis, thoughts and feelings take on a consistently negative overtone. The relationship your patient establishes with negative thoughts can be viewed as the *cause* of suffering. The analogy to use is the distinction between chronic pain and disability. Some people are able to live with chronic pain by realizing they now have new limitations and the job is to carry on with life. They accept the pain and continue their life's work, embracing challenges as they come. On the other hand, the chronic pain patient sees pain as a reason why life *cannot* go on, at least not until a cure is produced that will get rid of the pain. Many people in the grip of these chronic pain emotions and cognitions seem fixed on the idea that such a cure is somehow, somewhere available, and they suspend many aspects of their lives as they search, often futilely, or wait, often angrily, for relief. For these persons, pain becomes a reason for not working, not participating in family life, and avoiding intimacy. In the chronic pain mode, pain experiences usually worsen and ultimately become disabling. The pain is not accepted, and because of this it becomes the dominant theme in the person's life, a life that becomes increasingly less satisfying.

To be suicidal, a person must be unwilling to accept emotional pain and must see suicidal behavior as a way to get rid of unacceptable thoughts and feelings. Pain avoidance may be why suicidal behavior and other consciousness-numbing avoidance behaviors such as alcohol use, drug use, and eating disorders tend to occur together. They all serve the same purpose: to take the edge off pain. When acceptance is low, most of the person's resources are spent trying to eliminate suffering rather than making adaptive changes in behavior. In other words, like the functionally disabled pain patient, the suicidal patient is not doing what needs to be done to adapt to life's circumstances and uses language that implies negative thoughts and feelings are *responsible* (causes) for this dysfunction.

The objective is not to get rid of disturbing thoughts or feelings, but to teach the patient to make room for them *and* do what needs to be done to get on with life. This space gets created when your patient learns that negative thoughts or feelings do not block adaptive behavior. The two can coexist. Needed behavior change can occur even in the presence of ongoing suicidal ideation and emotional distress. The patient can learn how to accept negative private events without excessive self-evaluation. When the thought-feeling-behavior relationship has been recontextualized, your patient does not need to engage in a contest to see whether suicidal thinking can be eliminated or whether the urge to follow through on the thought can be resisted. By encouraging your patient to bring negative, ambivalent, and positive feelings into the problem-solving process while at the same time remaining committed to change, your patient learns that tolerance for emotional distress means seeing distressful thoughts and feelings for what they are (a covert influence on the way one behaves), not what they advertise themselves to be (monsters waiting to devour us if we allow them in the house).

Comprehensive Distancing

The act of *comprehensive distancing* is accomplished when the patient establishes a willingness to detach from active participation in suicidal thoughts or affective distress. A powerful strategy is the *willingness thermometer* exercise. Have your patient keep a daily diary, rating two dimensions of experience on a 1–10 scale at the end of each day. The first scale is willingness, or a noncritical openness to have whatever experiences occur during the day. This state is best described as being present for, mildly interested in, and observant of these experiences. The other scale is a *suffering thermometer,* or how much distress the patient feels in the presence of these experiences. Have the patient rate both scales each day, making short notes on any factors that seemed associated with an increase or decrease on either scale compared with the previous day. The two thermometers will typically reveal an inverse relationship between willingness and suffering. Generally, as willingness goes up, an active sense of suffering goes down. Use your patient's own positive experience with moments-of-willingness ratings as a jumping-off point to build willingness skills. These techniques help the patient develop a healthy skepticism about the usefulness of attaching to *hot* thoughts and feelings. For some better functioning suicidal patients, increases on the willingness scale can occur in treatment, often with strong clinical results in one or two sessions.

An additional advantage of comprehensive distancing strategies is that you are able to use them to both monitor and use recurring suicidal ideation as part of treatment. A difficult clinical task at any stage of treatment is finding a way to be attentive to the patient's ongoing suicidal experiences without inadvertently making that the sole focus of clinical intervention. Once comprehensive distancing becomes a viable strategy, suicidal thinking or behavior can be framed as just another example of low acceptance of certain emotions. In other words, suicidal thinking is designed to get rid of, rather than make room for, negative feelings. Remember, even when other problems are the current focus of treatment, suicidal behavior can easily be brought back into the mainstream in the event of a crisis. For the interested reader, Hayes et al. (in press) provides a much more detailed formulation of acceptance as behavior change, along with many highly useful therapeutic strategies.

Building Personal Problem-Solving Skills

During the intermediate stage, you will want to help your patient develop specific skills that can increase adaptive social and interpersonal behavior. Specific behavioral skills training can be delivered during individual therapy sessions or in skills-training groups. We find it to be a particularly effective model to couple skills-training groups with individual therapy sessions. This allows the patient to continue working on developing pain tolerance and problem-solving abilities individually while learning new skills in a supportive group environment. If skills training is delivered without also working on acceptance, the patient may see the skills as a new, more sophisticated tactic for avoiding or eliminating emotional pain. In other words, the skills will be put in the service of the same self-defeating agenda as before. It is often helpful to say, "The reason we are focusing on these skills is that you have a job to do in life while you are in pain. The better you know these skills, the more likely it is you will use them even while you are hurting."

Personal Problem Solving

Effective personal problem solving evolves through several discrete stages: 1) problem identification, 2) identification of alternative problem-solving strategies, 3) evaluation of the likely utility of different problem-solving responses, 4) selection of a specific problem-solving technique and the formation of a plan, and 5) implementation of the response and evaluation of its effects. Deficits in any of these skill areas may put your patient at risk for lingering problems and chronic life stress. This pragmatic approach to personal problem solving underscores the empirical, trial-and-error nature of effective efforts at addressing life problems. Teach your patient the absolute necessity of using *feedback* in approaching life's difficulties. Feedback emphasizes a "no failure" aspect in that all problem-solving approaches are viewed as "best guesses." The process of problem solving must be done repetitively until enough information is obtained to effectively overcome the obstacle. Given the well-established problem-solving passivity of the suicidal individual, this model offers a concrete, teachable alternative that will give your patient the tools to perform in an active mode.

Even when the specifics of this model are being taught in a group or psychoeducational format, you can and must simultaneously work with your patient on beliefs that undermine proactive problem solving. The use of active problem-solving homework assignments will stimulate the patient's feelings of hopelessness, predictions of personal failure and abandonment, and many other performance-stopping beliefs. You can then help the patient test out some of these negative predictions through the use of highly structured homework assignments that are based on the problem-solving model.

Interpersonal Effectiveness

In the interpersonal skills arena, you should emphasize an approach that integrates interpersonal, social, and assertiveness skills. The three key components of interpersonal effectiveness are conflict resolution skills, general social skills, and appropriate assertiveness. Conflict resolution skills generally emphasize finding a common ground around which a conflict with someone else can be worked out in a way that satisfies everyone's interests. Because of the suicidal patient's passive style and tendency to make black-and-white judgments, it is difficult for this person to imagine a resolution of some interpersonal conflict that would obtain the desired outcome, maintain the relationship, and enhance the patient's self-esteem. By learning negotiation skills, including techniques to develop a common best interest, your patient is more likely to steer this delicate course to an effective resolution. Again, a combination of individual therapy and skills-training groups is a very effective package. The therapist generally takes responsibility for working on personal issues associated with application of skills, and the group leaders focus on teaching basic component skills.

General assertion and social skills are also important. This can be a very difficult area of functioning for the suicidal patient, who often has poor skills (e.g., does not maintain eye contact, apologizes instead of saying no) and very negative beliefs (e.g., If I stand up for myself, my spouse will dump me.). When working with assertion skills, focus on the ability to maintain an assertive response in the face of strong opposition. The suicidal patient lives in interpersonal environments often marked by increased dysfunction and interpersonal conflict. The other players in this environment may not be particularly well put together either and may respond to healthy behavior with undermining, cajoling, or demeaning responses. It is important to confront the patient with these responses in skills-training groups so that the patient can develop a "thicker skin." There is often a person in your patient's social network who is consistently negative and problematic. Try to teach skills that will enable the patient to consistently set limits despite negative feedback from that dysfunctional person. The more realistically your patient is able to practice via role-play, the better he or she will be able to handle the real event. It is useful to do role reversals in which the patient plays the role of the dysfunctional person and has to model the reactions that person would have. The trainer then takes on the role of the patient and models limit-setting responses.

There are excellent books that can be used as a guide to such training. The interested reader is encouraged to consult these more comprehensive texts, some of which are listed at the end of this chapter. It is important to realize that skill deficits are important determinants of the patient's suicidal behavior. Skill deficits may have occurred because of faulty training from a dysfunctional family, specific cultural deprivation or aberration, or just plain lack of available role models. The keys to forming better adaptive relationships are the presence of effective cognitive and emotional perspectives, and the ability to act appropriately in your environment (i.e., do what needs to be done when you need to do it).

Clinical Pitfalls of the Intermediate Stage of Treatment

The major pitfall in this stage is the tendency to lose focus once the acute suicidal crisis has passed. The principal symptom of this pitfall is a lack of session-to-session continuity and more of a "what's on your mind this week" approach. Often, clinicians feel emotionally winded at this stage and prefer to let the patient direct the form and content of the therapy. This is unfortunate because this is the opportunity to address key cognitive, emotional, and spiritual issues. The therapist's goal is to increase both the patient's problem-solving flexibility and the patient's problem-solving view of the world. The optimal time for doing this is when your patient is not operating in the crisis mode.

A second error is to assume that the absence of crisis means that suicidal behavior has stopped. This phase often involves the persistence of chronic low-level suicidal ideation. Because it does not represent a crisis, it is not focused on in treatment. In fact, chronic low-level suicidal ideation is an ideal target for work in the intermediate phase. Because the pain associated with such experiences is not so intense, it is easier to get your patient to experiment with such things as emotional pain tolerance, observational interventions, and personal problem-solving plans.

A third and more subtle pitfall is a negative countertransference, which can be ironically linked to the patient's improvement. In other words, your need to rescue has been fulfilled and yet your patient has not finished therapy. This is dangerous if you begin to lose interest and become distracted. You can also begin to engage in subtle behaviors indicating a lack of commitment to continuing on to the end of the treatment. Behaviorally, it looks as if you are no longer concerned in your patient's quest to address different life problems. Because your attention is a powerful reinforcer, your patient may respond to this shift by resuming or escalating suicidal behavior.

Session Scheduling and Course of Treatment

The intermediate phase of therapy is more difficult to gauge in terms of both its beginning and ending points. Generally, this phase begins when the acute crisis has been defused to the point that the patient can talk about suicidal ideation, negative thoughts, and emotional distress as part of a single continuum. Some patients find it easier to adapt to this mindfulness approach, especially if they have had spiritual experiences such as prayer, meditation, or yoga that have given them some abilities to be distant from and contemplate events. Patients with strong obsessional traits or highly rationalized defense styles tend to move more slowly into the acceptance and commitment model. These patients rigidly defend against their negative thoughts; asking them to become more accepting can be perceived as quite dangerous (i.e., "If I let the thoughts in the house, they will burn it down."). Try to focus on developing *split perspectives* with such patients. This strategy sees each thought sequence as a *story*. The exercise is to have your patient tell the story over and over, each time with some different connotation. The goal is not to keep going until the patient gets the right story but to have your patient *experience* the reality of there being multiple outcomes to an ap proach to any life or mental obstacle. This approach will often help the more obsessive patient accept the mindfulness approach.

The frequency of sessions during the intermediate phase can be quite variable. Sessions can be as much as 2 or 3 weeks apart to accommodate experiential learning. The sequencing between sessions also may be highly variable. For example, there may be times when weekly sessions are indicated followed by a phase in which meetings every 2 or 3 weeks are better suited to the patient's pace of change. In some settings, weekly sessions are not consistently available. Here, a good plan is to move to a regular but less-frequent session schedule as soon as the acute crisis has been addressed. Try to collaborate with your patient around developing a schedule of sessions that makes sense, focusing on the work required between sessions and the amount of support your patient needs.

The intermediate phase of treatment ends when the patient truly understands and uses the treatment: the patient "gets it." Your patient is now reporting an integrated perspective that comes in the midst of situations that previously produced suicidal ideation. Look for situations in which your patient selects new problem-solving strategies even while acknowledging that the possibility of suicidal behavior occurred as one possible course of action. Another indicator is your patient reporting that, even though many of the same thoughts and feelings are occurring, they do not seem as credible or as demanding: they are not as *hot* as they once were. There are great variations among patients in movement through the intermediate phase of treatment. Higher functioning patients may complete the work in 1 or 2 months. Chronically suicidal patients with characterologic difficulties may require a year or more to integrate the concepts necessary to complete this part of treatment.

The Termination Phase of Treatment: Building Into the Future

The final phase in working with the suicidal patient is to develop a termination plan that addresses the longer term needs of your patient and that has a built-in, self-correcting component to prevent relapse.

At this point, your patient has established good problem-solving alternatives to suicidal behavior, although suicidal thinking may not have entirely disappeared. Your patient knows that suicidal ideation is a signal that low acceptance is present and old forms of avoidant problem solving are being used. The suicidal thinking is now used as a stimulus to initiate acceptance strategies and commit to proactive problem-solving strategies.

Although termination is always an issue in treatment, it is perhaps more so with the suicidal patient. Your patient has been through a crisis with you, and that simple fact creates a potential for dependency. Your patient may see you as a necessity, a major component for any future change. This dependency must be dealt with in the termination phase. It is important to lavish praise on your patient for effective problem-solving behaviors or spontaneous examples of heightened acceptance. Use explanations that discount the importance of therapy in this process and instead emphasize the many hours per week the patient is out of therapy. Point out that there is only 1 hour per week of treatment but 167 hours per week "in the field." It is vitally important to help your patient get into feeling good about handling tough situations. Your goal is to internalize the patient's self-praise and not to take credit for any changes that have occurred. At the same time, your patient has to accept that suicidal ideation could reappear and have a prevention plan for when that happens.

It is very important to help your patient identify the central features of a positive future and to begin shaping that future through goal setting. It is not an acceptable clinical outcome to simply weather a crisis and start out symptom free from the same basic spot in life. It is important to stimulate the patient to set valued life goals. One way to approach this is to ask, "What do you want your life to stand for? If you died tomorrow, what would be the most important thing you want to be remembered for?" Get the patient to specify in concrete terms some intermediate goals that would represent steps in the right direction. In general, the suicidal patient is overfocused on outcome and tends to underplay the importance of process. Express the idea that attaining life goals may not be nearly as important as what is learned on the way toward achieving those goals. Often, the patient will recall instances in which a goal is in sight, only to find it has been outgrown. Another way of saying this is that the work of striving toward one's goals in the here and now is what life is all about. Applying this strategy with the chronically suicidal patient can be at the high end of the difficulty continuum because these individuals may be all but completely absorbed in what has not been accomplished in life and may have great difficulty placing value on the hard work of goal setting and problem solving. For many patients, however, enduring significant interpersonal or material losses as a consequence of the suicidal crisis makes the notion of building into the future very reassuring and allows for a constructive approach to what comes next.

The Role of Relapse Prevention

Preventing or reducing relapse potential is accomplished by preparing your patient for likely tests of his or her commitment to non-suicidal problem solving. This involves development of early risk warning systems as well as development of a clear response plan that incorporates skills and techniques that have already worked. It is helpful to dovetail this activity into the intermediate-term life-planning process. In this way, the potential recurrence of suicidal behavior can be reframed as one of many potential obstacles your patient will need to move through. It is important to tell the patient to expect a crisis that will be an invitation to suicidal problem solving. Ask your patient to think carefully about the earliest signs of increasing suicidal potential. These might be social withdrawal, self-preoccupation (i.e., attaching more than usual to certain types of thoughts) or low acceptance of feelings. Walk through the process of treatment to identify which skills and techniques are most compatible with your patient's coping style. Encourage the use of skills and techniques that most closely match this style. Skills that are compatible with a patient's personality or world outlook are much more likely to be remembered and used than skills that seem artificial, contrived, or remain persistently uncomfortable to use. Rehearse the response plan and ask your patient to imagine any obstacles that might get in the way of implementing this plan. Have your patient imagine and rehearse strategies to overcome those obstacles and then get to the point of implementing the response plan. Table 5–5 lists elements of a typical prevention and intermediate-term life plan.

Putting a New Frame on Termination

Your patient should view termination as a process of field experiments built around a model of session tapering. This involves

Table 5–5. Sample suicide prevention plan

1. What are the *first* signs of trouble in the way I believe, think, feel, or behave (e.g., sleeping less well, avoiding social situations, getting more depressed or anxious)?
   a.
   b.
   c.
   d.

2. How do I plan to monitor myself to watch for these signs? If I plan to watch for the above signs, when and how do I plan to check for them?

   If I plan to rate my suicidal thinking, when and how will I do this?

3. What are my most important goals for the next year?

4. What stresses do I anticipate in the next year, both ongoing (e.g., job problems, sick older parent) and new (e.g., move to a new house, Christmas at my house), and how do I plan to cope with them?

5. What is/are the most valuable idea(s) I have learned in treatment up to now, and how do I plan to remember it/them?

6. What is/are the most valuable coping strategies I have learned in treatment, and what and how and when do I plan to use it/them?

7. What hurdles might occur that would get in the way of using these coping strategies, and how would I overcome them (e.g., too tired to cope, get down on myself for having problems)?

decreasing session frequency in a sequence of progressively longer gaps. For example, a typical session-tapering schedule might involve meetings at 1, 2, 3, and 6 months. The goal in each meeting is to review the results of the previous field experiment with reference to the relapse prevention plan and life goals. Establishing prearranged meeting times allows the patient to return for a booster session even if his or her life is going very well. Encourage the patient to go as long and as hard as possible before making an unplanned visit. The fact that an additional session is already on the books is reassuring to the patient and tends to promote a sense of a safe environment in which to experiment with new pain tolerance or problem-solving strategies.

Ideally, your patient should terminate therapy. In the natural flow of the session-tapering model, your patient may suggest that a return visit really is not needed. This, of course, is the optimal form of termination because your patient is initiating breaking the bond rather than you. On the other hand, some patients may want to stay connected, even at the level of checking in once a year. This is a very efficient use of your time and can be an important part of relapse prevention. In this scenario, your patient may fail to return for the yearly visit but eventually contact you and want to discuss how things are going. In this case, immediately praise the patient for testing an even longer period of time than to which was originally agreed.

Done properly, the session-tapering model decreases termination anxiety, enhances your patient's sense autonomy, and keeps the door open for a return to therapy in a cost-effective way. Avoid the scenario of the suicidal patient viewing termination as a test of whether the problem has been cured. This can cause your patient to see a return to therapy because of suicidal thinking as an indication of failure. By developing a model that makes a suicidal crisis part of an ongoing learning paradigm, you can avoid situations in which the patient needlessly avoids treatment. Always be available for "tune-up" visits, and always stress that you can be much more helpful early in the game. It is much more efficient and gratifying to intervene early than to deal with a patient who returned to the suicidal mode some time ago and struggles with an even greater sense of failure.

When your patient returns because of a setback, put a positive context around the decision to come back into therapy. Suggest that your patient has picked exactly the right time to come in for help. Express admiration for the courage and wisdom needed to make that decision. It is important to discuss the new crisis in a way that suggests it is a new learning situation and not the patient's failure to remember things past. Learning acceptance and problem-solving strategies is an incremental task. There are periods in which any of us will exhibit fewer skills than were evident the week before. Not only that, but the makeup of life challenges is complex and ever changing. It is not always clear to your patient how particular skills may apply, given the new properties of stressful situations. If your patient is willing to approach therapy early in the new suicidal crisis, it is often amazing how quickly crises are solved the second, third, or fourth time around. What has taken several weeks or months to achieve in the first episode of care is achieved in only one or two sessions. Go to great lengths to point out how quickly your patient seems to be responding to the need to apply new skills. In other words, always build self-efficacy when dealing with a relapse by the patient.

If your patient has simply not used the relapse prevention plan, you should avoid resistance interpretations. Instead focus on obstacles that may have gotten in the way of implementing the plan. You should take the blame for failing to get a clear enough vision of the potential obstacles. Apologize and then work with the patient to troubleshoot the plan. The goal is to empower your patient and to build a better future over time. This is not achieved through blaming but through shaping, practice, and reshaping.

Clinical Pitfalls of the Termination Stage of Treatment

The most important pitfall to avoid at the termination stage of treatment is creating a situation in which your patient feels abandoned and cut off by you. This most often occurs because you have not begun dealing with the issue of ending treatment early enough. Unfortunately, it is not unusual for a clinician to decide at the end of one session to end therapy at the conclusion of the next session. When this happens, the issue has not been integrated into the treatment process. A good general strategy is to discuss the time-limited nature of the therapy contract in the early part of the intermediate stage of treatment and to form some agreements about how your patient and you will know that therapy can be moved into a field experiment phase. The more directly or matter-of-factly this reality can be approached, the easier it will be to actually move to the field-trial and session-tapering phase.

A second pitfall is the development of a tacit understanding between the patient and therapist that the therapist's brilliance is responsible for the patient's clinical improvement. The patient begins to fear life without the therapist as the termination/field-trial phase nears. To avoid this pitfall, you should consistently put responsibility for positive changes back in the patient's lap. This can be done very effectively by being both pleased with and curious about the methods your patient uses to accomplish a variety of goals, even little ones, in the process of therapy. The emphasis in these discussions is to get your patient to accept the credit for what has happened and to make this progress a part of your patient's self-concept.

The heart of every therapist's rescue fantasy is the encounter with the eternally grateful patient who attributes miraculous properties to the therapist. To let go of ownership of miracles, you need to remain mindful of the real limits of personal persuasion and influence over others. The therapeutic community is somewhat to blame for this problem in promoting the idea that therapists cause patients to change. In Chapter 7, in which we discuss recurrent suicidal behavior, we note how this destructive mythology can play a prominent role in negative treatment outcomes. For the present, remember to take responsibility for all failures and give your patient credit for all successes. This stance is humbling but, most importantly, it works.

Conclusion

Conducting therapy with the suicidal patient is a complex process that often brings out the best and the worst in us. We have chosen disciplines that involve helping others, but what is helpful in this particular circumstance? The answer to that question is at the heart of many of the mixed feelings we have when working with acutely suicidal patients. It also explains the tremendous range of negative feelings that are elicited by the person who is unresponsive to and critical of our efforts, such as the chronically suicidal patient. Avoiding the temptation to promote treatment as a way of getting rid of emotional pain or disturbing thoughts seems like a good place to start. Unfortunately, our patients ask us to do just that. This is not only impossible, it is an unrealistic portrayal of our contract with life. What we can do is help our patients focus on the inevitability of tragedies and setbacks *and* personal failures as well as the joys and challenges of continuing into the future. We can do this by being clear about the values that guide our understanding of life-and-death matters. Our most valuable resource is our capacity to respond to our patient's emotional pain. What will help lead our patients through that pain and into the future is our ability to collaborate and learn together. We should not assume that what we would do is automatically what our patient needs to do. This is a matter of individual discovery and it can only be aided by our acceptance and commitment.

Helpful Hints

♦ The major goal of treatment with the suicidal patient is to change one or more of the Three *I*s (pain that is intolerable, inescapable, and interminable).

♦ The problem-solving approach reframes suicidal behavior as a form of problem solving.

♦ Remember to always validate the patient's emotional pain.

♦ Focus on teaching the patient methods for tolerating emotional pain.

♦ Focus on using real-life problems to teach the patient better problem-solving skills.

♦ Use ongoing suicidal behavior as a jumping-off point to teach problem solving.

♦ Try to adopt a collaborative, personal scientistic approach with the patient.

♦ Teach the patient that negative thoughts and feelings can be accepted and adaptive responses can still be made.
♦ Focus on developing interpersonal, problem-solving, self-control, and stress management skills, either in individual or group settings.
♦ Focus on reconciling conflicting beliefs that support the patient's ambivalence about life and living.

Selected Readings

Ascher M (ed): Paradoxical Procedures in Psychotherapy. New York, Guilford, 1989

Beck A, Rush J, Shaw D, et al: Cognitive Therapy for Depression: A Treatment Manual. New York, Guilford, 1979

deShazer S: Clues: Investigating Solutions in Brief Therapy. New York, WW Norton, 1988

Jacobson N (ed): Psychotherapists in Clinical Practice: Cognitive and Behavioral Perspectives. N. New York, Guilford, 1987

Hayes S, Strosahl K, Wilson K: Acceptance and Commitment Therapy. New York, Guilford (in press)

 Chapter 6

The Clinician's Attitude and Behavior

The Medium Is the Message

In this chapter, we discuss your role in the effective treatment of suicidality. Both your emotional state and behavior are of tremendous importance, and in this chapter we underscore both the negative and positive potential of the transactions that occur between you and your patient. Although the patient's suicidal potential is certainly a potent force in determining the course of treatment, nothing is more dangerous for producing a negative outcome than a clinician who is out of control in relation to suicidality. Our purpose in this chapter is to provide you with concrete, workable strategies that are likely to have a positive effect on the working relationship between you and your patient. First, we focus on behaviors to avoid, behaviors that can subvert all your clinical efforts. Second, three attitudes are discussed that can have a major impact in terms of reassuring your patient and enhancing your credibility in dealing with suicidality. Third, we describe several attitudes that are useful to develop in dealing with any patient, whether suicidal or not.

Understanding Your Troublesome Emotions

To be successful as an intervener with a suicidal patient, it is absolutely essential that you understand your own *hot buttons*.

These refer not only to moral, ethical, and legal pressures that you experience but to very personal issues such as unreasonable rescue fantasies and unwarranted assumptions about your power to make people change. Just as suicidal crisis is heavily marked by the patient's difficulty with making room for and accepting negative thoughts and feelings, you must also learn to let go of desires and fantasies that will interrupt the process of working with the patient. The fact is you are not going to save your patient by some brilliant slight of hand. This is not a time for heroes; it is a time for common sense and a consistent and caring approach to someone else's painful sense of emotional desperation. This may mean that the patient does things that you find objectionable in trying to cope with emotional pain. Your job is to let go of your objections—even, sometimes, your outrage—and instead find a way to work with your patient to find an approach that makes sense and works. You need to realize that loosening up and modifying your agenda will often allow your patient to benefit in the long run, even when short-term consequences seem less than desirable. You may be tested in this process, for allowing your patient to solve problems means doing so without expressing anger or resentment when your advice is not followed. Remember, learning and accepting your limits is not only the best way to help your patient; it also gives you a feel for reality that will serve you well in the difficult moments of treating suicidality.

The *Don'ts*

Suicidal ideation and behavior elicits an ambivalent emotional response from caregivers. These responses can evolve (or degenerate) into hostility, mutual mistrust, and confrontation. This can be a particular danger on inpatient services, where suicidal patients sometimes receive the least-intensive and least-preferred modes of treatment. Furthermore, the rate of premature termination from inpatient or outpatient therapy has been reported to be as high as 50% for suicidal patients. These findings suggest that many clinicians are uncomfortable working with an acutely suicidal patient and may project that ambivalence into therapeutic interventions.

The technical steps in intervening with suicidal behavior are relatively straightforward. The hard part is for you to implement these steps and at the same time accept the *suicidal bind*. The suicidal bind is the inescapable fact that the power to commit suicide or engage in suicidal behavior is finally and completely in the hands of your patient. No amount of coercion, restraint, persuasion, or pleading is going to change the fact that your patient in the long run controls destiny. The suicidal bind can leave you feeling powerless and simultaneously feeling responsible for doing something miraculous. When these competing attitudes get tested in a suicidal showdown, negative outcomes can occur in very short periods of time. Sometimes, the patient simply quits therapy, often to the relief of the therapist. In other circumstances, the clinician can feel strongly pressured to have the patient committed as a way of showing who really is in control. Clinicians can cancel appointments, routinely make the patient wait, or become increasingly less responsive. There are, in fact, a variety of ways that the therapeutic relationship can be jettisoned.

The first and most important principle is not to match your patient's anxiety level. The suicidal patient is very concerned about self-control and is hypersensitive to therapist comments or actions that signal a lack of confidence in the patient's self-control functions. When you fidget nervously, seem overfocused on suicidal potential, and ask indirect or vague questions about suicide intent, the patient often reads this as an indication that the situation is out of control. A second rule of thumb is not to moralize about the act of suicide. Your moral outlook is not very relevant to your patient's decision-making process. In addition, moralizing often carries a good versus bad overtone with it, and most suicidal patients are worried about whether being suicidal is good or bad in the first place. Morals, by their very nature, have a black-or-white, yes-or-no, either-or connotation to them. Operating at this level only plays into the either-or view of the world that creates contradictory belief systems and fuels the patient's ambivalence. Although you certainly need to be in touch with your moral beliefs about suicide, this cannot substitute for the implementation of effective interventions *even* when the patient is apparently inviting a morality-based response.

A third rule of thumb is to avoid using coercion as a means of reducing the risk of suicidal behavior. Threatening the patient with involuntary hospitalization can be a particularly destructive practice. For example, the statement, "If you don't stop thinking about suicide, I will have you committed," is often not helpful. Equally damaging is threatening to kick the patient out of therapy or withdrawing emotional support because of suicidality. Some therapists refuse to take their patients back into therapy after a suicide attempt. The suicidal patient already feels that the world is punishing, full of abandonment, and loaded with unpredictable rejection. It is hard to justify using withdrawal of support or access to help as a way of curing suicidal behavior. Even when this approach seems to work, the aftermath can be quite destructive. After the suicidal behavior has passed, the patient discovers that the therapist is no longer available and can become acutely suicidal once again in response to the sense of rejection.

Another behavior to avoid is lecturing your patient about the negative consequences of suicidal behavior. If the patient were going to respond to lecturing, this would probably have happened long before therapy started. Realize that almost everyone in the patient's social network is busy lecturing as well. Lecturing is almost always based on consequences the lecturer feels will accrue if the forbidden behavior occurs. This set of consequences may be entirely irrelevant to the patient. Consequences labeled bad by the lecturer may in fact be construed as good by the patient. For example, you say, "Just think about how devastated your wife and kids would be." Your patient says (or thinks), "Fine. They've never been there for me when I needed them. Maybe it'll do them some good to hurt the way I have."

Most of us have encountered chart notes using such terms such as *suicide gesture, manipulative suicide attempt, token suicide attempt,* and other terms that suggest that the patient's intent is to control someone else. Be careful. Using pejorative labeling can destroy your capacity to relate to the real human suffering of the suicidal patient. Such labeling ignores the fact that at this moment the problem-solving technique is to try, perhaps desperately, to get other people to pay attention, to sit up, and to take notice. Your patient is in real emotional pain and is trying hard to solve difficult life problems. The suggestion behind many pejorative labels is that the person has intentionally selected this behavior, knowing that it is "bad," and it will cause other people to suffer. This can lead the therapist to view suicidal behavior as malevolent, a perspective that automatically generates an adversarial relationship. A frequent response of the clinician operating from this position is the use of limit setting as the principal way of managing the suicidal patient. This limit setting can be a projection of the intervener, who is most likely expressing irritation over suicidal behavior, powerlessness, and anger at the suicidal bind. We have found it helpful to keep the following thought in mind: "This person is doing the best he can do right now. It may not work very well, and it may make me angry, but it is the best available option. My job is to find new options."

The Triad of Effective Intervention

There are three central characteristics that define an effective clinician: 1) taking a matter-of-fact approach, 2) encouraging and modeling openness and honesty, and 3) being consistent in the application of the treatment approach. Remember, your patient's ability to exercise self control over anxiety vis-à-vis suicidal impulses is enhanced when you act in a calm and professional manner. You need to convey through your attitude and behavior that it is work you are comfortable doing, even in the face of highly evocative disclosures about suicidal impulses. This matter-of-fact attitude is not to be mistaken for a lack of caring. You care, and you are accepting your patient's emotional disclosures without communicating discomfort or anxiety that would reflect negatively on your ability to help. Your demeanor must indicate that you are comfortable hearing any and all communications. Good treatment means good listening and well-considered treatment strategies. Do not load up on hasty interventions simply because your patient's expressed suicidal potential is high

You must initiate honest and candid dialogue with your patient about the nature and extent of suicidal thinking or behavior. This requires being comfortable hearing anything and everything your patient has to say about the issue of suicide. This includes what your patient may feel most shameful about, such as having made a suicide attempt that nobody knew about, currently practicing the steps of a suicide plan, or being convinced of the need to die in spite of everyone's advice about how wonderful life is. You must take these communications in stride and ask straightforward questions in return. These questions convey a true sense of caring and concern about your patient's pain and world view. For example, instead of immediately using the standard suicide risk triad (plan, method, lethality), you might instead ask, "How do you think this whole situation will end up for you?" In other words, you use honest inquiry and directness as the best way to access your patient's plans and predictions. Honesty allows you to empathize with the fact that your patient is experiencing the world in a way that would look bleak to any sane person. You then acknowledge that most people can and will get suicidal when they feel their situation is inescapable, intolerable, and unending.

Another way to encourage rapport is to ask candid questions about your patient's suicidal behavior and thinking. By routinely and briefly checking in on occurrences of suicidal ideation or behavior since the last session, you are building a bridge between the patient's self-imposed exile in the land of suicidal secrecy and shame, and the more satisfying and accessible world of problem solving. Open communication is enhanced when you maintain good eye contact while asking questions about suicidal thinking and behavior. You should use candid nonevaluative terms for suicide that do justice to the roughness of suicidal crisis (e.g., offing yourself, croaking, checking out) when this fits the language patterns of the patient.

Consistency is essential because your patient needs to rely on you taking the same stance with respect to suicidal behavior on a day-in, day-out basis. This is true even in short episodes of treatment and is absolutely critical in longer term work with the repetitiously suicidal patient. Consistency is a key building block in working through an upturn in suicidal potential. Your patient gains reassurance when you can be counted on to take the same position on central issues, that you follow through on collaboratively generated agreements, and that you do not change your position when a crisis occurs. Consistency also applies to how sessions are structured and how your patient helps manage the work flow. You can build session agendas with your patient and follow the same template each time a session is held. In doing this, you make sure the agenda is flexible and that new topics can be added by your patient at anytime. Overall, there is a regular progression from one session to the next. The main thing that changes in crisis is that the steps in the progression of treatment will typically be smaller.

Other Stylistic Attributes

Many of the specific qualities discussed in this section characterize effective clinicians generally and are certainly important when working with the suicidal patient. To a great extent, these characteristics involve conscious decision making. They are not automatic responses for most therapists. For example, in an attempt to rescue your patient from a suicidal outcome, you might take too much responsibility for solving problems and inadvertently develop an adversarial relationship with the patient. When your patient does not comply with your vision of healthy functioning, you can end up feeling frustrated and unappreciated.

Build a Collaborative Set

Your most important general attribute is your desire to build a *collaborative set* with your patient early in the process of addressing suicidal behavior. Often, both you and your patient have exaggerated ideas about your capacity to alleviate your patient's sense of suffering. You need to undermine idealized expectations in a way that has a rapport-building feature to it. Building a collaborative set involves recognizing that, by virtue of your training, you possess special sets of information about how people change in difficult circumstances. However, the actual process of behavior change will have to be a team effort, a "we" effort. You and the patient need to work as a team to discover which strategies will work best at resolving the dilemmas that have precipitated the suicidal crisis. Your role in the team project is first to help your patient see the value of a problem-solving format, and second to act as a *resource* when your patient is ready to use your knowledge in some constructive way.

Develop the collaborative set with a suicidal patient in the initial session and build upon it regularly. This is best done by constructing an alternative reality to the likely viewpoint of the patient. This reality includes many important messages about how the collaboration will unfold. Specifically, acknowledge that your patient may reengage in suicidal behavior during therapy. If this happens, it will be an opportunity to collaborate and learn what would work better for your patient. Make it clear that the recurrence of suicidal behavior in therapy is not an indication that the treatment is failing and does not compromise your continued commitment to your patient. As we have stated before, most people do not stop troublesome behaviors just because they enter treatment. It is unfortunate that some clinicians make this assumption and are surprised, hurt, or angry when proved wrong.

Your patient should be fully involved in developing meaningful task assignments between sessions. You should sympathize with the many obstacles that your patient must confront and overcome on the way to enacting meaningful behavior change. Encourage your patient to imagine and discover obstacles that would get in the way of valued change, and jointly discuss solutions to these obstacles. These actions, and others you can think of, have the effect of creating a sense of team and a shared sense of responsibility.

Be Emotionally Validating

This essential process can be difficult with the suicidal patient because you must make sure that validating an emotional state is not also seen as validating a cognitive set. Many of your patients feel bad about their emotions (i.e., feel bad about feeling bad) but will be uncritical of the way they are approaching problems. Your approach is the opposite: "You have every right to feel the way you do. Almost anyone in your situation would. I understand how you feel, but I am concerned about how you are thinking this through." Make ample use of emotional validation by making a conscious effort to "walk in the patient's shoes," even when you feel your patient may be overreacting. This provides your patient with useful feedback and is a way of both connecting with the patient and diffusing the ever-present stigma associated with being hopeless and suicidal. Validate emotions, but always be cautious about accepting the cognitive interpretations that may lead to these intense emotional responses. A useful technique is to start with your patient's interpretation (accept it as a hypothetical truth) and then work backward into understanding feelings. This reverses the usual perceptual set of the patient, namely, that negative feelings are the "problem" and the thoughts are accurate. Although potent negative feelings clearly are uncomfortable and difficult to tolerate, they may in fact be entirely appropriate, given the patient's interpretation of life circumstances. A simple summary of this is as follows: Your patient sees his or her feelings as wrong and his or her thinking as right. You see feelings as right but question the thinking process.

A second aspect of effective emotional validation is to empathize with suffering while not buying into the notion that suffering is intolerable or that suffering can be expressed in only one fashion. When a therapist has trouble with validation, it is usually because the therapist believes that the patient has made a mistake in interpreting events and therefore should get rid of suffering. In other words, the *therapist's agenda* is that the real cure for suffering is to get rid of it. You will be more effective when you are willing to let suffering be there and are able to encourage different perspectives on suffering. This may take the form of building strategies to tolerate, rather than eliminate, pain, or designing strategies to capitalize on natural variations in pain acuity. For example, when your patient says, "I can't stand it," you can often find examples, even recent ones, when your patient did stand it, did weather the storm. Find out how. Find out what worked. Emphasize your patient's strengths and abilities in getting through difficult life moments.

Be Concrete and Specific

Another stylistic attribute of the effective therapist is the capacity to be concrete and specific about situations that are related to changes in the patient's functioning. You must operationalize what may be viewed by the patient as a global problem. Be specific and concrete by developing intrasession work assignments that are tangible and have a specific behavioral reference. Instead of focusing on a global concept such as "changing your attitude," pinpoint what a change in attitude would mean in terms of the patient's behavior, speech, and internal state. Specificity and concreteness are extremely reassuring to the suicidal patient, who by nature is often global and diffuse in the self-evaluation process.

When an intervention is not working, a concrete and specific approach is more effective at revealing the true cause of setbacks than trait-level characterological interpretations. A related consequence of being specific is most useful: *You can take the blame*. You can jump in and take responsibility for setting a situation up poorly so that your patient did not experience a sense of success. Presumably, you are in a better emotional position to accept failure than your patient. The last thing you want to promote in the course of therapy is yet more failure on the part of the patient. Such failure is often due to vagueness and generality. A concrete and specific approach to events that led to a failed assignment will reveal information that otherwise would have remained hidden at a more general level of inquiry. Always remember the *personal scientist* approach. Assignments are experiments, and we do not know if they will succeed or fail. Either way, we will learn something from them and move on.

Steal the Point of Resistance

The effective therapist gets to the point of resistance before the patient. You need to anticipate your patient's objections to a particular intervention or strategy and co-opt those objections. For example, the suicidal patient is usually interested in feeling better *now*.

The patient may not believe a particular behavioral objective is going to create better feelings immediately, and he or she is probably right. You know that effective problem solving is usually less oriented to immediate gratification, so you may preface the intervention with the caveat that it probably will not affect how the patient feels right away, but might solve a problem.

Anticipate the arguments for and against doing something healthy and be willing to play the devil's advocate. By doing this, you mirror your patient's own internal struggle with the difficulty of changing. For example, your patient may tell you he has collected medication for a possible overdose but may balk if directly asked to give it up. The point-of-resistance maneuver would involve you examining the need to keep the medication. You could point out, for example, the possible important psychological benefits of having a stash. The possession of the medication might be a comfort to the patient, a sense of a last resort if all else fails. As one of us was once told, "Thoughts of suicide have gotten me through many a bad night." The issue with the medication might be one of control. Your patient might feel powerless in many aspects of life, "but this stash [by damn] is something I am in charge of." Stealing the point of resistance is not a paradoxical intervention in which your secret intention is to get the patient to oppose you and thereby surrender the pills. Your goal is to anticipate places in which control and counter-control processes might arise. In this example, the best way to give up the stash is to give up the idea of needing it by examining its purpose and then developing alternatives to meet the same ends. Ideally you want your patient to give it up because it is no longer needed, not because you have forced the solution.

Communicate Sincere Caring and Attention

A final stylistic attribute of the therapist is the ability to communicate sincere caring and attention. Your attention, in both nonverbal and verbal forms, is a powerful reinforcer of behavior. This attention is almost always there when your patient is in crisis. You are riveted to every move and every word the patient makes. Unfortunately, you may look bored and inattentive when your patient is not in crisis and is actually doing things that work. You will be more effective by being less attentive (but not inattentive) during times when the patient is in the "suicidal rut." Be ready to spring to life and be full of encouragement when the patient begins articulating more positive, constructive responses. Your caring and concern is *most evident* during those stretches in which the patient is talking about things that work, things the patient has done to solve problems, and so forth. The goal is not to punish the patient when suicidal behavior is prominent in the session. It is simply to show your patient that you care about positive problem behaviors and better outcomes.

Take Care of Yourself

You must understand that working with suicidal patients is very hard and emotionally taxing work. You should regulate the number of such patients on your caseload to keep you maximally effective. Our rule of thumb is that no more than two or three repetitiously suicidal patients can be dealt with at any one time. Episodically suicidal patients are usually easier on a therapist's resources than the hardcore, chronically suicidal patient, so you may be able to concurrently treat more of these individuals. A second yardstick for managing case overload is the intensity of the suicidal crisis. Generally, as a case becomes more acute, more time is consumed in after-hours contacts and care coordination. Even in a caseload of well-functioning patients, two concurrent suicidal crises are usually more than enough for the average clinician. On the other hand, you may have the capacity to deal with a larger number of patients who are not acutely suicidal.

When case overload occurs, it is easy to spot the signs. The therapist typically is more short-tempered and will report feeling burdened by the unreasonable demands of suicidal patients. It is ironic that at times like this, telephone calls almost always come at the wrong time, crises occur at 5:00 P.M. on Fridays or just before leaving with the family for a vacation. The clinician may react by provoking a confrontation with a particular patient, more out of an attempt to get some needed distance from the problem rather than from some clinical rationale. The advice is simple: Estimate the number of patients that can be handled at any one time and do not exceed that estimate.

Helpful Hints

- ◆ Understand your own *hot buttons* in relation to suicidal behavior (usually rescuer fantasies, moral outrage, religious prohibitions).
- ◆ Manage the number of suicidal patients on a caseload at any given time to avoid emotional overload. Remember, working with a suicidal patient is more than a "9-to-5" job.
- ◆ Be honest, straightforward, and consistent in your approach.
- ◆ Repeatedly validate the patient's sense of emotional pain and desperation.
- ◆ Be as concrete and specific as possible in your approach to the patient's problems.
- ◆ Be pragmatic and emphasize a "what works" approach to solving difficulties.
- ◆ Be collaborative and emphasize a "team" approach to the client's problem.

Selected Readings

Chiles J, Strosahl K: The suicidal patient: assessment, crisis management and treatment, in Current Psychiatric Therapy. Edited by Dunner D. Toronto, Canada, WB Saunders, 1993, pp 494–498

Meichenbaum D: Cognitive Behavior Modification: An Integrative Approach. New York, Plenum, 1977

Strosahl K, Jacobson N: The training and supervision of behavior therapists. The Clinical Supervisor 4:183–206, 1986

 Chapter 7

Crisis and Case Management With Recurrent Suicidal Behavior

In this chapter, we discuss how to manage a suicidal crisis in a way that is both collaborative and leads to good results. We also show you how to coordinate care across different parts of the same delivery system or across different service delivery systems. We have included a separate chapter on crisis and case management because we feel that these are the most demanding aspects of your work with those suicidal patients who are prone to slip in and out of crisis over the course of treatment. Dealing with episodically or chronically elevated suicidal behavior puts most providers ill at ease. In contrast to the traditional notion of crisis intervention, *crisis management* refers to the act of planning a response to recurring suicidal behavior in collaboration with the patient. The goal is to establish a framework that rewards alternatives to suicidal behavior and minimizes the short term reinforcements if and when suicidal behavior occurs.

Some patients you see will be nearly always suicidal, although the intensity level varies from week to week. It is not productive to view repetitive and intractable ideation as a suicidal crisis. For a

125

substantial number of suicidal patients, suicide ideation is a daily reality—it is an ever-present symptom. These patients are often assigned to case management systems. The case manager and therapist must continually balance their crisis intervention response to the recurring suicidal behavior, ongoing treatment, and the community resource needs of the patient.

Case management is best defined as the effective coordination of care in a variety of settings. As a case manager, you address liability issues, overcome system-level obstructions, communicate a clear treatment plan, and deal with resistances other providers may experience in following through with case management strategies. Another goal of case management, and sometimes the most difficult, is to resolve the potential conflict of interest between the social control goals of treatment delivery systems and your own sense of what is in the patient's best interest.

Whereas crisis intervention is largely a matter of interaction between you and your patient, case management is your attempt to influence the behavior of others to support your patient. These two missions often converge with the less treatment-responsive patient. Typically, difficult suicidal patients require more episodes of behavioral management as well as more frequent and active case management. When these demands intensify, you must be aware of a tendency to drift away from a problem-solving focus. In effective treatment, problem solving and emotional tolerance need to be pursued consistently, regardless of recurrent crises or the amount of case management.

Working Through Suicidal Crises: Principles

Whenever a patient needs help with a suicidal crisis, successful intervention relies on five fundamental principles. First, remember that suicidal behavior is designed to solve specific problems that the patient views as inescapable, interminable, and emotionally intolerable. Any of us can become suicidal when faced with these conditions. Successful crisis intervention helps the patient work through the suicidal crisis by using both short- and intermediate-term problem-solving strategies. Second, your demeanor plays a critical role in accelerating or decelerating the crisis. Approach the suicidal crisis in a direct, matter-of-fact, and candid fashion and avoid appearing nervous, scared, or apprehensive about what may happen next.

Third, remember that nearly all occurrences of suicidal behavior are nonfatal. Most suicidal crises do not lead to suicide. Furthermore, there is little evidence that any form of crisis intervention, be it counseling, psychopharmacology, or both, will prevent suicide. Most of the therapeutic maneuvers that count are based on the assumption that the patient will be alive tomorrow. The patient should learn from this crisis and by this experience be less vulnerable to subsequent crises. If your only motive is to keep the patient alive, a precious opportunity for human growth will be missed. With the chronically suicidal patient, you will do little but react to a never-ending stream of suicidal episodes.

The fourth principle is that real suicidal crises are self-limiting. Few individuals can maintain an acute crisis for more than 24–48 hours without going into an adaptive period of emotional exhaustion. Your treatment should be focused on getting through the next 1–2 days, while anticipating that the episode will soon give way the underlying problems that provoked the crisis. Fifth, the final objective in crisis intervention is to help the patient solve problems in nonsuicidal ways. Your intervention techniques should never reinforce suicidal behavior. Your goal is neither to punish nor reinforce suicidal behavior but to make it a "neutral valence" event. By achieving this valence, the suicidality will lose any advantage it had over other more adaptive problem-solving strategies.

Working Through Escalating Suicidal Behavior: Strategies

There are specific strategies to use when working with an acutely suicidal person. These techniques can be put into play with both new patients and individuals in ongoing therapy; they are described in Table 7–1.

Overall, you need to remain calm, direct, and methodical. Your demeanor promotes the gathering of certain important pieces of information, such as your patient's perception of the problems that have precipitated suicidal behavior, the range of problem-solving responses that have been considered, and mood and cognitive factors that will influence short-term problem solving.

Assess your patient's problem-solving flexibility and monitor for the presence of psychotic or thought-disordered symptoms. Generally, the more disordered a patient's thinking, the less workable is a self-directed problem-solving plan. The psychotic illness should be addressed. This type of patient may benefit from the increased structure of a short-term hospitalization or a longer term hospitalization targeting the underlying psychotic symptoms.

Mood symptoms are important. They heavily influence a patient's motivation and energy level. A severely depressed patient is likely to have trouble following through with a problem-solving plan because the energy is not there to accomplish it. A highly anxious, agitated patient has plenty of energy to expend but may experience trouble focusing on a plan of attack. Mood is the highway to a reading of your patient's suffering and desperation, a reading that will help decide whether the initial plan is aimed at lowering suffering or focuses on solving the problem(s) that triggered the crisis.

It is important to assess your patient's current use or potential for abuse of alcohol or drugs. Many suicidal people use alcohol or drugs

---

Table 7–1.   What to do when the crisis heats up

A. Be direct in questioning about suicidal behavior.
B. Be calm and methodical—remember functional analysis.
C. Review mental status. Ask about psychotic symptoms, mood symptoms, and drug and alcohol abuse.
D. Schedule extra contacts if necessary but beware of reinforcing suicidal behavior—emphasize problem solving, not "feeling better."
E. Try to help the individual generate short-term objectives.
F. Now is a great time to make a "random" support call.
G. Negotiate a positive action plan.
H. Review the crisis protocol.

as a way to treat emotional pain. If drug or alcohol abuse plays a role, avoid lecturing or moralizing about the negative effects of substance abuse. Instead, form a problem-solving plan that is incompatible with the passive approach that leads to drug or alcohol abuse. For example, schedule constructive activities during the time your patient is prone to drink or take drugs, or consider follow-up calls at a time when your patient might be tempted to use. It is useful to probe for high-risk times when drugs or alcohol were not used. Find out how your patient was able to devise better solutions, then focus on the increased use of these strategies. It is often useful to enlist the aid of others in your patient's social network to help restrict access to alcohol or drugs or to support or initiate activities that are incompatible with heavy use.

Do not assess your patient's potential for suicidal behavior by limiting yourself to the use of traditional suicide risk assessment questions. Evaluate beliefs about the efficacy of suicide as a way of solving problems (see Chapter 2). Reframe suicidal behavior in the problem-solving context so that your patient's first impression of treatment is oriented toward solving real-life problems. This approach destigmatizes the suicidal behavior per se and gets your patient thinking about symptoms from a different perspective. Work hard to get the initial message across that suicidal behavior is not a sign of abnormality. It is an outcome of a legitimate problem-solving process. This tactic alone will often defuse a suicidal crisis.

The Positive Behavior Action Plan

The outcome of effective behavioral management is a short-term plan that has been *collaboratively* generated by you and your patient. The plan addresses what actions need to be done in the succeeding days to solve the problem(s) that precipitated suicidal behavior. A good plan is easy to define. It is concrete, detailed, and within the patient's ability level.

The two most common mistakes are forming a plan that the patient is unable to accomplish, and pushing a plan that is not formed by a collaborative effort. Given the pressure inherent in the

crisis situation, you strongly want the outcome to be good. Unfortunately, good might be defined by solely what you think the patient
ought to be doing to solve difficulties. This type of good may not be
something that the patient agrees with or is able to do. It is not
necessary to do heroic things to solve problems. Achieving a *small
positive* step will have a big impact. Remember, the psychology of
suicidal behaviors is that the situation is viewed as unchangeable
and inescapable. Any positive change can bring these often rigid
assumptions into question. When you have developed a workable
short-term plan, you have done your best to ensure that your patient
will succeed. Measuring a plan to a patient's real capacity is the key
ingredient of success. If the plan is unachievable, your patient will
give up and have one more failure to deal with. The plan must be
seen as workable and, if successful, as a positive step forward. Two
key questions are, "If you were able to do x in the next few days,
would you see that as a sign of progress?" "Do you think x is
something that you can actually do in the next few days, given the
way you are feeling?"

What follows are some typical goals for the short-term problem-
solving plan. Look for ways to decrease your patient's social isolation, increase pleasant or reinforcing events, and reengage your
patient with some activity in which success is likely. An isolated
person may have a competent social support network but worries
about being a burden and so avoids interactions. In this situation, a
short-term behavioral plan might emphasize initiating a social contact with one or more helpful persons but limiting the amount of
time spent talking about personal problems. You can work on ways
to get your patient to resume a pleasant activity that has somehow
dropped out of the weekly routine. This might be scheduling one or
two walks in the park over a 5-day period, going to a movie, or
taking an aerobics class. Notice that the scale of these interventions
is not large and the interventions themselves may not directly target
suicidal ideation or behavior. The important point is to choose
interventions that are likely to be done. Initially, actually experiencing some success is much more important than struggling to solve
huge problems. Wherever possible, this short-term, constructive plan
should be written down and a follow-up contact should be sched-

uled so you and your patient can assess how the plan is working. This follow-up is usually conducted 1–3 days after the initial intervention.

The No Suicide Pact: Who Is the Beneficiary?

In recent years, the no suicide pact has made its way into clinical lore as a way to remove the threat of suicide. Patients are asked to state in writing that they will not engage in suicidal behavior for a set period of time. This approval has some utility, but we prefer, as discussed in more detail in the next chapter, a time-limited, *positive action plan*. The no suicide pact was originally conceived as an inpatient management technique. It has subsequently been used in other settings and situations, often, unfortunately, with scant effort to evaluate efficacy or even examine theoretical underpinnings. Some systems unfortunately have used this pact as a hospitalization criterion (i.e., one has to promise not to be suicidal to be admitted). Other systems use a patient's refusal to sign as a criterion for involuntary hospitalization. Additionally, the no suicide pact may actually deceive the clinician into believing that the patient is better. Pointedly, there is no indication that suicide is less likely in people who have agreed to a no suicide pact or that this strategy serves a preventive function. Theoretically, it may actually increase risk if the patient is not able to abide by the agreement, feels guilty, and does not disclose this fact to the therapist. The alternative is the positive action plan. In brief, patients are asked to engage in positive, constructive behaviors for a defined interval. This change in emphasis, from what you *should not* do to what you *should* do, becomes a critical part of an effective problem-solving set. Remember, *no* strategy guarantees the removal of suicidal potential, so the goal is to at least create a positive context for short-term problem solving.

The no suicide pact has been used as a requirement for a patient to be discharged from one treatment system into another system. This is like requiring the depressed person not to be depressed in order to go home from an outpatient therapy session. If the depressed person was able to be nondepressed simply because of that type of pressure, would not the patient have done it already? If the suicidal patient were really able to agree not to be suicidal, would not it seem reasonable to assume that the patient would have done it already? Patient flow between parts of a comprehensive system of care needs to be based on an assessment of level of intensity and need, not on the extraction of a statement that can have a misleading and soporific effect on clinicians.

The Emotional Tone of the Intervention

Although the technical goal of crisis intervention is to develop a problem-solving set and formulate a plan, it is extremely important to remember that the underpinnings of suicidal behavior are emotional desperation and intolerable and inescapable pain. You need to validate these difficulties and provide emotional support. Crisis intervention sessions can go bad when the therapist's anxiety to do something leads to a disconfirmation of the patient's sense of pain and distress. The "just do it" motif might work well in the locker room, but it is anathema for the suicidal patient who may interpret this as belittling. The patient may actually become more suicidal. When this happens, the patient is saying to the provider, "No, you don't quite understand just how badly I'm really feeling. Let me show you a little more directly!" As frequently as you can, validate your patient's sense of emotional pain and your understanding that he or she is considering suicide as an option to stop that pain. At the same time, confidentially state your belief that if the two of you work together, better solutions can be found. There are many technical steps that can be taken with a patient who is suicidal, but the emotional tone of the session is by far the most important mediator of overall success. The patient who feels listened to and accepted is more likely to carry through with a collaborative problem-solving plan.

Managing Suicidal Behavior During Treatment

Any patient may become suicidal again during the course of therapy given the right set of life events or a predisposition to use suicidal behavior as a problem-solving device. Although this seems obvious, some therapists implicitly assume that the act of entering therapy causes suicidal behavior to disappear. If suicidal behavior reappears, the therapist is often unprepared and angry, and will confront the patient. The art of successful therapy is to collaboratively anticipate and plan for the recurrence of suicidal ideation or behavior at some point in the therapy sequence. The act of coming for treatment is not to be confused with solving real-life problems. Acknowledging this fact puts the clinician-patient relationship on a realistic level rather than perpetuating an idealized image of therapy. Use any recurrence of suicidal behavior as a "learning laboratory" for problem-solving skills and emotional pain tolerance. This technique gives the patient permission to bring everything into the therapy session, rather than withholding information that the patient believes will displease the therapist.

Suicidal Behavior Protocols

Table 7–2 lists some of the most important points to cover when developing a behaviorally based protocol for managing suicidal behavior. Most of the protocol is established in the initial session. Two things are important: 1) that the protocol is well understood and agreed to by your patient, and 2) that it is consistent with your beliefs and values. The bottom line is, "What are you the clinician

Table 7–2. Protocol for managing suicidality during therapy

A. Prevent alcohol and drug use.
B. Reward appropriateness.
　　1. Do not reinforce suicidal behavior with increased attention.
　　2. Reward attempts to address crisis without suicidal behavior.
C. Establish a specific crisis protocol for each patient—the crisis card strategy.
D. Remember that suicidal thinking and behavior continue after hours—consider crisis clinic, social support network.
E. Establish conditions under which the individual may seek hospitalization.
　　1. Emphasize self-control behaviors over acting-out behaviors.
F. Make clear your own policies regarding involuntary hospitalization.

going to do if I the patient become acutely suicidal?" Your patient may, for example, be concerned that you will use involuntary hospitalization and so will be reluctant to mention anything about a suicidal crisis. Accordingly, you must state your beliefs and values regarding a potential suicidal crisis. There are legal, ethical, and moral cross-currents here that can influence the success or failure of therapy. This information should be discussed openly. Any jointly agreed-to action plan must reflect principles that you are willing to follow in the midst of a suicidal crisis.

Your strategies about how to use hospitalization should be laid out as well. This might include discussing the issue of short-term acute care, voluntary admissions to evaluate diagnostic issues, and the use of involuntary admissions. For example, you may present the value of voluntary, short-term, "time-out" admissions over longer term, vaguely defined admissions. The goal is to build a scenario in which effective decision making can occur in the event of a crisis by including your patient in the advanced planning and thereby maximizing the sense of his or her self-control.

Additional sessions may be needed in the event of a suicidal crisis. However, scheduling additional sessions may inadvertently reinforce suicidal behavior by making your extra attention seem a reward for being suicidal. This is a perennial problem with many of the usually unscheduled interventions that occur during periods of elevated suicidal behavior. In general, it is more helpful to schedule additional sessions when positive problem-solving behaviors are occurring and your patient will benefit from more intense work. If additional contacts are required because of a crisis, try to make it as minimally intensive as possible. This might include brief phone call follow-ups rather than 1-hour, face-to-face visits, for example. You should focus efforts on reinforcing and building constructive problem-solving behaviors. Encourage your patient to develop self-sufficiency in crisis, that internal ability to weather the storm.

Establish very soon in treatment when and under what conditions you will receive unscheduled calls. Once the patient has *initiated* suicidal behavior, limit your participation in crisis phone calls. A good strategy is to indicate that in the event suicidal behavior has already occurred, you will undertake an assessment of medical lethality. If you believe the patient is in medical danger, an emergency aid car will be sent to the location immediately. Indicate that this is not an appropriate time to discuss more effective problem-solving options, and reinforce your interest in discussing the situation at the next regularly scheduled session. Encourage your patient to make mental or written notes concerning the handling of this particular crisis, and strongly state your belief that there is much to be learned from this situation. If your patient calls regarding thinking about a suicide attempt, always offer the opportunity to dispose of the means and engage in a brief problem-solving discussion. Again, instruct your patient to make notes and bring them to the next session, and praise your patient about calling you instead of pursuing suicidal behavior. Never be abrupt or imply that you are punishing your patient because of misbehavior. Many practitioners cringe at the thought of cutting short a phone call, fearing the liability implications if the patient ever committed suicide. This is exactly the dilemma that "liability-based" treatment puts us into. The issue here is to look at what *works clinically* in this situation; document the basis of your decision and the steps you have taken to help the patient.

In general, a crisp handling of phone calls coupled with the capacity to turn the context of the phone call into a homework assignment is far more constructive than lengthy unstructured conversations.

A problem in taking phone calls is that you, like anyone else, need rest, time away from work, and the ability to pursue other activities. You want your patient to call you prior to initiating suicidal behavior. This approach builds self-control and personal responsibility. When your patient complies with this protocol, you should be available to consult at any hour of the day. It is important, however, to remind your patient that clinicians, like all people, have nighttime and after-hours activities that are not a part of their daytime work. If these activities are underway when a patient calls, indicate that you are busy, instruct your patient to follow the self-support plan on his or her crisis card (see the next section in this chapter), and schedule a time to talk that will work for both of you.

A more perplexing situation is when your patient calls, is suicidal, has the means immediately present, and tells you, "I'm going to do it!" In this case, instruct the patient to remove the means from immediate access by turning it over to a friend or otherwise disposing of it. At times like this, it is helpful to say something like, "I want to help you, but it is going to be hard for us to talk if you are thinking about killing yourself at the same time. Let's put that stuff aside so we can work together to sort out what is going on here." If your patient will not adopt this stance, then any phone-based problem solving is likely to be a melodrama, and a bad one at that. You have already indicated what your stance is in situations like this. Now is the time to follow through.

The Crisis Card

The last and most important crisis protocol strategy is developing a crisis card. The goal is to teach your patient to use existing social support and community resources and to depend less on you as time goes on. Identify one or more competent social supporters that could be contacted in the event of a crisis. A competent social supporter is a person who will not lecture, cajole, or moralize about problems but will provide emotional validation and a safe atmosphere. Once these social supporters are identified, your patient writes their names down as well as their phone numbers on a card. Next, identify community resources that can be contacted in the event of a crisis. This might include the local crisis clinic, a mental health center emergency services unit, or a local emergency room social worker. These resources are written down along with their corresponding phone numbers. The last name on the card is yours, with associated work and home numbers. Your patient is to first contact all of the social supporters, followed by the community resources. If those resources fail, your patient contacts you. You jointly agree that you will be as available as possible for such contacts if your patient has followed through with attempts to contact all of the above mentioned resources. If your patient has not followed the protocol, then (directly and in a supportive way) ask your patient to proceed through the card and call back if all attempts at contact fail to ameliorate the crisis. If your patient is unable to do this, proceed as described above but emphasize the need to reexamine the protocol at the next session.

A second aspect of the crisis card is self-support strategies. Two to four instructions can be quite helpful. If substance abuse is an aggravating problem, the card item could be, "Don't drink. If I am drinking, STOP." Simple tactics for affect regulation are useful, "Take 10 deep breaths and count to 50." Positive statements, to be repeated several times, can be useful, "I am a strong person and have weathered moments like this before." Lastly, and perhaps always, evoke the problem-solving perspective: "I need to step back and look at the problem I am having right now."

Random Support Calls

Inform your patient that from time to time you will be calling to see how things are going. The random support call strategy is designed to remove the association between escalating suicidal behavior and your attention. The random support call neutralizes this association and can be a precipitant for some major movement in therapy. The random support call is usually very short, no more than 2–3 minutes. The essence of the message is, "I care about how you're doing. I hope the behavioral homework assignment is going well. You were going to pay particular attention to x. How is that going? I really look forward to seeing you next week. Take care." In other words, do not perform therapy on the phone but rather support your patient in whatever activities are occurring that week. To make this process truly random, it is advisable to randomly draw numbers and then set up a schedule 3 months in advance. These calls will be made regardless of your patient's functional status. Random support calls do not have to be made often; one a month can often have a positive impact. When your patient is in a crisis, you can bend the rules a bit and make a random support call in a not-so-random fashion. Even though your patient is in a crisis, the message is essentially the same, and the duration of the call is short (2–3 minutes). This strategy creates a new kind of relationship. The issue of mattering to someone and being understood can be so central to your suicidal patient's view of the world that a simple 2-minute call may be a major event in treatment.

Growing Through Suicidal Behavior

There are two key principles that can make any occurrence of suicidal behavior a productive event. First, *suicidal behavior in the midst of therapy is not evidence that the treatment is failing*. It simply means that the behaviors that brought the patient into therapy in the first place are still present in the patient's problem-solving hierarchy. The clinician who insists that the patient refrain from suicidal behavior in order to continue therapy is doing a disservice. You must learn to harness your disappointment regarding a patient's suicidal crisis. A good place to start may be to remember that the power to influence is great; the power to control is nil.

Second, *the basic goal is to neutralize the reinforcement of suicidal behavior*. When your patient presents you with suicidal behavior, you have a golden opportunity to directly modify the behavior. This means that you arrange consequences so your patient will not experience suicidal behavior as a potent problem-solving strategy. For example, if the patient uses the hospital to escape his or her environment (i.e., I am suicidal, let me in), then develop other forms of respite. If suicidal ideation or behavior helps to relieve anxiety, then devise strategies to install alternative methods for achieving anxiety reduction. If your patient is dependent on you and uses suicidal behavior to maintain an unhealthy intensity of treatment, then adhere to a regular session schedule, and do not reinforce suicidality with additional contacts.

These interventions depend on your assessment of how suicidal behavior is being reinforced. What does this patient get out of being suicidal that allows the behavior to stick around even with its longer term negative consequences? Remember, despite the social stigma attached to suicidal behavior, it is a very powerful short-term problem-solving strategy with strong internal and external consequences.

It is very important to be consistent with the problem-solving model. The clinician who abandons a treatment model during suicidal crises has a much greater likelihood of failure, either through unsuccessful therapy or through premature termination. The key is to show the patient that everything comes down to problem solving whether a crisis is present or not. The more matter of fact, candid, and upbeat you are when confronting recurrent suicidal behavior, the more likely it is that your patient will adopt a problem-solving set and get task oriented instead of focusing exclusively on emotional pain. Use the assessment strategies described earlier. Build homework assignments around tracking suicidal ideation or behavior. Identify trigger situations. If your patient can experientially verify these concepts, then his or her view of suicidal behavior will change.

Your patient can get demoralized over the recurrence of suicidal behavior, believing it demonstrates that things have not changed for the better. The more direct, matter of fact, and accepting you are of the suicidal behavior, the less likely it is that your patient will take any of these negative interpretations to an extreme. Many a patient has dropped out of therapy in an effort to avoid the disappointment of, or confrontation with, the therapist.

You must distinguish between working with the suicidal behavior and inadvertently reinforcing it. Accomplish this by focusing on problem-solving communication and pain tolerance as twin frameworks for therapeutic transactions. Pay less attention to suicidal behavior per se, except as it relates to experiments in problem solving. This can be difficult to do because of the power of suicidal communications. It can be hard to remain as interested in problem-solving communications as suicidal communications. Do you sit perched on the edge of the seat when the patient is talking about suicide but relax and sit back when problem solving is the focus of exchange? To combat this phenomenon, assess the amount of time spent talking about effective problem solving versus suicidal behavior. The general rule is that at least 85% of the session should be spent in the former pursuit and no more than 15% spent focusing directly on suicidal behavior.

When suicidal behavior recurs, you need to execute agreements that were formed in the initial session. This is a test of your belief in the treatment protocol because it is being challenged under real-life conditions. This is where "the rubber hits the road," especially with the chronically suicidal patient. If you have a soft spot, it will be revealed now. If you promised the patient that no involuntary hospitalization will be used but now invoke this intervention, you have jeopardized the working relationship. When soft spots appear, modify the treatment plan to be consistent with what you really believe. You must be genuine. Admit your mistakes and ambivalence, renegotiate the plan, and push on.

To Hospitalize or Not To Hospitalize: That Is the Question

No examination of crisis intervention or case management principles would be complete without addressing the issue of voluntary or involuntary psychiatric hospitalization as a treatment for suicidal crisis. Hospitalization is overused for suicidality, and in Chapter 8 we address the plethora of factors that must be understood to appropriately use this modality. These factors dictate a cautious approach to the use of hospitalization as a behavior management tool. The emphasis should be on whether psychiatric hospitalization is the preferred treatment for an underlying mental disorder that is related to the patient's suicidal potential. For example, the schizophrenic patient who is experiencing command hallucinations to commit suicide would profit from a secure environment so that medications could be started, with the expectation that the command hallucinations would begin to dissipate with effective treatment. The focus is not suicidal behavior per se but the underlying mental disorder. When a person is hospitalized to treat the mental disorder and suicidal behavior is present, it is imperative to closely monitor reinforcement patterns on the unit so that suicidality is not being exacerbated.

Emphasizing Responsibility and Self-Control

Patients who take responsibility for hospitalizing themselves before engaging in suicidal behavior not only experience more self-control but tend to be viewed favorably by inpatient staff. It is important to work to place responsibility for the admission in the hands of your patient, so that the admission is an act of self-control. Your patient can be instructed that it is a positive act of self-control to acknowledge that a time-out is needed. In the event a patient wants a time-out hospitalization, the patient should go (not be taken) to the appropriate emergency or intake unit, request a short-term stay with an anticipated discharge in 48–72 hours. The goal is to minimize time away from the environment where the real problems are occurring while at the same time allowing the patient to form a problem-solving plan. This approach encourages using personal responsibility and self-control to offset the potentially negative effects of a hospitalization.

There are too many situations in which clinicians treat their anxiety about a patient's suicide risk rather than securing appropriate treatment for the patient. Often inpatient staff feel that suicidal patients have been "system dumps" because clinicians up the line simply are too anxious to deal directly with the problem. This results in a lot of anger being directed at the patient for being the one who caused the mess in the first place. The charge to outpatient clinicians is to seek appropriate consultation to reduce anxiety about a particular patient and to gear treatment strategies to the best interest of the patient. Therapy is not the business of clinician anxiety; it is the business of helping patients solve problems using clinically effective strategies.

Case Management, Crisis Intervention at the System Level

When a patient receives medical or mental health treatment from different systems, or is seeing more than one provider within a single system, case management concerns almost inevitably arise. For example, a suicidal patient may first visit a family practice doctor's office, then be transferred to an emergency room for an assessment. At this point, the patient is either hospitalized or referred to the outpatient mental health system for counseling. Each of these contact points represents both an opportunity for coordinated care and a potential for conflicting, disjointed, and idiosyncratic responses.

Effective case management attempts to ensure that treatment is consistent as the patient crosses between systems or moves between levels of care within a system while at the same time keeping each service delivery entity working within its own area of expertise. In other words, each of the players knows exactly both what his or her role is and what he or she is not supposed to do.

As systems work more closely together, case managers will play a crucial role in coordinated transfer planning. Local delivery systems are part of a coordinated and interconnected network that will provide various services to the suicidal patient. Case management is responsible for coordinating the patient's smooth transition between systems. The inpatient psychiatric facility shares responsibility for the patient's continuous and coordinated care in the outpatient system. Outpatient treatments are likewise coordinated through the inpatient stays in a way that ensures consistency in the care models that are being used with the patient. When the emergency room transfers a patient into inpatient or outpatient care, it is responsible for ensuring that the patient follows through with the referral. Likewise, it is responsible for coordinating its delivery of services with any outpatient or inpatient unit that has previously worked with the patient. This model may bedevil those risk managers who want to protect their agencies but do not have a clue about what constitutes quality clinical care. However, this model sees the community of systems as the treating agent, and thus creates a very efficient managed care format.

The irony is that there are many examples where drawing an arbitrary line between systems or departments invites negligence. Had the facility in question seen itself as part of the treatment community, that extra phone call might have been made to ensure that the patient had followed through with an appointment at another facility. The potential negligence was not the patient's state of mind on leaving the facility, the negligence was that the facility did not follow through and ensure that the patient arrived at the next destination. When the patient makes a coordinated transfer between and within systems, quality of clinical care increases exponentially. Providers in different systems can talk with one another without feeling put on the spot or exposed to unacceptable risks. Not only does the patient benefit, but fewer resources end up being expended in the process—better outcomes, lower costs, less litigation: sounds like a good equation.

The Case Manager Role

Most effective case management systems have a single person who is accepted as being in charge of coordinating treatment and transfers. This person may be the therapist, or it may be the crisis interventionist/mental health professional who is attempting to move the patient to various needed treatment locations. Case management can be time consuming. It is a legitimate and indispensable component of effective treatment. This means you must talk with other health and mental health practitioners so that they understand the rationale of treatment and are willing to follow the role that is scripted for them. This is particularly true with the suicidal patient because everyone not only has strong reactions to suicidal behavior but has a variety of ideas on how to work with the patient. This can lead to an array of conflicting treatment approaches that leave the patient bewildered and confused. Similarly, the pressure to fix the patient can lead to dissension among providers who conflict about the right way to treat a suicidality.

In many treatment settings, case management is not viewed as part of legitimate clinical service delivery. It is often counted as administrative time by the clinic directors. This puts the clinician in the position of being negatively reinforced for implementing perhaps the most important aspect of treatment. In effect, the time spent comes out of the clinician's hide; caseload expectations remain the same despite the difficulties associated with managing a particularly suicidal patient. This organizational stance not only invites negligence claims but also reduces general quality of care.

Qualities of the Effective Case Manager

There are three pivotal qualities that lead to being an effective case manager with the suicidal patient. First, you need a clear approach to the problem and need to be willing to articulate the approach and how it will produce clinical benefit. Second, you need to state in concrete operational terms what various players need to do to support a coordinated treatment effort. Third, you need to provide frequent feedback about how the plan is working, and you need to deal with the concerns of the various providers.

The dearth of literature on how to treat the suicidal patient causes many to have vague case management goals. This vagueness results in confusion among other providers or among clinical team members, who will not understand the objectives of the treatment nor what they are supposed to do to support those goals. In the worst case scenario, this lack of clarity does not surface until suicidal behavior escalates and the patient begins traveling within or across systems. When this movement occurs, providers initiate their own personal strategies and are unwilling to abandon their own strategy in favor of ones they do not completely understand or endorse. Effective case management requires that you be absolutely clear about the treatment strategies that will produce a good clinical outcome. This is often best done using a written case management plan that is distributed to all concerned parties. Figure 7–1 provides a model case management planning sheet that helps begin to address this and other questions that go into an effective case management plan.

Armed with a therapeutic strategy, the therapist still needs to convert that strategy into concrete instructions for different health and mental health care providers. These instructions need to be consistent with the skill and background training of the providers. For example, instructions for emergency room doctors might focus more on issues related to medical evaluation and short-term instructions about transferring care of the patient if further assistance is needed. Expecting emergency room doctors to perform social work services or psychotherapy with a suicidal patient is usually not realistic.

It is important for you to provide a constant flow of feedback, both positive and negative, to key points in the system. Ironically, most case management discussions occur when things are not working. There is a tension associated with these discussions that could be ameliorated if there was a balance between positive and negative feedback. You should take the time to call back providers who followed instructions and show them how this has helped produce a good clinical outcome. If a provider's efforts supported continuity and coordination of care, the provider should be made aware of that fact. In other words, try to avoid circumstances where the only communications with other providers occur when there are disagreements about treatment strategies or a failure to follow through on a specific plan.

A good example is when you develop a strategy to make suicidal behavior a neutral valence behavior. This will require the providers who contact the suicidal patient to respond neither with excessive attention, caring, or concern, nor with punishment, confrontation, or

---

Patient name: _____ Primary provider: _____

A. Target behaviors and frequency of occurrence (Describe the behavior, not your evaluation of it.)

B. Location/settings where target behavior occurs

C. Factors rewarding/maintaining target behavior
   1. Response of staff
   2. Response of significant others
   3. Changes in the patient's mental or emotional functioning

D. Behavior modification plan
   1. Who will do it (list all staff and departments involved)?
   2. When will it start?
   3. What is to be accomplished?
   4. What will be done to accomplish this (list specific behaviors)?
   5. What will be measured to determine whether the plan is working?
   6. How long will the plan be implemented before the results are reviewed?
      a. Scheduled review date: _____

Note. The primary provider is the person to contact if there are any questions. The primary provider is the person responsible for the treatment of this patient. In case of a patient emergency, the primary provider should be contacted immediately at the number(s) listed below

---

Figure 7–1. Sample suicidal behavior management protocol.

cajoling. This is a difficult task in the heat of the moment. When there is follow-through at an emergency room, it is very important to let providers know that they did a good job.

An equally important goal of effective case management is to have the patient understand that the case management umbrella will be user friendly so long as the patient stays underneath it. Frequently, patients with character disorders or other oppositional attributes test out the timbre of a case management system. The patient presents with suicidal ideation or behavior at various points in the case management system to see if there is a consistency in the response. If the patient has collaboratively developed the case management plan with the therapist, there will be less testing. However, it is important to have the patient understand the limits of the case management system. For example, it is difficult to link every emergency room or hospital to a particular patient's case management plan. The patient needs to understand that presentation at an uninvolved facility could result in unpredictable outcomes such as involuntary hospitalization or the use of restraint and seclusion. The patient must understand that the therapist cannot control what will happen outside the umbrella. The goal is to get the suicidal patient to present at service delivery sites where the practitioners have been prepared to respond in a clinically effective manner.

Just as is the case with providers, it is important to praise the patient for staying within the case management umbrella. The therapist might bend over backward to be available for a crisis call in such a circumstance. This extra attention will reinforce the patient for sticking with the case management plan. Although this may be an inconvenience, it generally takes a lot less time than managing a care plan that is being continuously tested by the patient.

Suicidal patients differ in the extent to which they require case management services. Clearly, the difficult patient requires much more case management. These patients tend to be more disordered, multiproblem patients who may have developed a lifestyle of chronic suicidal crisis. If you are willing to follow the principles outlined in this section, there is a greater likelihood that service delivery systems will respond in a way that not only helps the patient but will also make life easier for the therapist.

Helpful Hints

During Crisis

♦ The two key skills in effective crisis intervention are validating emotional pain and forming an effective problem-solving plan with the patient.

♦ Remember, the goal of effective crisis intervention is not to prevent suicide but to help the patient learn how to move through problems and tolerate negative affect.

♦ The goal in crisis intervention is to stay consistent with the problem-solving model while focusing on short-term goals.

♦ Try to defocus on a suicidal behavior per se while increasing emphasis on solving specific problems that precipitated crisis.

♦ Remember that almost all true suicidal crises are very short lived, no longer than 48–72 hours.

♦ Beware of using psychiatric inpatient treatment for suicidal behavior per se as it may inadvertently reinforce the behavior.

In Therapy

♦ In therapy, directly address and plan for the possible recurrence of suicidal behavior during the initial session with the patient.

♦ When planning for crisis, emphasize steps that reinforce the patient's responsibility and self-control in seeking help.

♦ Analyze the reinforcements for suicidal behavior so that interventions do not inadvertently reinforce suicidal problem solving.

♦ Effective case management with other service delivery systems requires a clear statement of treatment goals, concrete instructions for other providers, and providing frequent feedback.

Selected Readings

Bancroft J, Skirimshire A, Casson J, et al: People who deliberately poison themselves: their problems and their contacts with helping agencies. Psychol Med 7:289–303, 1977

Blumenthal SJ: Suicide: a guide to risk factors, assessment, and treatment of suicidal patients. Med Clin North Am 72:937–971, 1988

Chiles J, Strosahl K: The suicidal patient: assessment, crisis management and treatment, in Current Psychiatric Therapy. Edited by Dunner D. Toronto, Canada, WB Saunders, 1993, pp 494–498

Chiles JA, Strosahl K, Cowden L, et al: The 24 hours before hospitalization: factors related to suicide attempting. Suicide Life Threat Behav 16:335–342, 1986

Newscom-Smith J, Hirsch S (eds): The Suicide Syndrome. London, UK, Croom Helm, 1979

Chapter 8

Inpatient Treatment of
the Suicidal Patient

We state our bias immediately: hospitalization is overused for suicidality, and when it is used, it is often for the wrong reasons. Society has given the hospital a pivotal role in dealing with a suicidal person, and yet, as a treatment for suicidal behavior, hospitalization has limited usefulness. There is little evidence that a stay on a psychiatric unit has a long-term beneficial effect on suicidal behavior. No reasonably well-controlled studies have demonstrated that hospitalization will reduce suicide potential. Further, there is little or no agreement about what set of criteria should be used for hospitalization. In some settings, the majority of suicidal patients referred to emergency rooms are not psychiatrically hospitalized, whereas in others, most are. More and more, hospitalization because of suicidality is driven is by legal concerns, concerns that are predicated on a rather vague notion of what one must do to avoid malpractice litigation. This approach is unfortunate, because hospitalization is an extremely important component of a multitiered psychiatric response system to crises, including suicidal crises. Hospitalization is one of several essential tools to have in your treatment tool box. Hospitalization can become problematic when it is viewed as the *only* response you, the clinician, can make to a suicidal patient. An old adage is pertinent: if all you have is a hammer, you must treat everything as if it were a nail. In this chapter, we examine the negative and positive aspects of hospitalization, describe treatment principles, and discuss alternatives to inpatient treatment.

All states have some sort of mental health statute that requires a clinician to initiate hospitalization or other strong protective measures if a patient is deemed to be an *imminent risk for suicide*. Although there is a wide range of personal opinion about a person's right to commit suicide, this is not expressed in state statutes. There is no doubt that the social control function of the law is strongly in favor of stopping the individual from committing suicide. Further, the assumption behind most state statutes is that hospitalization, whether voluntary or involuntary, represents the most effective short-term preventive treatment for suicide. Individuals who are deemed imminently suicidal are thus deprived of their civil right to be free of incarceration so that a short-term treatment for their suicidal crisis can be provided. Several questions are raised by involuntary treatment. First, does placement in a psychiatric unit prevent a person from engaging in or succeeding at suicidal behavior? Second, does hospitalization represent an effective treatment per se for a person who is suicidal at the time of admission? Third, are there longer term consequences associated with being psychiatrically hospitalized that can be potentially detrimental to a suicidal person (i.e., can hospitalization make things worse)?

Do Hospitals Prevent Suicides?

There is very little conclusive evidence to suggest that being placed on a psychiatric unit reduces the person's chance of committing suicide in either the short or long term. Suicides occur more often on psychiatric units and in jails than in any other location. Inpatient suicides account for up to 5% of all known suicides. If you add to this the events of the first week following hospital discharge, up to 11% of all suicides will be accounted for. Interestingly, both jails and psychiatric inpatient units contain troubled individuals who may well consider the setting and its restraints as an intense invasion of their personal freedom. The fact that the suicide rates in psychiatric units are not the *lowest* in the land suggests that individuals who are intent on the act are able to complete it even in the midst of staff concern and close observation.

Almost all mental health care workers have heard anecdotal reports of inpatient suicides. Mental health professionals with some expertise in this area frequently get legal requests to be expert witnesses in situations in which patients on psychiatric units have succeeded in killing themselves. Many of these anecdotes and descriptions are reminiscent of scenes from movies such as *Stalag 17* or *The Great Escape,* in which the central theme of the film is the incredible cunning and resourcefulness of individuals who are bound and determined to escape observation and do what they feel they have to do. Although most psychiatric hospitals have fairly elaborate protocols for close observation of at-risk patients, the inability to accurately predict risk levels means that many of the closely observed patients are not those who commit suicide. Almost all mental health workers with inpatient experience know of patients categorized as at low or declining risk who have gone on to attempt or complete suicide.

Does Hospitalization Work?

The second question has to do with the efficacy of hospitalization in dealing with suicidal ideation or suicide attempt. There are no outcome studies that show that the inpatient location per se is a critical factor. Researchers who have looked at the treatment of the suicidal patient in the inpatient setting tend to confound the setting with the type of treatment actually delivered. Often, these treatments could just as well be delivered in an outpatient environment. Inpatient clinical outcome reports are at best equivocal and at worst do not support this level of intervention. Germane to the potentially negative impact of hospitalization is a variety of research that shows that the suicidal patient tends to be received in a less than favorable way by hospital staff. The patient receives less-preferred forms and amounts of treatment, and tends to have interactions that are hallmarked by confrontation and hostility. These negative reactions may help explain the elopement and/or discharge against medical advice that occurs with as many as 50% of hospitalized suicidal individuals. A problem in reviewing articles on efficacy is the lack of clear clinical characteristics of those suicidal persons who are hospitalized versus those who are not hospitalized. Probably crucial to the successful use of a hospital is a judicious process for selecting admissions. When hospitalization occurs because no other options are available, a variety of bad reactions can set in. The patient can feel abandoned, the staff can feel angry because it appears that outpatient clinicians are not doing an adequate job, and both patient and staff can feel frustrated, disconnected from both what went on before and what should go on after. These reactions can produce their own ill effects and muddle the meaning of outcome information.

Iatrogenesis

Last, there are unintended side effects of hospitalization. As a rule, the most invasive treatments have the most invasive side effects, and hospitalization is no exception. First, labeling can determine behavior. People live up or down to the labels that are attached to them. The label of *psychiatric patient* can lead to a negative view of self that is then confirmed in subsequent behavior. The experience of being in an inpatient facility is something the patient may never forget, even when the stay is positive. Second, when a patient is admitted, the issue of autonomy comes into play. When the essence of a suicidal crisis is a struggle with one's sense of self-control over suicidal impulses, then the decision to hospitalize can be an extremely potent communication that the patient is out of control, confirming his or her worst fears. This makes it extremely important to present hospitalization as a component of a rational multimodal treatment plan, not as a last ditch effort because all else has failed.

Third, hospitalization can act as a reinforcement for suicidal behavior. By providing short-term relief from long-term problems, hospitalization can reinforce the patient's sense that suicidality works (i.e., "I made a suicide attempt and things got better"). This happens because hospitalization removes the individual from a stressful situation, and the subsequent anxiety reductions can be a reinforcer for the recurrence of suicidal ideation or behavior. The patient moves from an environment marked by hostility, criticism, or confrontation into one of some caring and concern. In the hospital, much of the conflict the patient has been experiencing is carefully governed in the hope that this will protect the patient's psychological stability. Troubled relationships seem to get better. For example, someone admitted for a suicide attempt is suddenly reconciled (at least temporarily) with a formerly hostile, alienated spouse who may feel blame for the way things have gone. Following an adolescent's suicide attempt, a dysfunctional family can be galvanized around the patient's suicidal behavior in a way that feels like the family is coming together. Because most of the possible negative conse-quences in these scenarios are longer term (e.g., other people avoid you, spouses get even more angry) and therefore not readily appar-ent, the patient may feel empowered to solve problems using suicidal behavior again. Most inpatient units are struggling with the growing number of repetitive suicide attempts. In one study, we found that the mean number of prior suicide attempts among hospitalized suicide attempts was more than two (Chiles et al. 1991). As the number of attempts builds up, staff often feel more pessimistic about their interventions. This can be a factor in the unfortunate conflict and hostility discussed earlier.

Is This a Hospital or a Prison?

In addition to the psychological and interactional elements discussed in the previous sections, the architecture of the unit can be another major factor in determining inpatient efficacy. Some hospital wards, particularly older ones, are designed to maximize isolation rather than to promote observation. Can nurses be aware of activities from a central station? Is staff at ease about patient location and behaviors, so that therapeutic work can be done? Without a spacious, commo-dious, and eminently viewable unit, there is danger that ward staff will overuse suicidal precautions as a means of patient control. Wards full of nooks, crannies, and blind spots (and many of them are) create a near guard/prisoner relationship between patient and staff. This atmosphere does not promote, and in fact demotes, the goals of successful treatment of suicidality: autonomy, efficacy, and self-control. Keep these components in mind. If you have a choice of inpatient services, visit them. When you are involved in hospitalization, try to get your patient to the unit that is the most efficiently unobtrusive. If you are fortunate enough to have a say in new unit construction or old unit remodeling, *insist* that clinical criteria be incorporated into design.

Will I Get Sued if I Do Not Hospitalize?

You cannot predict completed suicide, and there are not enough beds to hospitalize everyone troubled by suicidality. Almost every clinician working in an area of mental illness treatment has close knowledge of suicide occurring during treatment. For a therapist directly involved, the death can have a devastating effect. "What could I have done differently?" can become a painful and obsessive question for the clinician, just as it can be for friends and family. The accusation, "You should have hospitalized," can feed into troublesome second guessing. The fear of a lawsuit starting at this point haunts many health care providers. Of course, a dispassionate reading of the literature can equally support an accusation of, "Why did you hospitalize?" followed by a powerful self-doubt, "I should not have hospitalized." Can you be sued for inappropriately hospitalizing? It does not happen often—not yet—but this could become another worry.

Mark Twain once noted that the ethics of legality are the ethics of scoundrel. Performing legally sanctioned interventions may not be the same as performing good treatment. There can be a discrepancy between what is stated in the law (a legislatively conceived attempt at health care) and what seems the best and most appropriate clinical way to approach the problem. Decisions made *primarily* to address liability issues are often not good treatment decisions. In the litigious climate of the United States, lawsuits can happen at any time and for any reason. The question is not, "Will I get sued?" The question is, "Have I used my training, experience, knowledge, and expertise to devise a treatment plan that can help my patient deal with the problem of suicidality?" Think clearly and document your thinking. *If you don't write it down, it did not happen.* Have a reasonable treatment plan and stick with it. If you are worried about malpractice suits, increase your malpractice insurance.

When Hospitalization Goes Sour

The case report literature is full of examples of individuals who are hospitalized because of suicidality. This literature contains little or no long-term follow-up statements about the benefits of hospitalization. The following is a case report of an individual whose suicidal behavior escalates following hospitalization.

Ms. T, a 28-year-old, white female, worked in a laboratory in a major medical center. Soon after beginning employment, and 2 years before her first hospitalization, she sought treatment for depression and relationship difficulties. At that time she spoke of her parents' strictness and told of a difficult childhood. She was born and raised in a small town, the oldest of six children. Her parents were active members of a fundamentalist church. The family was often in financial difficulty, and Ms. T was working and giving her paycheck to her parents by the age of 13. Both parents demanded that she take over a number of child-rearing duties, and they frequently blamed her for troubles with her younger siblings. The parents would often go to religious retreats, leaving her in charge. She had little time or inclination for a social life and worked throughout her high school and college years. When she reached adulthood, her parents continued to demand that she support the family, including buying clothing for her siblings. At one point she took over payments for her father's truck. Just before she entered treatment, her parents had gone on a prolonged trip. When they returned they found that some of their other children had gotten into difficulty. They called their older daughter, now living in another city, blamed her for her failure to "come home and look after her brothers and sisters."

Ms. T was treated with antidepressant medication, and sup-portive psychotherapy was conducted at a rate of about one

session every 2 weeks. Her first visit to an emergency room came
when her physician was on vacation. She complained of increased
depression, anxiety, and suicidal thoughts. She was living alone
but had supportive friends, several of whom had urged her to
come to the emergency room. She had tried but could not get hold
of the individual covering for her vacationing caregiver. The emergency room physician evaluated her as being in "imminent danger
of suicide" and strongly recommended hospitalization.

Ms. T did not do well in her first 4 days of inpatient treatment.
She became quite distressed over the needs of the other patients.
Her psychiatric symptoms did not improve. When asked, she stated
she still "felt" suicidal. Her antidepressant medication was continued, and benzodiazepines were added to her regimen. On day 5
she demanded to leave, stating she needed to return to work. At
that point, she was involuntarily committed at a state hospital. She
was there for approximately 1 week and then discharged to her
outpatient provider. The psychotherapy was continued in the
original format; supportive sessions every 1–2 weeks. In about
1 month, she called her psychotherapist at night stating that she
had cut her wrists. An ambulance was dispatched and she was
again admitted to a local hospital. She argued about staying and
was transferred involuntarily to the state hospital. The patient was
released after about 3 weeks. Ten days later, she once again
contacted her psychotherapist stating she had made a suicide
attempt. This time she had taken approximately 1500 mg of a
tricyclic antidepressant and severely slashed her right arm. Her
medical treatment required several days of inpatient cardiac monitoring. Her self-inflicted wound required 28 stitches.

We do not know what would have happened to Ms. T if that first
emergency room visit had gone differently. Would an alternative
plan have provided adequate health maintenance until her regular
doctor returned? We do not know, and hindsight is often not fair.
However, in this case, hospitalization of this suicidal person did not
decrease the behavior and in fact may have had dramatic negative
consequences. Did Ms. T suffer a devastating loss of self-control? Did
social stigma and loss of civil rights have a profound effect on her
identity? Were suicidal precautions and one-to-one close observations invasive and counterproductive? Was the sense of intense

scrutiny that comes from ubiquitous staff presence experienced as oppressive, and did that scrutiny induce restlessness and frustration? For Ms. T, did any of these negative emotions and behaviors outweigh any benefit than suicide precaution might have in providing a temporary aura of safety? Was Ms. T received less favorably by staff?

Remember, staff/patient interactions can be confrontational and abrasive, with mutual hostility, anger, and mistrust. This intense environment can effect the judgment of both staff and patient. For many staff, it is difficult to analyze provocative behavior and at the same time try to rapidly respond to it. One staff member can act in a way that other staff disagree with, and staff/staff conflict can ensue. Considering these factors, there are times the hospital atmosphere does not engender good therapeutics.

So, When Should You Hospitalize?

A decision to hospitalize should be carefully weighed. Remember, there is no evidence that hospitalization reduces longer term suicide risk or that hospitalization is an effective treatment for suicidal behavior per se. In other cultures in which hospitalization for suicide attempt is less of an option, there may be less overall repetitious suicidal behavior. Psychiatrists need to be aware that there are no medication regimes that have been proven to reduce suicide risk. Medications should target psychiatric syndromes that are known to respond to those medications. With these caveats in mind, we recommend three criteria that can be used to decide about hospitalization: the presence of a serious psychiatric illness, the need for short-term sanctuary, and the use of hospitalization to reshape suicidal behavior.

Psychiatric Illness

The most easily justified reason for admission is the presence of a serious psychiatric state that requires the intense therapeutic and evaluation milieu of a hospital setting. Schizophrenia, severe affective disorders, and psychotic depressions are just a few of the psychiatric conditions that could benefit from the around-the-clock management that only hospitals can provide. Another plus for hospitals is the concentration of diagnostic facilities that can be rapidly brought to bear. This array of services can be crucial in understanding a severely disturbed or distraught person who might be experiencing one of a number of illnesses or toxic states. Last, more than one thing can be wrong. It is increasingly common to find individuals who have two or more conditions contributing to their distress. Most common is the combination of a psychiatric illness and substance abuse disorder. Inpatient services have the capacity to put several treatments into action at the same time and the capacity to do so at a time of crisis and urgency when a person might be most amenable to change. This ability to implement treatment quickly is a notably good component of units that are able to take this dual (or more) diagnostic and holistic approach.

Short-Term Sanctuary

A second reason for hospitalization involves the concept of sanctuary, an idea that has been with us for a long time. For centuries, individuals attempting to escape intolerable circumstances have been given respite in temples and churches. In our times, hospitals are being asked to perform this service, and often the admission ticket is a statement of suicidality. This is certainly not the best use of hospital resources. On the other hand, the hospital is often the only resource. In several parts of the country, treatment programs are starting to reexplore the notion of providing sanctuary outside of a hospital setting for an individual whose functioning is compromised by overwhelming stress. For now, respite care for suicidality is a legitimate use of the hospital. At the time of admission, it is important that both staff and patient understand what is being done. The patient needs to agree that the current stress level is overwhelming and that the hospital can be useful by providing a safe place with plenty of help available to develop a plan to deal with the discomfort and dysphoria. The stay should be described as brief (no more than

48–72 hours) and as the first step in a process of dealing with the stresses. This use obviously effects the types of services provided to the patient. There is much less emphasis on diagnostic studies and medication trials and more emphasis on crisis support and problem solving.

Reshaping Suicidal Behavior

A third reason for hospitalization occurs when admissions are planned as part of a long-term shaping strategy, a strategy that can be helpful with repetitiously suicidal individuals who have a history of multiple hospital use. Almost always, hospital admissions have occurred on a *mental breakdown* basis. The strength of a planned admissions strategy is that it puts future hospitalizations on a *health maintenance* basis. The technique is as follows: A review of prior records will determine the frequency of hospitalization. Future admissions are planned, generally at the end of a hospitalization, based on this pattern. If admissions are occurring at 4-month intervals, the next one should be planned at approximately 4 months and for a period of time somewhat under the average length of stay of previous hospitalizations. The outpatient therapist can use this in several ways. One of the most important is to demonstrate to the patient that emotional pain can be tolerated, knowing that a period of respite is planned. Once the first planned admission is accomplished, the next admission should be negotiated for some period longer than the usual interval between hospitalizations. The hospital stay should be somewhat shorter in length. Repeating this process over time can result in both less use of the hospital and in enabling your patient to develop better coping skills.

> Ms. B is a 32-year-old woman who has been treated with both medications and psychotherapy for (diagnosis of mixed personality disorder) for approximately 10 years. A planned admissions strategy was incorporated into her treatment approximately 3 years ago. Up to that point, the patient had been hospitalized about every 3 months, with a length of stay of 3 days to 2 weeks each time. Hospitalization was planned for 3 months after discharge for

a length of 5 days. During that 3 months, the patient reported distress on several occasions but agreed to wait for the hospitalization. At one point she appeared in the emergency room. She was asked to hold on until the date of the hospitalization. She was able to do so, and the planned admission went according to schedule. There was no crisis at the time of the first admission. For 5 days, the patient focused on building a more competent, social support network. The next planned hospitalization was placed at 5 months for a period of 3 days. During that 5 months, the patient went through several distressful emotional periods and once asked to be admitted. Other strategies were evoked (see Chapter 6), and she had less trouble agreeing to wait until the upcoming hospitalization. The third hospitalization was placed at 7 months for a period of 3 days. As that date approached, the patient stated that she felt she did not need to be hospitalized and that it might interfere with her life. Her therapist argued about this with her, saying the hospitalization was an important aspect of health maintenance program. In the end, the patient agreed to the hospitalization but only for 2 days. The next hospitalization was set for 10 months once again, but at this time the patient successfully argued that this was no longer a necessary part of her treatment plan.

A Hospital Treatment Package

Table 8–1 lists a seven-point plan for conducting treatment for suicidal behavior in a hospital. The first point is probably the essence of psychiatric hospitalization: start treatment for psychiatric disorders

Table 8–1. Seven-point hospital plan

1. Start treatment for psychiatric disorders if indicated.
2. Validate emotional pain.
3. Discuss ambivalence.
4. Provide encouragement.
5. Develop a problem-solving plan.
6. Get the longer term responsible person involved.
7. Evaluate and mobilize the social support network.

as indicated. Psychiatric illness is painful and can be disorienting, and can certainly contribute to suicidality. The second point, validate emotional pain, is a reference to Chapter 6 in which you begin reframing the pain using the technique of the Three *I*s: the pain is inescapable, intolerable, and interminable. In the hospital, it is most important to validate the pain, to agree with the individual that he or she is suffering, and to convey your understanding of that suffering. Reviewing the pain from the Three-*I* point of view will provide your patient with the problem-solving framework. The goals are to attack situations, tolerate associated emotional discomfort, and be oriented to long-term change. This is most important work, as it will set the stage for both further inpatient activities and for the structure of treatment following discharge.

Ambivalence needs to be addressed with any suicidal individual: one part wants to live, one part wants to die. An excellent tool for exploring ambivalence is the Reasons for Living Inventory (Appendix 3). The factors derived from this instrument (i.e., survival and coping beliefs, responsibility to family, child-related concerns, fear of suicide, fear of social disapproval, and moral objections) can provide a focus for a discussion of the positive side of ambivalence. This discussion of ambivalence will provide a context to move to initial work in problem solving, for it will show your patient that there are a range of feelings and a range of concerns with which to deal.

Providing encouragement has as much to do with attitude and demeanor as what is said. The hospital staff needs to have confidence in the ward treatment scheme for suicidality and be assured that it is a process that will work. The organization of the team around a coherent plan is most important. Most inpatient services conduct daily team meetings to review progress and coordinate treatment. At each of these meetings, the question should be asked, "Are we providing the proper encouragement?" Suicidality is always capable of producing negative emotions in staff. A discussion about encouragement is an excellent way of getting at and dealing with these difficult provider feelings. Staff "brainstorming" on providing encouragement to a difficult patient generally produces both good ideas and some needed attitude adjustment.

The *positive action plan* is a useful clinical alternative to the traditional *no suicide contract*. A no suicide contract asks the patient to agree to no suicidal behavior for a set period of time. In the no suicide contract, the patient is asked to define a period of time in which they would be comfortable not engaging in suicidal behavior. Although useful in helping with pain tolerance, a contract like this does not allow the treatment team to use all the treatment modalities at their disposal. Converting the no suicide contract to a positive action plan is more productive. A positive action plan is a way of negotiating a series of small constructive responses to suicidal ideation. These responses can be self-care, exercise, interpersonal contacts, and the like. The focus is on developing tolerance for and diversion from emotional pain. These behaviors have the effect of riding out an acute suicidal crisis. Like the no suicide contract, it is most important to negotiate a time limit. The time limit should be brief: hours to a few days. It is useful for staff to argue for a shorter period of time than the patient initially identifies while negotiating the plan. Define with the patient what specific actions need to be taken if an obstacle to plan implementation arises, and set up periodic check-ins to evaluate how the plan is working. Be absolutely certain that a staff member is there when the contractual time runs out. At this point, the strategies are reviewed, those that did not work are tossed out and new ones instituted, and a new contract is written.

Outpatient treatment is always a factor in inpatient treatment. Either the individual hospitalized is in a treatment program or such a program should be initiated. From the first day of hospitalization, the outpatient plan should be part of the discharge plan. If the outpatient therapist is already involved, make sure he or she has input into the inpatient program. Seek the outpatient therapist's advice and solicit his or her ideas. If there is no ongoing outpatient treatment, it is the job of the inpatient team to initiate it.

The last point in the hospital plan is to evaluate and mobilize the social support network. If at all possible, interview family and friends, and make an evaluation of the competency of the aid they can give. Often, other individuals would like to help, but they feel overwhelmed or burned out. Hearing them out and then making their job a possible one is most important work.

The Trouble With Discharge

Suicidal patients require coordinated and coherent care across systems and among levels of care. A problem in moving between systems is the act of *discharge,* a term that is often taken to mean both release from care and severance of further responsibility. From the continuity of care point of view, far too many hospitals operate independently from outpatient treatment systems. Care is not finished just because the most intensive and expensive mode of treatment is no longer in effect. Arranging for outpatient treatment is a necessary part of the hospital plan, but *participating* in a system of care should be the goal of current planning. *Coordinated transfer planning* is a much better phrase for describing what needs to be done to move the patient from the hospital to the next step in treatment. The inpatient service should be part of a coordinated and interconnected network that provides various services within the context of a longer term and coherent plan. This *integrated treatment and crisis response system,* the focus of the last part of this chapter, also offers exciting and positive alternatives to the use of the hospital in treating suicidality.

Integrated Treatment and Crisis Response System

A major challenge facing the mental health system is to produce efficient and effective care for suicidal individuals. The use of hospitalization as a principal option for these people requires careful examination. We have already discussed the lack of efficacy; hospitalization does not deliver on the assumption that it will reduce suicidality. Furthermore, it is very expensive. Health care dollars are scarce, and dollars spent on hospitals are not available to develop better alternatives. This is particularly true in the public sector, where it is absolutely essential to get the most out of each dollar spent. Patients stabilized in an inpatient environment are more likely to decompensate unless they receive continued outpatient support. Destabilization adds to the demand for crisis services and an increased demand for hospital care. If the dollars remain the same and hospital care goes up, this can only lead to a further reduction in outpatient resources. This is a downward spiral, and the mental health system cannot afford it. Crisis management in general, and the treatment of suicidality in particular, suffer. Hospital care is a precious and expensive resource and must be reserved for those people who truly need it. An array of less-expensive, more-efficient, non-hospital alternatives must be developed. To meet this end, independent elements must work together. Emergency centers, hospitals, and outpatient facilities need to vigorously attack the current barriers to effective long-term care. The work is not easy. There are philosophical, administrative, and legal impediments to be overcome. Each community will face a different challenge, and each state will need to review its civil commitment and other mental illness processes. What follows is an outline of an integrated, five-component system, a system that is within the grasp of many communities.

1. You Must Have an Emergency Center

An emergency center is a hospital-based facility. It offers acute care for a variety of trauma and illnesses, and is an entry point to either the hospital or outpatient clinic. Emergency psychiatry is a significant player in any such center, and mental health workers in this system deal with a great variety of difficulties. The complexity of the evaluations can be enormous, requiring input from multiple medical specialities. An example, and a common one, is contained in the workup that might be required for a person brought in by the police "found down" and "acting confused and psychotic." The evaluator needs to look for many things including head trauma, psychotic illness, acute substance abuse, and innumerable medical conditions such as thyroid dysfunction and diabetes. Has this person overdosed? Is this toxic condition deliberate (a suicide attempt) or an accident? Individuals like this are often unknown to the emergency evaluating staff, and no information about prior medical or psychiatric history is available.

To evaluate this patient, psychiatric, general medical, and neurological assessments must be done. In addition, staff must scramble to find out what they can: Is this person in treatment anywhere? Can we tap into that database? Often this information is hard to get, especially at night and on the weekends. This information can be difficult to get from patients, especially if their psychiatric state and/or the sequela of a suicide attempt make effective interviewing impossible. At that point, assuming you know the patient's identity, you should have ready access to the facts about him or her. In this information age, emergency centers can be linked via computer with state hospitals, mental health centers, and other sources. The fact that most of them are not is a sad comment on our multifaceted inability to cooperate between systems, especially when it comes to addressing our pervasive medical, legal, and liability fears. The legitimate sticking point in information exchange is patient confidentiality. Mechanically, this is dealt with by computer safeguards. At the crucial level, this is dealt with by interagency agreements that each agency is part of a system dealing with the same people and their problems over time. Unless we all strive to develop these tools, case management will come to its limits of efficacy fairly quickly.

In addition to acquiring information quickly, a second and powerful case management tool in an emergency center is appointment authority. Too often, psychiatric patients leave emergency centers with at best a phone number to call. This "wish-and-a-prayer" approach to follow-up is not effective. What should happen, and is now technically feasible, is this: A patient is evaluated and observed in an emergency setting, and treatment is initiated. If outpatient follow-up is the next logical step, the patient is given an appointment with an identified clinician. Two things should happen before that appointment. First, the provider on the receiving end needs to have available, in advance, all this information obtained from the emergency center evaluation. Second, a case manager must work to get the patient to the appointment. This can involve a range of action, from a phone call (most of us know how good dentists are at this) to picking up the patient and transporting him or her to the follow-up appointment.

2. Psychiatric Emergency Centers Need 24-Hour Holding Beds

The suicidal patient described above might well need a lot of work done before a rational disposition from an emergency center can be made. Admission to an inpatient unit (the expensive option) is often done because the emergency center is busy, patients need to be moved on, and the workup is incomplete. Having 24-hour holding beds can often obviate this need for admission. Tests can be run, information gathered, observations made, and response to treatment observed. Having a bed for the patient and a calendar day to work with is much more satisfactory than feeling pressure to get the patient "somewhere, anywhere" within a maximum of 4–6 hours.

3. Psychiatric Emergency Centers Need Disposition Options: First, a Brief Stay Inpatient Service

For all the reasons given earlier in this chapter, a psychiatric unit is a critical part of an integrated crisis system. We define *brief stay* as anywhere from 2 to 21 days. Let us take our "found down" patient and flesh him out a bit. Like many psychiatric patients, he has more than one thing wrong with him. In the emergency center we learn the following: He is 43 years old and was diagnosed as schizophrenic 20 years ago. He is followed by a mental health center but has not been seen for 6 weeks. He has been prescribed antipsychotic medication, but he does not like the side effects and has been noncompliant. He is alcoholic and is in the mental health center's newly formed dual diagnosis program. He has insulin-dependent diabetes and is often in poor control. A year ago he was knocked unconscious and robbed, and his behavior has been more erratic since then. A week ago he was kicked out of his boarding home because of drunkenness.

The emergency center evaluation reveals an acutely psychotic gentleman who is also intoxicated. He talks of needing to kill himself before "the demons" kill him. His diabetic state requires immediate management. Over 6 hours, the staff have an adequate diagnostic picture, and medical and psychiatric treatments are started. It is clear this gentleman needs hospitalization, and he is admitted.

But for how long? His acute psychosis might be well on the way to resolution in 3–6 days and his diabetes brought under control even more quickly. As with most patients, his acute suicidal ideation will probably abate in 5 days. He might well be transferred to a nonhospital option at that point, or continued problems might necessitate more time in house. For many patients, even with the complexity noted in our example, the time in hospital after a week of treatment is determined less by some absolute need to remain an inpatient and more by the quality of other options.

4. The Emergency Center and the Hospital Ward Need a Crisis Residential Unit

We discussed earlier the need for sanctuary, for a sheltering, safe environment where an individual can be housed and cared for and get a respite from overwhelming daily hassles of life. With regard to our "found down" patient, he is now physically and mentally better. However, he needs continued monitoring regarding his medication, a place to stay, and integration with his mental health clinic's intensive outpatient programs. As his psychosis resolves, his suicidality becomes more clearly related to his loss of shelter and uncontrolled addiction disorder. Problems have been identified, and problem-solving therapy is initiated. All of this can safely be accomplished in a residential milieu.

5. An Integrated Crisis Response System Needs a Crisis Stabilization Outpatient Program

Our suicidal patient will have his crises resolved, and he will return to long-term treatment for his chronic illnesses. Some neuropsychological deficits that are found have been the result of the blow to his head. Rehabilitation from this injury has been added to his therapy regimes. Other patients, however, will not have a chronic or longer term illness. Their crises, including suicidality, can be dealt with in a 1- to 3-month crisis intervention clinic. Such a clinic consists of mental health personnel trained in individual, family, and group support and crisis resolution techniques. Crisis case management has a major role in this clinic (see Chapter 7), lending a firm hand to establishing or reestablishing a comprehensive system of support. Equally important is an understanding of the brief and judicious use of medications, especially when suicidal potential is involved.

Keep All the Doors Open

If an integrated system is to live up to its name, the suicidal patient must be able to move easily between components. Each part of the system has an unlocked door to every other part. Movement is *not* failure. It is based on clinical appropriateness. Inpatient services are the place for most intensive diagnosis, observations, and treatment. Outpatient services deliver definitive therapy and integrate patients back into the community. Residential services are of intermediate intensity and provide sanctuary. Each component can function best knowing the other components are available. For example, an acute residential setting, if it has immediate hospital backup, will be much more comfortable taking a suicidal patient who is a little better but still is in a state of some disrepair. The outpatient setting can use a residential setting in lieu of the hospital. If information flows freely around the system, the only major impediment to movement through the doors is that peculiar medical paranoia: the fear of dumping.

Dumping, pushing the problem to someone else's bailiwick without concern for the patient's welfare, is the death of system development. Fight it like the plague. Feedback loops among all the components, which allow for open discussion about problems, will help. The *key* question for feedback discussion is, "Are we working in the best interest of the patient?" The second question is, "Was transfer done to treat the patient, or was it done to treat our own difficulties, be they anger, a sense of failure, job burnout, or whatever?" As important as feedback is having individuals who work both sides of the fence. Spending time, for example, in the emergency center and in the residential setting will provide a perspective on how the two units work together that is far richer than working one place and speculating on how another place functions. In an integrated system, it is not us and them. It is all of us.

Helpful Hints

♦ Do not rely solely on the inpatient unit to treat suicidality; hospitals are overused and have no proven efficacy.
♦ When you use a hospital, make sure it is for the treatment of a psychiatric illness, for short-term sanctuary, or for reshaping suicidal behavior.
♦ Do not let your fear of malpractice litigation override your clinical judgment.
♦ Do your best to establish an integrated crisis response system in your community.

Selected Readings

Bond B, Witheridge T, Wasmer D, et al: A comparison of two crisis housing alternatives to psychiatric hospitalization. Hosp Community Psychiatry 40:177–183, 1989

Chafetz L: Issues in emergency psychiatric research, in Emergency Psychiatry at the Crossroads: New Directions for Mental Health Services. Edited by Lipton F, Goldfinger S. San Francisco, CA, Jossey-Bass, 1985

Crammer JL: The special characteristics of suicide in hospital inpatients. Br J Psychiatry 145:460–476, 1984

Drye RC, Goulding RL, Goulding ME: No-suicide decision: patient monitoring of suicidal risk. Am J Psychiatry 130:171–174, 1973

Sunqvist-Stensmann UB: Suicides in close connection with psychiatric care: an analysis of 57 cases in a Swedish county. Acta Psychiatr Scand 76;15–20, 1987

Section III
Special Clinical Problems

 Chapter 9

The Repetitiously
Suicidal Patient
A Health Care Dilemma

F ew patients represent more of a challenge to mental health and
medical practitioners than the repetitiously suicidal patient.
Whether the suicidal behavior is repeated sublethal overdosing or
near-lethal attempts at killing oneself seems to make little difference.
Health care systems have difficulty in dealing with these patients;
they are a source of conflicts between providers. Practitioners often
diagnose them as having character disorders or personality disorders, both terms synonymous with trouble. These patients can
challenge a practitioner's theoretical and practical assumptions, and
they can reveal gaps in service delivery systems. Repetitiously suicidal patients present their suicidality in a host of different encounters
within both the general health and mental health care systems.
Emergency room physicians deal with and feel frustrated by these
people as much as seasoned psychotherapists do. The primary care
physician is just as likely to feel overwhelmed by such a patient as is
the inpatient attending psychiatrist. In other words, there is something universal about the dilemma presented by this type of suicidal
patient. Our system response to a chronically suicidal patient often
does not work well, and this is in part due to a singular focus on

suicide prevention and liability reduction that can limit effective treatment. This chapter provides a balanced and holistic approach to the problem of repetitious suicidal behavior.

Suicide, Attempted Suicide, and Parasuicide

Much has been made in recent years of a possible distinction between patients who will ultimately commit suicide, patients who make suicide attempts, and parasuicide patients. The term *parasuicide* was originally coined by Norman Kreitman (1976), a British researcher/clinician who noted that there seemed to be clinical differences between patients who are attracted to suicidal behavior for reasons other than the purpose of dying and those who are intent on dying, whether they succeed or not. In psychiatric parlance, the latter group are suicide attempters; the former group are parasuicide patients. A variety of speculations have been forthcoming about how these groups might differ. For example, parasuicide patients are thought to be characterized by using methods of limited lethality, such as drug overdosing, and acting in a context in which discovery is highly likely. Conversely, suicide attempters have been described as using more lethal means of attempting, even if drug overdosing is involved, and make efforts to elude detection. A major clinical milestone would be achieved if research could isolate those characteristics that distinguish parasuicides from attempted suicides. From this, clinicians could identify patients who are most likely to engage in lethal forms of suicidal behavior.

Unfortunately, the utility of this distinction has not been substantiated. For example, there is very little evidence that a patient's suicidal intent (i.e., intent to die, attempts to avoid discovery, preplanning) is related to the medical severity of the attempts. High-intent patients may not be the same as the patients who end up in intensive care units. Clinical judgment has not been very accurate in separating these populations. With the exception of perceptions regarding the problem-solving value of suicide and the patient's ability to tolerate emotional pain, research has revealed very few differences between states of suicidality, even between patients who simply think about suicide and those who engage in some form of behavior.

In a recent study that included repetitious suicide attempters on an inpatient unit, we noted subtle differences between low-intent and high intent suicide attempters. Low-intent patients appear to be more influenced by hopelessness, depression, and low reasons for staying alive than high-intent attempters. High-intent attempters report lower depression, hopelessness, as well as more life-sustaining beliefs. The key thing to remember in this study is that these assessments were obtained after suicide attempts. High-intent attempters may have experienced more anxiety relief from their behavior and therefore reported less depression, less hopelessness, and a sense of being able to move on with their lives. In other words, the suicide attempt worked. Conversely, low-intent attempters may not have experienced the same degree of anxiety relief and problem resolution, perhaps because the attempt was seen as not serious, negative labeling occurred, and the problems were either not helped or were made worse. Finally, recall that suicide intent itself, which is an assessment of the patient's self-reported intent to die, seems to have little to do with the probability of a completed suicide. In other words, these distinctions still do not reveal who is likely to die.

In a problem-solving framework, suicidal behavior is a method of managing distress. Many patients die because they were playing with fire. Their conscious intent to die might well have actually been ambivalent or even low. Conversely, high-intent patients discover that to commit suicide, everything has to work just right and there are a thousand things that can go wrong. Bullets aimed at the heart have missed, hanging ropes have broken, and inadvertent passersby have discovered and rescued many a near-dead individual. These factors lead to the following conclusion: Any form of suicidal behavior can be fatal; trying to label patients on the basis of lethality level is not only inaccurate but can also create major intervention errors.

Nevertheless, the concept of parasuicide has heavily influenced the British response to self-poisoning overdose (about 70% of suicide attempts) and has led to intervention techniques that have had positive outcomes. In Great Britain, parasuicide has been defined as a syndrome requiring a distinct form of treatment. This has led to the creation of innovative and effective alternative treatment strategies, such as "Self-Poisoning Centers" (SPCs). In SPCs, patients are only medically assessed and stabilized; referral and discharge are immediate. Inpatient psychiatric hospitalization is only one of a variety of placement options. This approach has helped to make suicidal behavior a nonreinforcing event and to return the individual to the natural environment where real-life problem solving can occur. Interestingly, the health care system in the United Kingdom has successfully used this low-intensity approach to repetitious self-poisoning and has violated some precepts of American risk management in doing it (Hawton and Catalan 1982, 1987)!

A Profile of the Repetitious Suicide Attempter

The repetitiously suicidal patient often has a multitude of psychological deficits known to be associated with suicidal behavior. The type of deficits may not be qualitatively different from those of the person who experiences a single suicidal crisis only. What makes the repetitious patient difficult to treat is the manner in which these multiple deficits interact negatively with both a world and self view to produce a suicidal lifestyle. The term *multiproblem patient* is another way to describe the person who constantly functions in crisis and relies extensively on suicidal behavior (see Strosahl 1991). This term is both less pejorative and more descriptive of the real problem. Multiproblem, repetitiously suicidal individuals often have a dysfunctional family background characterized by sexual and physical abuse, neglect, parental addiction or alcoholism, and/or parental abandonment. In other words, many of these patients matured in an environment that provided scarce opportunities to learn the necessary skills to survive and thrive in the real world. Table 9–1 lists some of the more common beliefs about both self and the world that can form the basis of a multiproblem patient's adaptation to the demands of life.

As can be seen in Table 9–1, there is very little that is elegant about the day-to-day reality of multiproblem patients. Their lives are characterized by emotional pain, a constant struggle to meet the demands of living, and interpersonal conflict and/or isolation. In a world producing continuous discomfort, the rule of survival is simple. If something helps lessen the pain of a situation, use it again and again. Never mind long-term consequences; that is for people who *have* a future. Adhering to this simple rule, there are few problem-solving behaviors that work as quickly and as effectively as suicidal behavior. It relieves pent-up frustration and anxiety, creates an environment oriented toward providing attention and caring, and helps the individual escape from what is often a painful and hopeless living situation. Make no mistake about it; suicidal behavior is a very effective problem-solving behavior if one is willing to risk possible (even if considered unlikely) death and is willing to ignore long-term consequences.

Table 9–1. World- and self-related beliefs of the multiproblem patient

I. Beliefs About the World
  A. The more important it is, the less likely it is to happen.
  B. When you expect good things, bad things will happen.
  C. Negative thoughts and feelings are destructive.
  D. Life cannot proceed in the presence of suffering.
  E. The only way to change is just decide to be different.
  F. Make a mistake and you will be punished for it.
  G. The goal with suffering is to get rid of it.
  H. Life is basically unpredictable and unfair.
  I. Do unto others before they do unto you.
II. Beliefs About Self
  A. I am flawed in a basic way.
  B. I don't deserve to be happy.
  C. If I can't do it well, I won't do it at all.
  D. I must understand why I am the way I am or I can't be different.
  E. I will end up killing myself.
  F. I don't "fit in."
  G. I am permanently damaged by my past.
  H. If I let my emotions go, I will go crazy.
  I. Killing myself is the easiest way out.

Polarities in Working With the
Repetitiously Suicidal Patient

For some individuals and in some situations, a clinician can cause a patient to perform in more adaptive ways by the exercise of personal authority. As an expert, you state what needs to be done, and your patient follows this advice. You are in a professional role, that of a healer, your suggestions are sound and your motive is to be helpful, and the individual seeking your help does what you say. Some individuals, however, do not respond to authority in this manner. They push the issue of who has control in the patient-clinician interaction. These patients may get labeled as having personality disorders; they are uncooperative because they have not accepted your treatment. If treatment gets stalled at this point, you can end up feeling defeated, powerless, and angry. These negative reactions can sometimes be transferred onto your patient in the form of pejorative labels, labels such as *borderline traits, manipulative, insincere, oppositional,* or *defiant.*

Given this dynamic in giving care to the repetitiously suicidal patient, it is important to note that there are many potential sources of polarization between you and the patient. The most initially troublesome is usually the acceptability/unacceptability of using self-destructive behavior to solve problems. In the normal world, individuals are taught to regulate their behavior primarily around an evaluation of long-term consequences. The clinician, coming from the normal world, has difficulty accepting the notion that someone will knowingly engage in repetitious suicidal behavior. Dangerously, the clinician may attribute malevolent intentions to the patient (i.e., the patient is deliberately doing bad things).

A second polarity relates to differences both in the perception of suffering and what to do about it. You may come from a world in which people are taught to endure their suffering while finding constructive ways to regulate and solve problems. Your patient often comes from a world that is strictly focused on getting rid of suffering. Your patient can be in the unenviable position of being unwilling to accept emotional pain while being told that the outside world does not accept the only available solution for getting rid of that pain.

A third polarity involves trying to get better versus trying to get by. You will usually emphasize that improvement is possible, whereas your patient's experience may be that trying to improve things does not work. Attempts at improvement may have backfired, especially if your patient comes from a dysfunctional family or a dysfunctional support network is present. Some therapists tend to link emotional validation and support to evidence that their patient is doing something constructive about problems. This attitude makes it hard to provide attention and caring in the face of destructive solutions for pain and suffering. The patient wants to be cared for even though the life plan is just to get by. Consequently, those actions that the patient is most likely to engage in to solve problems (e.g., suicidal behavior) are also the most likely to draw negative reactions from the therapist and therefore put the issue of the therapist's real caring for the patient on the table.

In addition to these polarities, some clinicians have unreasonable rescue and power fantasies that become activated in a showdown motif: Can the therapist stop the patient from using self-destructive behavior? The impasse that results over this issue can be fatal for treatment. It can produce increased episodes of suicidal behavior, treatment noncompliance, resistance interpretations, therapy drop-outs, and therapist "dumps" into different layers of the treatment system. Both the clinician and the patient can spend a lot of energy on feeling frustrated, angry, and misunderstood. In the uncontained case, the patient may begin to use suicidal behavior in an attempt to solve the impasse with the clinician, just as the patient would use the same problem-solving approach in the natural world.

An Alternative Approach to Repetitious Suicidal Behavior

The treatment goals with the chronic patient are the same as those with the more functional suicidal patient: develop better problem-solving skills and better acceptance and tolerance of emotional distress. The process used to reach these goals with the multiproblem patient is the difference. The approach to the chronic patient centers on the five polarities previously described and on the extent to which you and your patient can negotiate and accept basic rules for treatment. This acceptance involves a recognition that struggling over issues always makes those issues larger. *Acceptance* means that you and your patient have come to a joint understanding and mutual respect for your different personal histories. You, the clinician, must come to grips with the fact that your patient may continue to engage in suicidal behavior, that there is a small likelihood that the patient will actually commit suicide, that preventing suicide cannot be the sole focus of the intervention, and that the overriding context is not living versus dying even though the language of the presenting problem hints that this is so. The real issue is learning to live more effectively and with more satisfaction.

Reconciling Polarities

To reach the chronically suicidal patient, you must realize that the more pressure you apply to eliminate suicidal behavior, the more intractable suicidal behavior may become. The process that occurs between the push of the clinician and the push back of the patient needs to be harnessed for constructive purposes. Following the principle that the surest way to avoid loss in a tug-of-war is to drop the rope, this treatment approach focuses on techniques that allow you to drop negative polarities while making strategic use of polarizing processes.

Allow Your Patient "To Be"

The critical strategy in this regard is to give your patient room to make decisions, even decisions that are based on old and unhealthy behaviors. The fact is, your patient can be unhealthy despite your best efforts, so allow the patient "to be." For example, it is useful to preempt the issue of stopping suicidal behavior by predicting that it may well occur during treatment. While you need to be clear about related case management and crisis procedures, the important message is that a recurrence of suicidal behavior is not going to result in a power struggle. *If it happens, it happens. We will learn from it, and treatment will proceed.* Look for and reinforce positive elements in whatever your patient has done. Rather than criticizing a patient who has just overdosed, focus on any and all positive thoughts and actions that occurred during the suicidal episode. Search for problem-solving behaviors that occurred before the drug overdose, and strongly praise your patient for trying those things. For example, look for attempts to contact others for help, for maneuvers to reduce emotional distress, and for any techniques your patient may have used to get through the difficult period. Praise any effort to steer the episode toward more-effective problem solving. These techniques create an acceptance of suicidal behavior as a form of problem solving, an acknowledgment that your patient is struggling and trying his or her best, and an atmosphere that always encourages other ways to look at difficulties.

Steal the Point of Resistance

This strategy involves being the first to find the downside of any nonsuicidal problem-solving strategy. For example, in a dialogue with your patient about a way of solving a particular problem, occasionally play the devil's advocate by stating all the reasons why suicidal behavior would work better than the new alternative. It is important to develop a sense of timing with this intervention. Look for those moments when your patient seems to be losing a problem-solving focus and begins making superficial and poorly thought through comments about needing to find other ways to solve difficulties. Intervene by pointing out that suicidal behavior has been far too important to be whisked away in this manner. In general, anticipate a possible point of polarity and occupy the negative pole, so that your patient can either agree with you or take to the positive pole in an attempt to maintain polarity. At heart, this technique is based on the assumption that the chronically suicidal patient is a disappointed optimist—that is, the patient really wants to believe that things can be changed for the better but has had so many

disconfirming experiences that a *fear develops about being hopeful.*
When given the opportunity, the suicidal patient may unexpectedly
occupy the optimistic pole and may even express some disbelief or
confusion about your apparent pessimism. Ironically, when you take
the apparently negative, pessimistic position, your patient often feels
understood and validated. The act of embodying your patient's sense
of frustration and negativism is an act of empathy. The fact that there
is an ever-present potential for suicidal behavior can make you feel
constantly obligated to challenge the patient's negative world views.
Remember, taking the right occasion to identify with your patient's
negative world view can create a new context in which to discuss
persistent suicidal ideation and behavior.

Sympathize With Suicidal Impulses

This technique is designed to validate emotional pain while reframing what are often experienced as uncontrollable suicidal impulses.
When your patient is feeling suicidal, make a concerted effort to
identify all of the patient's problems and then add that almost
anyone would consider suicide if faced with such a multitude of
difficulties. Acknowledging that there is a universal connection
between feeling frustrated and blocked and considering suicide is a
way of slipping the problem-solving notion in the back door. In
other words, suicidal behavior is moved "off center" when you
empathize with your patient's sense of emotional pain and frustration while at the same time linking repetitious suicidal behavior and
unsolved problems. Many difficulties can mean suicidal behavior for
almost anyone. Let your patient know he or she is not alone in this
and that the need to face suicidality and get on with life can arise in
all of us and at any time.

Make Suicidal Impulses an *It*

One of the most effective ways to deal with destructive impulses is
to develop the capacity to comment about yourself as a person
having these impulses and to move out of your participant role and

into an observer role. A good image to suggest is this: "Put parentheses around yourself in this suicidal situation. Now step outside the parentheses and look at that person dealing with that problem. Describe what you see." The capacity to do this transforms suicidality to an *it,* an entity to be received, commented on, and changed. As an *it,* the suicidal mode of behaving automatically loses the aura of some overwhelming force to which your patient must succumb. When your patient reaches the point of stepping outside the situation at the moment he or she is in it, then a truly significant advance will have been made. Questions such as, "What do your suicidal thoughts have to say about trying something new in this situation?" help your patient externalize and encapsulate suicidal impulses. By giving them entity or *it* status, these impulses become endowed through linguistic association with their own motives. You can then place these motivations at odds with something your patient really wants, for example, "Do you think your suicidal impulses are really going to stand for you having a good time this weekend?" "What do you think they'll do to ruin it for you?"

The implicit goal of these maneuvers is to separate the patient from the suicidal impulses and to create a greater contrast between what the patient thinks and what the patient is. The capacity to extract the *I* out of suffering is a prerequisite for any acceptance.

Suicidal Feelings Are Your Friends

The chronically suicidal patient comes to rely on feeling suicidal as a way of gaining reassurance. Even though such feelings are experienced as uncontrollable and alien at one level, at another basic level they are familiar, predictable experiences in an otherwise chaotic world. If all else fails to create meaning, the patient can always fall back on being suicidal (e.g., "Thoughts of suicide have gotten me through many a bad night."). It is important to honor this relationship between your patient and suicidal impulses. Point out that gaining reassurance is an extremely vital human need, and nothing in therapy is designed to break that important bond. For a patient who has been repeatedly stigmatized for having such feelings, having the reassuring function of suicidal thoughts acknowledged and protected can be a major step toward viewing these experiences in a different context.

The ultimate behavioral goal of these reconciling strategies is to create a therapeutic moment where your patient does a *double take*. This indicates that your patient has just run into a piece of information outside of his or her operational frame of reference. When your patient has to form a new, more accepting context to relate to key issues, the pressure to engage in suicidal behavior is likely to diminish. This does not mean that existing skill deficits have been remedied, but the situation has become more amenable to developing other ways of adapting to circumstances. It is very difficult to promote behavior change in the face of unacceptable suicidal impulses and the consequent frequent self-destructive behavior. Change becomes easier as the impulses become friendlier, more amenable, more open to being dealt with.

Dealing With Downers

Working with the repetitiously suicidal patient is made difficult by the recurrence of communications that put you in a bind: any response you think of seems likely to make things worse. Most patients have been conditioned to expect failure and interpersonal disappointment, so their immediate reaction to almost any attempt to help is to downplay the sincerity or the competency of the helper. Your patient may tend to tenaciously cling to suicidality as if it were a security blanket, appearing so sensitized to failure and rejection that the encouragement to even experiment with alternative problem solving seems all too risky. The recurrence of these situations that seem set up for rejection can be traced to the ongoing influence of the polarities previously discussed. Although it is impossible to anticipate every variation on these themes, the overall success of treatment is in large part determined by the consistency and quality of your responses.

The Dealing With Downers exercise in Table 9–2 is designed to allow you to experiment with some likely responses to common

Table 9–2. Dealing With Downers exercise: patient statements and therapist sample responses

Patient statements

1. I really do want to die.
2. Everything is fine, I don't need to do anything.
3. It doesn't matter anyway.
4. Why don't you focus your time on helping someone who has a chance?
5. It's just too hard to do.
6. What would you do if you felt like I do?
7. I don't want to talk about it, it's stupid.
8. It will take forever to change.
9. I don't care one way or the other.
10. It would be nice if it were just all over.
11. That's baloney (in response to your statement of caring).
12. Nothing is working. Nothing is working. It just doesn't help.
13. There is only one way to feel better.
14. I don't know what I feel. Why do you keep asking?
15. This therapy isn't working. I don't feel any better than when we started.
16. I have pills and I'm going to use them.
17. (By a telephone call): I just want you to know that you are a very nice person. Whatever I do, I don't want you to take it personally. (This occurs at 3:00 A.M.)

Possible therapist responses

1. *It sounds like you've got a lot of problems, and, at least for now, you think suicide would solve them.*
2. **(If context is anger):** *It sounds like you are feeling fairly frustrated.*
   (If context is denial): *There is a lot going on in your life, and we both know there is much to be done. Maybe this is one of those times when you need to block everything out.*
3. *It sounds like you are down on yourself. What problems are you dealing with?*
4. **(If question based on hopelessness or worthlessness):** *I am. You do have a chance.*
   (If question is in the context of testing the therapist and can be rephrased as, "Do you care about me?"): *Regardless of what you think about your situation, I do care about the way it works out. I think we can work together and make things better for you.*
5. *It sure can seem that way. Change is not easy for anyone.*

(continued)

Table 9–2.   Dealing With Downers exercise: patient statements and
therapist sample responses *(continued)*

---

6. *I might well think about killing myself, and I hope I would be as smart as you were and get some help.*
7. *I know talking things over has at times not worked for you.*
8. *It can sure seem that way at times. Change is harder than most of us realize.*
9. *Let's imagine that you did care. Which way would you care?*
10. *What problems are going on that are causing you to feel that way?*
11. *Does that mean that most people who have said they care about you have had other motives?*
12. *It sounds like you are feeling defeated right now. What problems are defeating you?*
13. *Given the pain you are in, I can see how you might like not to feel anything (or you might not want to feel anything).*
14. *I know you have a number of bad feelings right now. I keep asking because the more precisely we can understand them the better we can deal with them.*
15. *Let's imagine therapy was working. What would you notice about your life that would tell that?*
16. *What happened? It sounds like things are going badly. What problems are you struggling with?*
17. *I look forward to seeing you at our next appointment.*

---

conundrums that are presented by your suicidal patient. The first part of the exercise lists the patient's statement. Your job is to generate a response that validates the patient's reality while eschewing a confrontation or disappointment. The second part contains sample responses that meet the criteria of being consistent, nonjudgmental, and confirming of the patient. As you complete this exercise, imagine that you are face-to-face with a suicidal patient. Also, keep in mind the following principles:

1. Beware of overly judgmental or defensive responses. Try to see this as a communication about your patient's view of the world, not as a criticism of your competence.
2. Find a way to validate the emotionally painful part of the communication in a way that is sincere and honest.

3. Try to think of these statements as predictions your patient is making about what is likely to occur in the immediate future.
4. Think of ways that you could move your patient from this declaratory state of mind into a more experimental and curious state of mind.
5. Avoid overinterpreting the underlying meaning of these comments in your response. Try to stay *on the surface* and respond directly to the affect that is being presented.

Remember, don't look at the sample responses until you complete this exercise.

The Moment of Truth: The First Crisis in Treatment

The moment of truth arrives when the issue of suicidal behavior is put directly on the table, and you are in the position of either accepting or rejecting your patient's possession of the final say over whether a suicide attempt will or will not occur. Usually, the moment comes when increasing stress precipitates an acute suicidal crisis. This can happen at any time with the repetitiously suicidal patient but is more common in the initial and intermediate stages of treatment. How you respond at this moment of truth will largely determine whether you and your patient can sustain a working relationship. You have to find a way to work together to employ a problem-solving approach, often in spite of seemingly uncontrollable suicidal impulses. This can be the time when treatment blows apart in a showdown over whether your patient will or will not engage in some sort of self-destructive behavior.

The moment of truth is best viewed as an inevitable conclusion of the various polarizing processes that are inherent in therapy with the patient. Consequently, you are as much an antagonist as a protagonist. An acute suicidal episode is an excellent opportunity for your patient to learn how to better tolerate distressing thoughts and feelings, to see suicidality in a different context, and to experiment with new problem-solving behaviors. Many clinicians will abandon the basic treatment plan and begin to react exclusively with suicide prevention behaviors. Therapists who abandon their plan of attack in these circumstances are very likely to see their patients terminate therapy, often following a suicide attempt and hospitalization. Once consistency and predictability is lost, the likelihood of the patient and clinician coming back together is low.

These moments require a special devotion to duty because your patient is usually too busy *being the problem* (instead of observing the problem) to be terribly helpful. In essence, it is important to execute the treatment plan exactly as agreed to, even with the specter of a suicide attempt lurking in the wings. The treatment is not failing. Remember that power is limited in such circumstances. You are like a riverboat gambler holding two deuces while your patient has a royal flush. The key is not to have your hand called. When clinicians crack during the moment of truth, it is usually because of some underlying lack of conviction in the treatment. Under the acid test of imminent suicidal behavior, beware of the impulse to do whatever you have to do to somehow save your patient. The more you try to assume control of the situation, the less likely your patient is to have an experience that promotes autonomy and growth. Be wary of setting up treatment plans that cannot be sustained under maximum stress. Many a clinician has been surprised by a phone call in the middle of the night concerning a patient's suicidal crisis. The answer to this situation is not an unlisted phone number or an impenetrable answering service. An emergency room physician, faced with no information from you and little knowledge of the patient will almost always act in an overprotective (i.e., sometimes not very helpful) manner. You must be prepared for a crisis and plan for a crisis with every suicidal patient with whom you work.

A well-formulated and mutually agreed-upon crisis protocol is essential. It gives both you and your patient an agreement to fall back on and each of you has clear responsibilities. Protocols that anticipate recurrent suicidal behavior are far more potent because they include and make legitimate suicidal behavior a part of treatment. The protocol spells out who is to do what in the event suicidal behavior occurs. A good protocol means you have very few *new* decisions to make when the moment arrives and can instead remain focused on executing the steps to which you and the patient have agreed.

By integrating a structured crisis protocol into treatment, your patient is able to learn experientially that you can make room for and work with suicidal behavior. With a planned, detailed, and matter-of-fact protocol in place, suicidal behavior begins to lose some of its luster, the counter-control communication process is neutralized, and your patient is left with a clear choice: whether or not to proceed with the behavior. As you move in a rational and controlled way into the process of responding to the patient's crisis, your patient can move in a rational and controlled way into the process of being in crisis. This approach allows your patient to cease struggling with a crisis and experience it in a more accepting way. Your patient learns to more rationally deal with things that are the inevitable consequences of being alive. One common phenomeno-logical report from suicidal individuals is the sense of struggling to remain normal in the face of an overwhelming sense of defeat and futility. Ironically, the sense of struggle leads to emotional fatigue that can be tied to the emergence of suicidal impulses. When the moment arrives, you can teach your patient to drop this internal tug-of-war and work with suicidal impulses. Rather than do nothing and try to look good, your patient learns to do something construc-tive *and* present the appearance of working hard at it.

Resistance: An Overused Interpretation

Traditional approaches to working with the repetitiously suicidal patient stress that the patient's resistance has to be overcome for the patient to get better. Resistance is an enormously tempting concept, in part because it can allow you to deny responsibility for impasses in treatment. From the polarization perspective, resistance poses an interesting paradox. Whereas your therapy emphasizes learning to recognize, accept, and work with competing and contradictory beliefs your patient may have, resistance implies the patient is consciously or unconsciously using these beliefs out of a desire to stay sick. Generally, clinicians use resistance interpretations when a stalemate exists. Often, one or more of the basic polarizing themes is involved. The resistance motif is often used when the patient tightens the grip on a dysfunctional belief as a counter-response to a clinician pushing a putative healthier way of thinking or feeling. Resistance interpretations may also occur at the behavioral level when, for example, the patient does not complete between-session homework assignments, misses sessions, or misuses prescription medication. There are clinicians who can effectively use resistance work with the suicidal patient, but the danger with many resistance interpretations is that they provide a pat answer to a difficult moment and, more important, do not lead to progress. When you are tempted to sum up a troublesome impasse in therapy by attributing it to your patient's resistance, remember: If all you have is a hammer, everything tends to look like a nail. It is much more helpful to view an impasse from a variety of perspectives.

An alternative that can be quite helpful is to view resistance as *your* failure: an immediate and direct result of your inability to fully recognize your patient's reality. When your patient does not follow through on a particular treatment task, you may have failed to fully appreciate the limitations imposed not only by cognitive and emotional processes, but skill deficits as well. For example, just asking your patient to go out and try something different, even as an experiment, requires your patient to have developed a particular outlook about risk taking. Why should you expect some follow-through if your patient views taking risks and potentially failing as just one more predictable defeat in life? Using the language of resistance at this point is not only inaccurate, it can be a significantly destructive communication.

Is there a suffering patient in the world who would not welcome less negative feelings? There are patients who sincerely expect failure or who believe they deserve to suffer because of past failures. This is not the same as *wanting* to hurt inside; rather, it addresses the fact that the patient has beliefs about getting better that may actually get in the way of succeeding. You can nonjudgmentally and objectively address a follow-through problem by *accepting blame* for failing to understand the obstacles that confronted your patient in the first place. It is hoped that you are in a better position to accept blame than your patient. Once you have avoided the resistance game, a collaborative process can be developed to identify trouble spots and generate troubleshooting strategies. On another level, this technique models effective personal problem solving for your patient.

Sample Dialogue: Accepting and Working With Suicidal Communication

The following dialogue, taken from a session with a repetitiously overdosing suicidal patient, demonstrates some ways to reconcile a potential transaction involving suicidal communications.

Therapist: So tell me, how has your last week been?

Patient: Well, I tried to do what you suggested. I stayed at home more and tried to find work to do that gave me more of a sense of completing things. I've been doing a lot of needlepoint work but I still don't feel any better. I've still got all the pills I told you about, those antidepressant pills and sleeping pills they gave me at the hospital, and I know just how many to take to do what I need to do. I also know just how to take them. I won't take them all at once because I'll have trouble keeping them down, but I'll take them one by one. That way they can't pump my stomach and keep me from killing myself.

Therapist: I'm really impressed by how thorough you are in the way you prepare plans like this. How did you learn to do that?

Patient: What? What are you asking?

Therapist: I'm just impressed by how you are able to look through to the end of a plan like this. Where did you learn how to prepare a plan so thoroughly? How did you learn how to do that?

Patient: I don't know. I've always been stubborn as a mule and I get what I want. When I think somebody is gonna try to keep me from something, I show them.

Therapist: I can tell you're a very determined person, and that you know how to stick with something and see it through when you really want to get it done. By the way, have you considered how you might be dressed if you did overdose?

Patient: What the hell difference does that make? If you're dead, you're dead.

Therapist: I know, it's just that arriving at a hospital looking all disheveled would be tacky, don't you think? Also, they need to know who to call to come and pick up your body. Have you thought about putting the name of somebody to contact in a pocket so that they would know who to contact?

Patient: What does this have to do with my problems? You're supposed to be helping me. This isn't doing any good at all.

Therapist: I'm really sorry. Some days I'm just not as sharp as I should be and I miss out on what is going on in a session like this. What could we do right now that would be more helpful for you?

Patient: Well, it sure doesn't help for you to be sitting here talking about me committing suicide, and what I'm gonna wear and how they're gonna notify my family!

Therapist: What else could we talk about that would be more useful, then?

Patient: I don't know.

Therapist: Should we talk a little while about what we could talk about that might be helpful? Does that make sense?

Patient: Well, I suppose so, but I don't think anything will help anyway.

Therapist: I know, thinking about all the setbacks and frustrations you've had to deal with, it makes sense to expect the worst.

In this dialogue, the clinician has moved suicidal behavior off center by reconciling the push-pull contest over overdose potential. Something positive is discovered about the suicidal threat and the patient is complemented in a general way. The patient does a double take, and the clinician immediately moves to the point of resistance. The point of resistance here is whether or not the patient will be allowed to "own" suicidal communications without drawing confrontation. The patient then moves to the positive point of resistance by indicating that talking about this negative content is not useful. The clinician accepts the blame for making this mistake but does not leave the point of negative resistance. The patient is asked for help in determining what would be more useful. The patient "doubles up" on the clinician by indicating that even talking about something else will not help. The clinician then moves to validate the patient's sense of hopelessness and to place it in a learning context. There is now the potential for the two of them to talk about what might work, circumventing a showdown over the patient's suicidal intent.

Providing Crisis and Social Support

The process of change for the multiproblem suicidal patient is usually slow. This does not mean that the patient requires weekly intensive psychotherapy. Change is a developmental process that can require episodes of therapy intermixed with linking up with more competent social support. The few research studies looking at treatment of suicide attempters suggest that longer term supportive treatment is effective at reducing the suicidal behavior per se but has little impact on underlying personality or behavioral variables. The most recent study by Linehan et al. (1991) indicated that a 1-year treatment program consisting of weekly therapy sessions combined with group skills training was effective in reducing the number of suicide attempts and related medical costs in a sample of women with borderline personality disorder. However, few changes were noted in other basic aspects of psychological functioning. This type of programming is difficult to implement in most community mental health settings because of the significant program costs being directed to relatively few patients. In addition, it is not clear how durable the treatment effects are in these more intense programs. Do patients revert to repetitious suicidal behavior after the program is withdrawn? How quickly do treatment effects deteriorate? An earlier study by Lieberman and Eckman (1981) indicated that using a skill-oriented treatment model in a group of hospitalized parasuicides did seem to affect suicidal potential per se but again did not seem to materially alter underlying personality variables such as depression, hopelessness, and problem-solving skills. Although these research efforts certainly are not definitive, they do suggest what practicing clinicians have long maintained: that the repetitiously suicidal patient requires some form of maintenance treatment that may well span the rest of his or her life.

In the typical case, the initial stages of treatment will consist of weekly sessions as you and your patient form a collaborative relationship and begin to reconcile polarities. Once this process has been completed, there is usually a reduction in or shift in the form and intensity of suicidal behavior. At this point, you can lengthen the interval between treatment sessions (e.g., one session per month). However, your patient should always understand that more therapy can be scheduled in the event of a personal crisis as long as this move does not reinforce going into crisis. You must remain ever mindful of the potential for explosive polarizing processes. The fact that your patient is spending more and more time out of therapy is not per se an indication that effective problem solving has been learned and suicidality is no longer an issue.

Effective Management: A Therapeutic, In-System Perspective

A major part of the formula for success with the repetitiously suicidal patient is to develop an effective approach to ongoing self-destructive behavior. To do this, you must effectively manage how adjunctive or ancillary services are delivered to your patient. Often, in working with the chronically suicidal patient you wear many hats: clinician, case manager, advocate, care coordinator. The more you plan out these roles, the less likely there is to be confusion and a critical change of course during a crisis.

Managing Chronic Crisis During Therapy

A well-known feature of the repetitiously suicidal patient is the capacity to slip in and out of crisis: the *crisis-of-the-week syndrome.* With some regularity, you are presented with a crisis by the patient that invites you to divert away from the treatment plan. These crises often occur in association with suicidal or self-destructive behavior. To some extent, this is the hallmark of the early phase of treatment.

Thus you need to assimilate these events into the flow of therapy without losing continuity or placing you and your patient in a confrontational or adversarial position.

Many of the important components of a behaviorally based crisis management protocol have been discussed in Chapter 7. The repetitious suicide attempter requires special attention to and stringent application of these principles. The reason is simple. You are going to be confronted with more suicidal behavior and you need to have a very potent yet flexible plan of attack. The issue of the patient engaging in suicidal behavior or experiencing severe crisis needs to be addressed at the outset of treatment. It needs to be predicted. You need to make very clear your particular stance with respect to intervening in suicidal behavior. The ground rules about after-hours phone contact or scheduling extra sessions in relation to suicidal behavior need to be clear and mutually agreed to. You must work together to develop a crisis card so your patient can begin learning to activate natural social supports. Encourage your patient to make therapeutic contacts *prior to* engaging in any self-destructive behavior. Create a structure in which you and your patient can effectively deal with the chaos and distress that often go along with suicidal behavior. It allows you both to hearken back to earlier agreements as a guide in managing your way through these difficult times.

A well-prepared crisis protocol will answer nearly all the questions in advance. This creates a higher level of comfort in the midst of suicidal behavior and generally promotes healthy interventions. The patient who is scared but locked in on suicidal behavior is drawn to a calm and purposeful clinician. An effective crisis plan can provide an experiential demonstration that selecting alternatives to uncontrolled self-destructive behavior can be rewarding. *Assimilation of crisis* is a major case management strategy. Many events that trigger suicidal crises in the chronically suicidal patient are small in scale and are better thought of as "the straw that broke the camel's back." If the suicidal response is taken off center stage, the patient might discover some straightforward and effective ways to solve the specific event. When the suicidal behavior *itself* becomes the focus of attention, then it is very difficult to solve primary problems, those problems that have pushed suicidality to the forefront.

Beware of Magical Assumptions

The clinician often communicates overtly or covertly an expectation that the patient's suicidal and self-destructive behavior will either disappear and rapidly diminish as a simple consequence of entering treatment. In this scenario, it is assumed that the "magic" of therapy will immediately effect a change in the patient's suicidal behavior independent of the therapy approach. Consequently, a recurrence of suicidal behavior is viewed as a signal that treatment is failing. Negative therapeutic processes can result from this error (e.g., resistance interpretations, anger and confrontation, ultimatums). The major philosophical cornerstone of effective case management is to use the suicidal crisis as an opportunity to promote growth in the patient. It is easy for the clinician's patience to wear thin when the covert expectation of decreased suicidal behavior is continually being violated. The act of planning and frequently reaffirming the crisis management plan in collaboration with the patient will help neutralize this potentially destructive dynamic.

Case Management in the Community

Case management activity is an essential ingredient of effective treatment with the chronically suicidal patient. It is important to case manage key contact points, particularly emergency room providers, who may not have the necessary clinical skills to independently implement an effectual treatment response to the repetitiously suicidal patient. Because suicidal behavior is potentially life threatening and raises legal liability issues, it is imperative that your case management plan be as specific and concrete as possible. For example, most emergency rooms have rotating shifts of personnel; the repetitious attempter may not see the same medical provider despite repeated contacts. The case management plan needs to transfer easily from one shift to another. That generally means that it is written in the patient's chart in concise and concrete language. It should identify who the patient is, the nature of the patient's suicidal behavior, a rationale for the management plan, and the specific steps providers are to take in the event they come into contact with the patient after suicide attempt.

Figure 9–1 presents a sample emergency room case management plan for a repetitious drug overdoser. As can be seen, the goal is to limit the amount of psychotherapeutic interaction that occurs with the patient after an index suicide attempt, in that this is a powerful reinforcer of suicidal behavior. Conversely, more attention, caring, and support is made available if the patient presents to the emergency room prior to engaging in the self-destructive behavior. The hardest part in forming such plans is to get health care providers to understand the rationale for, and importance of, stabilizing and then discharging a repetitious attempter after an index episode. This idea is both new and scary to most health and mental health profession-

---

TO: MSWs, RNs, MDs, Consulting RNs, Medical Clinics, Emergency Centers

RE: Protocol for S.L.

As most of you know, S.L. has made multiple medication overdoses. None of these attempts have been lethal, few have been serious. We are trying to modify her behavior without reinforcing it and without teaching her to be more lethal. We request that when she presents to you with an overdose, that you respond in the following manner:

1. Assess medical danger.
2. Treat her medically, as necessary.
3. Provide S.L. with a meal, but otherwise limit interaction to the bare minimum. Provide no positive nor negative feedback. No punishments, no lectures. Your contact with S.L. should be a noninteractive event.
4. Send S.L. home after treatment and a meal.
5. All therapeutic interactions are to be with N.S., S.L.'s primary therapist only.

For further concerns or questions, please contact N.S. If N.S. is not available, contact O.S., the clinical back-up in this case.

Thank you for your help with this difficult client.

Figure 9–1. Management protocol for S.L.

als, who often believe this flies in the face of risk management rules. The tendency is to hold the patient until mental health personnel eliminate all suicidal ideation or secure a no suicide contract, then discharge the patient. This results in a tremendous amount of interpersonal attention, which can promote a positive view of suicidal behavior in your patient.

Case management plans frequently require repeated contacts with both medical and mental health personnel at key contact sites. This is especially true when the patient tests the case management plan by increasing suicidal behavior and presentations for care. This makes providers uncertain and worried about legal liability. In such cases, it is important to teach providers about the learning theory concepts of extinction and spontaneous recovery. *Extinction* means that when suicidal behavior is neither positively or negatively reinforced, it will gradually decrease in frequency. However, well-learned behaviors undergoing extinction can spontaneously reappear at even a higher frequency for short periods of time. Suicide attempting may *initially increase* but will *gradually decrease* over time as the extinction plan is consistently followed.

When spontaneous recovery occurs with the suicidal patient, it often catches medical or mental health personnel off guard and is a critical point in determining the overall integrity of the case management plan. The more participating providers know what to expect in terms of the suicidal patient, the easier it is to draw attention to the fact that predicted events are occurring. This provides the reassurance that is needed for providers to drop their own biases about how to treat suicidal patients and can allay any risk management concerns.

Someone Has To Be in Charge

A final critical feature of effective case management is the identification of a single provider who makes the final decision about the patient's care. This individual also handles all psychotherapeutic transactions with the patient. Ordinarily, this individual is the patient's primary therapist. The goal of all such funneling actions is to restrain providers at other contact points from delivering uncoordinated treatment—often treatment that is incompatible with the approach being followed by the primary therapist. This is especially critical when a behavioral model is being followed and where reinforcements for the suicidal behavior are the all-important issue. In return for keeping interventions within set boundaries, the primary therapist needs to promptly respond to requests for help by participants in the case management plan. If the primary therapist is going on vacation, other members in the case management network need to be aware of this so they do not expect help that cannot be delivered. Case management plans often fall apart during a therapist's absence, insofar as the patient may interpret the therapist's departure as a form of abandonment and go into crisis.

Done properly, the funneling effect also allows the therapist to extend a wider umbrella of protection for the patient in the event the patient complies with the behavioral treatment plan. In other words, you can control the reinforcements offered at a wider variety of contact points (i.e., hospital emergency rooms, primary care clinics, CMHC emergency teams). When this occurs, the patient is not having two sets of response rules applied with regard to suicidal potential. This allows the clinician and patient to work from a consistent crisis management model.

To Hospitalize or Not To Hospitalize?

Our studies have consistently shown that about 50% of all suicide attempters in an inpatient psychiatric facility have a history of at least one prior suicide attempt. This suggests that inpatient staff deal with a revolving door filled with repetitious suicide attempters. This raises the question of how hospitalization should or can support the treatment process for the repetitious patient. Of all the subpopulations of suicidal patients, this one is probably the most difficult to deal with effectively during an inpatient admission. The patient is often not well liked by hospital staff and tends to be at disproportionate risk of an AMA discharge. The patient may be diagnosed as borderline personality before the first intake interview because repetitious suicidal behavior itself is strongly related to a diagnosis of borderline personality. Very few inpatient units can offer the long-term treatment programs that could even begin to address the many cognitive and emotional needs of the multiproblem borderline patient.

An equally important consideration is that the repetitiously suicidal patient is often dumped into the inpatient system by a frustrated therapist who just wants the patient to go away. When we talk about a therapist "cracking" in the moment of truth, this is one of the cardinal manifestations. The clinician is tired of the patient and hands over care to an inpatient staff who then may be negatively disposed toward the patient because of the dump and the out-of-control gestalt that develops around poor planning. Consequently, the suicidal patient can evoke a high level of hostility and confrontation during even a brief hospital stay. This patient may well get less-preferred and less-intensive forms of treatment available on the unit. The patient may be started on a medication regime that has little chance of succeeding. Often, diagnostic and treatment disputes can erupt on the treatment team that will be blamed on the patient (i.e., "splitting") rather than on the real culprits: interpersonal conflicts, disciplinary jealousies, and turf struggles among members of the treatment team.

Even when none of the above negative consequences occur, consider also the possible reinforcing effects of the hospitalization per se on the individual's suicidal problem-solving potential. The patient is removed from a stressful environment and is exposed to a very structured setting where all basic needs are cared for. Positive caring and attention is forthcoming from the unit staff. The individual feels looked after and supported because of the suicidality, and, accordingly, the behavior is reinforced. In all, hospitalization potentially offers negative and positive reinforcement scenarios. Given the frequent use of hospitalization for the suicidal person, this may be a factor in the relatively high risk of suicidal behavior noted in the United States.

There are certainly circumstances in which a patient is bound and determined to land in some type of intensive care facility. The clinician cannot ignore this possibility in effective treatment planning. It is therefore critical to attempt to develop alternatives to traditional inpatient treatment in the event the patient ends up in that part of the treatment system. This might involve contracting with a local hospital to allow the patient to elect a 72-hour voluntary time-out with an automatic prearranged discharge plan. If the local community has an acute care crisis facility, the patient can be directed to seek admission to that facility, with prearranged, short-term problem-solving goals. The goal is to eliminate the reinforcement potential from any intensified treatment and, as soon as possible, get the patient back into the natural environment and to solve problems.

Continuity in case management is particularly critical during the transition between inpatient and outpatient mental health treatment. When a suicidal outpatient enters a psychiatric hospital in the context of a suicide attempt, there is an even greater need to coordinate in a way that supports the basic outpatient treatment plan. The reason for this is simple: Psychiatric units can deliver an enormous array of services in a very condensed time period. If these services are not synchronized with the outpatient treatment regime, long-term treatment can suffer. Psychiatric inpatient staff have their own way of dealing with suicidal patients and often do not coordinate with the outpatient system. Coordination usually occurs at the initiative of the primary therapist. Because the very act of admission to a hospital is a potent reinforcer of suicidal behavior, the primary therapist must make efforts to arrange for appropriate treatment at likely inpatient sites.

It is important to provide a sound rationale to attending psychiatrists to gain support for a treatment plan that may be different than the normal milieu plan of the unit. For example, if the plan calls for automatic discharge within 48–72 hours and a minimum of psychotherapeutic contact, the responsible physicians need to understand why that is the best way to care for the patient. The primary therapist needs to initiate the dialogue about how best to coordinate the interface between outpatient and inpatient care. There are myriad reasons why this type of coordination and planning may not happen, and it is sometimes particularly difficult to effectively work together with the repetitiously suicidal patient. To deal with this, try to establish a consistency of purpose with at least one inpatient psychiatric site, and direct the patient to that site in the event of a suicidal crisis. Discourage admissions to hospitals where staff seem unwilling or unable to coordinate care. Hospitalizations are helpful when they reinforce your long-term strategy, but they are harmful when they subvert it.

Helpful Hints

- ♦ The repetitiously suicidal patient differs in degree, not kind, from episodic and more functional patients.
- ♦ The goals in treatment with the repetitiously suicidal patient are the same as those of the acutely suicidal patient: teach acceptance and tolerance of emotional pain and problem-solving skills.
- ♦ With the repetitious patient, the therapist must reconcile polarities that develop over who is in control.
- ♦ Effective treatment avoids confrontations with the patient over a variety of issues related to ongoing suicidal behavior.
- ♦ Typically, the repetitiously suicidal patient will require ongoing intermittent crisis and supportive care because beliefs and behavior are very slow to change.
- ♦ In case management, it is important to establish an open direct dialogue with the patient about how suicidal behavior will be responded to in the course of therapy.
- ♦ Intersystem case management is a basic therapeutic function and requires collaboration with emergency rooms, crisis units, and inpatient psychiatric units.
- ♦ In general, inpatient hospitalization is not helpful for the repetitious patient; consider using short-stay, acute-care alternatives.

Selected Readings

Beck A, Freeman A: Cognitive Therapy of Personality Disorders. New York, Guilford, 1990

Farmer RDT: The differences between those who repeat and those who do not, in The Suicide Syndrome. Edited by Farmer R, Hirsch S. Cambridge, Cambridge University Press, 1979, pp 192–204

Hawton K, Catalan J: Attempted Suicide: A Practical Guide to its Nature and Management. Oxford, UK, Oxford University Press, 1982

Hayes S: Comprehensive distancing, paradox and the treatment of emotional avoidance, in Paradoxical Procedures in Psychotherapy. Edited by Ascher M. New York, Guilford, 1989, pp 184–218

Liberman RP, Eckman T: Behavior therapy vs insight-oriented therapy for repeated suicide attempters. Arch Gen Psychiatry 38:1126–1130, 1981

Linehan MM, Armstrong HE, Suarez A, et al: Cognitive-behavioral treatment of chronically parasuicidal borderline patients. Arch Gen Psychiatry 48:1060–1064, 1991

Strosahl K: Cognitive and behavioral treatment of the personality disordered patient, in Psychotherapy in Managed Health Care: The Optional Use of Time and Resources. Edited by Berman W, Austad C. Washington, DC, American Psychological Association, 1991, pp 185–201

Chapter 10

The Suicidal Patient in General Health Care

Geneeral health care practitioners need to be effective at treating suicidal behavior in their patients for at least three compelling and clear reasons. First, and most important, the recent Epidemiologic Catchment Area Study (Narrow et al. 1993) contained a somewhat startling revelation about the role of general practitioners in delivering mental health care in the United States. Specifically, nearly *half* of all patients with mental disorders received their mental health care *solely* from a general practitioner (see Narrow et al. 1993). Although suicidality is certainly not limited to people with mental disorders, knowledge of suicidal behavior is part and parcel of dealing with this population. Second, the type of mental disorder treated by the general practitioner is important. Studies of the prevalence of mental disorders among medical outpatients have consistently shown that anywhere from 6% to 10% meet diagnostic criteria for major depression, panic disorder, generalized anxiety disorder, or somatization disorder. The recent Medical Outcomes Study (Wells et al. 1988) showed that mental disorders are generally underrecognized in general health care settings. A common mental disorder in such settings is *depression,* and one of the diagnostic symptoms of depression is *suicidal ideation or behavior.* Third, many suicidal medical patients do not have access to mental health care. There are both rural and urban parts of the United States that have poor health care resources. There may be few, if any, mental health providers. Even when referral for mental health care is available and acceptable to a suicidal patient, significant travel time may be required to attend sessions, and access to the mental health provider may be severely limited. In these situations, if a crisis develops, it is going to be the initial responsibility of the general practitioner to manage it. In sum, in a large number of cases, the patient will receive all treatment in that general health care practitioner's office, the major de facto mental health system in the United States (Narrow et al. 1993).

If this is the first chapter you are reading in this book, please look now at Chapter 2, Examine Your Attitudes: Affective, Ethical, and Legal Issues in the Treatment of the Suicidal Patient. The general health care clinic can be a most difficult arena in which to properly address suicidality. There is much going on, decisions must be made quickly, and the data base is often incomplete. The situation is usually emotionally charged, and the push to do something quickly can often seem overwhelming. Suicidal patients do not always fit easily into a setting that relies on evaluation, focused treatment, and long intervals between follow-up visits. To deal with suicidality, health care providers must have a thorough understanding of both their personal and clinical response to the suicidal patient.

Many general health care practitioners believe that it is very difficult, if not impossible, to conduct anything resembling an effective intervention with the suicidal patient within the confines of a busy schedule with patients spaced one-quarter hour apart. They point to the full 50-minute session used by mental health providers and rightly wonder how a 15-minute (or even 5-minute) intervention can be done when trained specialists take up to an hour. The key difference is the context; the general health care setting is one in which things happen rapidly, and most patients have a certain readiness for this. The mental health context is oriented toward the process of deliberate and detailed discussions, focused on producing change in many aspects of the patient's life. At times, the general health care provider has a distinct advantage over the mental health therapist, notwithstanding the fast pace of primary health care visits. Both practitioner and patient are acclimated to a setting when action is expected, the instructions are crisp, and compliance is high. This evolves from the long-term, sometimes lifelong, relationship the primary care doctor has with the patient and the fact that he or she is seen as a trusted friendly physician, not an imposing, inquiry-driven stranger. Despite the strengths of this special kind of leverage, many general practitioners still routinely respond with a not-in-my-office approach and try to refer the suicidal patient to some form of psychiatric treatment. This action is often based on the premise that the patient needs to be discharged from the general health care system and admitted to a mental health care system. It is a premise not always fulfilled. Many times, a gap of days and even weeks occurs between the patient's leaving one system and entering another, if the transfer happens at all. In some clinical settings, up to over half of the patients referred from general health care never arrive for a mental health appointment. A common referral practice, and one that sometimes seems set up to fail, is to give a patient a phone number with instructions to call for an appointment. The patient may not call. It is one more impersonal task to perform. Your patient may get one (or more) busy signals and become discouraged. Even worse, a recorded message intervenes, and your patient runs the risk of getting lost in the infamous phone mail jail. Almost as discouraging is to be told by a harried clinic clerk that nothing is available for a month or so. In these eventualities, your patient remains in limbo, and you remain in a position of potential liability for a negligence suit in the event of an adverse outcome. Our recommendation is to solidify your transfer relationships, with documented confirmation that continuity of care has been accomplished. In addition, develop your procedures for managing that period that is so overlooked and so important, the *in the meantime*. The remainder of this chapter discusses those procedures, and we hope it will give you the tools you need for treating these patients within your clinic structure.

A detailed discussion of the assessment of suicidality is to be found in Chapter 3. These assessments occur in a variety of settings, take differing amounts of time, and gather various types of information. One essential rule pertains to any assessment procedure: *It is part of treatment.* A reasonable and caring assessment, even a

10-minute one, leaves a patient with the understanding that the problem has been taken seriously and that help is on the way. Assessment in general health care should be proactive regarding suicidal behaviors. All patients should be screened for suicidal thoughts and behavior as part of an initial health care assessment. Questions about suicidality should be a regular part of the screening exam and not be linked to statements about particular psychiatric states such as depression or anxiety, particularly in the increasingly popular structured interview format with its skip methodology. A common error in screening is to ask about depression and, if the answer is no, to skip questions about suicidal ideation or behavior. Suicidality occurs in many patients who have no diagnosable psychiatric disorder, and some patients who are ultimately found to have a psychiatric disorder initially deny (do not reveal on direct questioning) their symptoms. In other words, suicidal behavior, ideation, or threats can accompany any psychiatric condition, and they can be present when no psychiatric condition is diagnosed. Accordingly, these behaviors need to be routinely asked about in a health care assessment.

As a general practitioner, be aware of two conditions in which the assessment of suicidality is particularly important. The first is *age*. Although there has been much made in the literature of suicides among the young, especially from adolescence through the middle twenties, the most lethal group is the elderly. Rates of suicide above the age of 75 are some two to three times greater than in the teenage and young adult population. The second condition, often linked to age, is *general state of health*. Both chronic poor health and recent deterioration of health should immediately set a suicide risk assessment in motion. These factors, especially when combined with a current mental disorder such as depression, present a potentially lethal mixture. Many people who have committed suicide have seen a general physician shortly before their death, and these patients are often defined by advancing age and poor health.

Appendix 4 presents a short Suicidal Thinking and Behaviors Questionnaire that can be used to assess suicidal history, intensity, causality, and efficacy.

This questionnaire provides you with a good basic data set

regarding suicidality. There are three areas of general psychological functioning pertinent to suicidality that can be quickly assessed. All of these areas have some long-term (not short-term!) predictive power for suicidal potential and are helpful in developing a treatment plan. The first, *efficacy* (see item six in Appendix 4), concerns whether your patient believes committing suicide will solve his or her problems. When a person feels that suicide would definitely be effective in dealing with troubles, his or her potential to use suicidal behavior is increased. Second is the concept of *hopelessness*. This involves a patient's lack of faith that the future will be any better than the present. Hopelessness has been shown to have some predictive value for long-term suicidal behavior, especially among depressed persons and especially in Western cultures. The Beck Hopelessness Scale is an excellent instrument to systematically assess this variable (Beck et al. 1974). Do not equate hopelessness with depression. This state of mind can come from a variety of conditions, including a generally reasonable assessment of one's life circumstance and environment.

The third function to assess is the relatively new area of *survival and coping* beliefs. These are the positive reasons for staying alive that your patient may use to buffer the impact of suicidal impulses. The lack of strongly held coping beliefs may remove some resistance to going ahead with suicidal behavior. Recent work has shown that the importance a patient attaches to survival and coping beliefs can be an important predictor of suicide intent. Survival and coping beliefs are more thoroughly discussed in Chapter 7.

The Role of Diagnostic Screening

Because suicidality, in about 50% of cases, is associated with an underlying psychiatric disorder, an assessment for these disorders is important. Treatment of a specific disorder is important in its own right, but you should not assume that the suicidal crisis is taken care of because the psychiatric disorder is being treated. Much of the suicidality in persons with a psychiatric disorder occurs in spite of treatment. Also, recall that a significant percentage of suicidal patients do not meet criteria for *any* psychiatric diagnosis. The assumption that suicidality automatically means the presence of a mental disorder can lead you on a diagnostic wild goose chase (most often depression is the goose). Make sure diagnostic criteria are met before you administer psychoactive medication. It is very difficult to justify prescribing pills that are subsequently used in an overdose when a solid basis for the prescription is not found in the clinical records. Our tact is to advocate for treatment both of the psychiatric disorder and of the suicidality, and to view these as separate goals of good management. Table 10–1 contains a series of questions that are useful in screening for psychiatric illness. A positive answer to any question should lead to further evaluation of that psychiatric condition. You can use this instrument to help you determine whether further consultation may be helpful in diagnosis or treatment.

Focused Interventions

The general health care physician must also make an assessment of urgency; that is, does the patient require immediate hospitalization or some other form of intensive crisis intervention? Hospitalization certainly has its place in the care of a suicidal individual but can be unnecessary and therefore potentially counterproductive. Sometimes, the patient is not committable and will not agree to hospitalization, often because of the perceived stigma and/or sense of loss of control. The chapter on hospitalization offers a detailed decision-making process that should lead to rational use of this intensive and expensive treatment modality.

In this chapter, we are going to focus on a *seven-step intervention strategy* (see Table 10–2): a program designed to help your patient weather a suicidal crisis. You can follow these steps to support your patient until transfer to another system of care is accomplished. When this is not possible, these steps will give you a framework to address suicidality for a longer term. These interventions flow from the information gleaned from the assessment described earlier in this chapter and are designed to initiate and promote nonsuicidal problem solving in your patient.

Table 10–1. Screening for psychiatric illness that may have co-occurring suicidality

Yes ○ No ○	1.	(Panic disorder/agoraphobia with panic attack) Has pt. ever had spells like a heart attack when became suddenly frightened, anxious, and had chest pain, tightness, trouble breathing, etc.?
Yes ○ No ○	2.	(General anxiety disorder) Has pt. ever had a period of 6 months or more when most of time nervous, anxious, with bodily symptoms such as weakness, fatigue, stomach problems, muscle aches, etc.?
Yes ○ No ○	3.	(Depression) Has pt. ever had a period of 2 weeks or more when felt sad, blue, depressed, loss of interest, loss of energy, hopeless, helpless, worthless, etc.?
Yes ○ No ○	4.	(Dysthymia) Periods of depressed days with symptoms not every day for 2 weeks over a 2-year period (sporadic symptoms).
Yes ○ No ○	5.	(Posttraumatic stress disorder) Does pt. have a history of traumatic event or experience that has led to reexperiencing the trauma?
Yes ○ No ○	6.	(Mania/hypomania) Has pt. ever had a period of 1 week or more when so happy, excited, irritable, or "high" that pt. got into trouble, or family or friends worried about it, or a doctor said pt. was manic?
Yes ○ No ○		Has pt. ever had a period of at least several days when irritable, "high," or excited, very energetic, very impulsive or confident, or needed less sleep?
Yes ○ No ○	7.	(Schizophrenia) Has pt. ever heard voices or seen visions?
Yes ○ No ○		Has pt. ever believed people were controlling, spying on, following, or plotting against pt., or reading pt.'s mind?
Yes ○ No ○		Has pt. ever believed pt. could actually hear or feel other people's thoughts or that other people could actually hear or feel pt.'s thoughts or put thoughts into pt.'s mind?
Yes ○ No ○	8.	(Alcohol-substance abuse) Has pt. ever had problems from drinking alcohol?
Yes ○ No ○		Desire to **C**ut down use?
Yes ○ No ○		Have others been **A**nnoyed at pt.'s use?
Yes ○ No ○		**G**uilt about use? "Paranoid"
Yes ○ No ○		"**E**ye opener" to avoid withdrawal symptoms?
Yes ○ No ○		Has pt. ever used marijuana, LSD, cocaine, stimulants? CAGE Alcohol C___ A___ G___ E___ CAGE Substance C___ A___ G___ E___
Yes ○ No ○	9.	(Antisocial personality) Does pt. have history of discipline problems in school, delinquency, running away from home, persistent lying, thefts or vandalism, frequent initiation of fights, alcohol or drug abuse, or school grades much below expectations, *before* age 15?

Table 10–2.   Seven-step intervention strategy

1. Validate emotional pain.
2. Discuss ambivalence.
3. Provide encouragement.
4. Develop a crisis card.
5. Get the longer term responsible person involved.
6. Arrange at least two supportive phone calls.

Step 1: Validate Emotional Pain

The first of the steps is to validate emotional pain. In Chapter 5, we discussed framing the pain a person feels during a suicidal period by the Three *I*s: the pain is inescapable, intolerable, and interminable. Communicating an understanding of the pain and legitimizing it for the patient is critical to defusing suicidal impulses. Many suicidal individuals do not see this pain as legitimate. They see it as a flaw, somehow a product of their own weakness. Validating pain is not the same as agreeing that suicide is the only option. If anything, providers are often so worried about inadvertently increasing a patient's suicidal intent that the overall approach can be unnecessarily brusque, leaving the patient with a feeling of lack of empathy. In the midst of a suicidal crisis there is a terrible sense of isolation, stigmatization, and shame. It really helps your patient when contact is made with someone who is nonjudgmental and understands the fear and sense of desperation. Validate the pain and at the same time understand that your patient is having trouble thinking through various approaches and solutions to problems. You need to emphasize that the pain is quite understandable given the circumstances but that the method of dealing with the circumstances is faulty. Remember, your patient is often doing the reverse. He or she is assuming that the pain is not legitimate but that the methods of dealing with it are.

Step 2: Capitalize on Ambivalence

An assumption all health care workers should make is that every suicidal patient is ambivalent: there is both the desire to live and to die. If your patient were absolutely intent on committing suicide, he or she would. Lethal means abound. But this is not the case. Your patient is here in the clinic talking to you. Some degree, some glimmer of ambivalence has brought this about. In other words, your patient has *regretfully,* and in an uncertain manner, come to the conclusion that death is the only way out. This is probably based on the belief that less extreme solutions have already been tried and have failed. The problem for you to address is that either your patient's goals were unrealistic (e.g., to stop feeling bad in the midst of a drawn out antagonistic divorce), poor solutions were used, or good solutions were not used long enough. It is important to come down unequivocally on the positive and life-sustaining part of the patient's ambivalence and to do this *without taking a moralistic stance.* Your first task is to give voice to your genuine optimism that problems can be solved and that there is more than one way out. A good way to quantify this ambivalence is to use the Reasons for Living Inventory (see Appendix 3). You can have your patient fill out the inventory, or you can familiarize yourself with the questions and use several of them in the interview. It is most helpful to find an area or two of ambivalence and point these out. If all else fails, you can use the fact of the patient's presence: "You are here. I take your being here as an indication that you are struggling with this. Our job is to take the time to look at that struggle. I know it seems very difficult right now to think through things and produce changes, but part of you wants to do that. Certainly, I want to do that. So let's get started."

Step 3: Provide Encouragement

Validating emotional pain and discussing ambivalence creates a context in which it is possible to provide healthy encouragement. The proper use of this technique has as much to do with your attitude and demeanor as it does with what you say. By truly understanding both your patient's pain and your patient's sense of no way out, you will come across as a caring person who can be trusted. If you do not make this connection, your own uncertainty and ambivalence is liable to shine through. Many individuals, in the midst of their distress, are quite perceptive, especially to nonverbal clues. Your words, the sense of organization you portray, the ability you have to understand what's going on, and your overall confidence level about this approach being the right way to go are major factors in reassuring and encouraging your patient.

Step 4: Establish a Crisis Plan

The crisis card is one of the more useful tools in the management of suicidality. Your patient may actually have used effective strategies to deal with past crises or can brainstorm with you and come up with some new ones. However, when the moment is at hand, the patient cannot remember what was discussed or does not follow through in any sort of step-wise fashion—hence, the *crisis card*. Table 10–3 provides a sample crisis card. Although this sample contains points that are pertinent to many people, it is most important to tailor this card to the individual. The development of such a card usually takes 3–5 minutes at the end of the office visit. It should contain no more than five or six points. Your patient should be encouraged to carry it, make copies, and tell friends and family of the approach. The copies can be put in convenient places around the house, taped to locations such as the medicine chest or the refrigerator. The moment the pain seems to be increasing, the card should be consulted, and these steps followed.

Table 10–3.   Crisis card sample

1. Do not drink, or, if I am drinking, stop drinking.
2. Sit down and take 50 deep breaths.
3. Say to myself 10 times, "No matter how bad things are right now, I am a strong person and I will survive."
4. Contact one of my friends who has said they will help me, and talk for 5 minutes about our joint interests.
5. Write down why I became upset and how I dealt with things so that I can discuss this episode with Dr. _____ at our next contact.

Step 5: Link to Social and Community Resources

This strategy allows your patient to walk away from the office visit with something tangible: a plan of immediate action. In this phase, the physician acts as a case manager, a critical function discussed in Chapter 7. This work is easier if professional community resources are available. Who in your clinic or community can work with this individual? Seek them out, and discuss referrals with them. Ideally, you should be able to schedule an appointment for your patient. Remember, requiring the patient to do the leg work can be difficult and discouraging. The suicidal patient already feels stigmatized and may resist making arrangements for outpatient follow-up. Be as helpful as you can. Get your office personnel on the case to make things work smoothly. Remember that even when a referral is set, the problems continue. For this reason, the use of the telephone to deal with the interim support is quite important. You may, however, be in a location without such professional help. Get creative. Use family, friends, community centers, church groups, social organizations, and whatever else you and your patient can think of. A strength of small towns and rural centers can be a greater willingness to help than that found in the more chaotic and anonymous world of a larger city.

Step 6: Arrange Telephone Follow-Up

Arrange to initiate at least two supportive phone calls in the time between your evaluation and your next visit or the point where your patient is scheduled to begin longer term treatment. You, your nurse, or other office personnel should organize the call to keep it brief and focused. Use the format outlined in Table 10–4. These calls are not meant to be therapy sessions. They are meant to display ongoing support and encouragement by following up on points that were made in the initial evaluation. Has your patient had the opportunity to use the crisis card? Have arrangements for a specialty mental health appointment been made? Make your patient understand that you are confident that things will get better if the patient follows

Table 10–4. Supportive phone call structure

---

1. State that you are calling as part of our initial plan of treatment.
2. Ask about details of treatment: for example, arrangements for future appointments, taking medication as prescribed.
3. Ask about emotional states, use of crisis card. Has card been effective? Discuss changes if it has not.
4. End with encouraging statement.

---

through on the plan. Remember that the crisis plan can be modified. If some aspect is not helpful, change it. Get your patient to come up with ideas. Develop a sense of partnership in this. Give a technique a fair trial. If it does not work, change it.

Step 7: Initiate Appropriate Medication Treatment

The last intervention is to start medication treatment for any mental disorder you have properly diagnosed. This can be a tricky issue with the suicidal patient, and some general health care providers are better trained and more comfortable doing this than others. Remember, medication in and of itself is not a sufficient treatment for suicidality, although it may be highly effective in providing symptom relief. However, this is *not* the time to prescribe medications to your patient if psychiatric symptomatology has not been demonstrated. As noted above, this tactic can backfire. Medications cannot produce change in other people, and they do not serve their intended purpose when taken all at once. A good technique is to develop a crisis card *before* writing a prescription. The pain tolerance and problem-solving techniques embedded in the card directives may be a better and more permanent solution to your patient's difficulties than adding a pill to the mix.

The most common disorder dealt with is depression. However, suicidality is only one symptom of depression and *not* sufficient to make the diagnosis. You need to carefully review the other diagnostic symptoms of this disorder before assuming that antidepressant medications are the way to go. The most important consideration in prescribing medication for the suicidal depressed patient is the total amount of medication given. Tricyclic antidepressants have been a significant issue in lethal overdosing for several decades. A large number of completed suicides and suicide attempts involve overdosing on antidepressants. A 2-week supply of a typical tricyclic is a lethal dose for many individuals, and yet prescriptions are commonly written for between 2 and 4 weeks. Our strong recommendation is to prescribe no more than a 7-day supply of tricyclic antidepressants and evaluate drug effects, compliance, and the patient's suicidality before prescribing a refill. A safer alternative is to use a selective serotonin reuptake inhibitor (SSRI), such as fluoxetine, sertraline, or paroxetine. These medications require little or no titration for most patients. Their overdose potential is quite small, and they can be prescribed for intervals that match up with your patient's overall treatment program. The claim that these medications cause elevated suicidality has been intensively researched and found to be without merit. These medications are appropriate for use in the *depressed* and *suicidal* patient.

Antianxiety agents, in particular benzodiazepines, are of limited usefulness in treating suicidality. These drugs often produce sedation, a state that is usually *not* conducive to increased autonomy and self-efficacy. Benzodiazepines do effectively treat anxiety *if* you have established that an anxiety disorder is present. These agents can treat insomnia if you are convinced that the short-term treatment of sleeplessness would be helpful. The dangers of extended use are well known: the development of tolerance and the possible need for increasing doses, dependency, and the sometimes horrendous problem of withdrawal after longer term use. So think about these agents carefully. We have found them overused with suicidal individuals, and often their short-term palliative effects on highly aroused patients do not provide sufficient benefit to justify use.

Helpful Hints

♦ Even in the context of a busy practice, the general health care provider can create an atmosphere in which good things happen for a suicidal patient.

♦ Use the tables in this chapter to set up an assessment of suicidality as part of your screening procedures.
♦ Train your staff to use telephone follow-up in a brief, focused, and empathic manner.
♦ Develop your referral sources. Make your office part of a system that cares for the suicidal patient.

Selected Readings

Beck A, Steer RA, Kovacs M, et al: Hopelessness and eventual suicide: a 10 year prospective study of patients hospitalized with suicidal ideation. Am J Psychiatry 142:559–563, 1985

Beck A, Weissman A, Lester D, et al: The measurement of pessimism: The Hopelessness Scale. J Consult Clin Psychol 42:861–865, 1974

Chiles JA, Carlin AS, Benjamin GAH, et al: A physician, a nonmedical psychotherapist, and a patient: the pharmacotherapy-psychotherapy triangle, in Integrating Pharmacotherapy and Psychotherapy. Edited by Beitman BD, Klerman GL. Washington, DC, American Psychiatric Press, 1991, pp 105–118

Hawton K, Catalan J: Attempted Suicide: A Practical Guide to its Nature and Management, 2nd Edition. New York, Oxford University Press, 1987

Michel K, Valach L: Suicide prevention: spreading the gospel to general practitioners. Br J Psychiatry 160:757–760, 1992

Murphy GE: The physician's role in suicide prevention, in Suicide. Edited by Roy A. Baltimore, MD, Williams & Wilkins, 1986, pp 171–179

Narrow W, Regier D, Rare D, et al: Use of services by persons with mental health and addictive disorders. Arch Gen Psychiatry 50:95–107, 1993

Von Korff M, Shapiro S, Burke S, et al: Anxiety and depression in a primary care clinic. Arch Gen Psychiatry 44:152–156, 1987

Wells K, Hays R, Burnam M, et al: Detection of depressive disorder for patients receiving pre-paid or fee for service care. JAMA 262:3293–3302, 1988

Chapter 11

Special Populations, Special Settings, Special Techniques

O ur goal in writing this book is to prepare you, the health care provider, with the tools you need to deal with the suicidal patient. To this end, we have discussed techniques by which you can examine your own attitudes and philosophies about suicidality, a most necessary step in working in this challenging area. We then developed a series of comprehensive and specific techniques for treating the suicidal person. We realized this can occur in a variety of settings, and so we have addressed this work in the major treatment settings: the family practitioner's office, the outpatient mental health clinic, and the psychiatric hospital. The approach outlined in this book can be helpful with almost any suicidal patient and in almost any setting. However, everyone is different, uniqueness abounds, and no amount of reading can fully prepare you for special situations.

In this chapter, we examine groups of patients that may call for the use of special techniques on your part. This includes the patient who is prescribed psychoactive medication, the substance-abusing patient, and the patient with a psychotic disorder such as schizophrenia. Finally, we take a look at two age groups that pose some special dilemmas in terms of their elevated risk for suicidal behavior: adolescents and the elderly.

Medication and the Suicidal Patient

Many patients are treated with medications for their psychiatric illness. Most commonly, patients are treated with benzodiazepines and/or antidepressants, and they are treated less frequently with antipsychotic and/or neuroleptic medication. Several things are important here. First, you need to understand how these medications might affect suicidality. Second, when a patient is working with several health care providers, you must review the challenges and complexities that occur when a patient is working with two clinicians: one who is prescribing medications and the other who is delivering psychotherapy. Finally, you need to become aware of the possible pitfalls associated with polymedication regimes, especially with the repetitiously suicidal patient.

For the past two decades, benzodiazepines have replaced barbiturates as the medications of choice for treating anxiety and agitation, and for producing sedation. Benzodiazepines offer a major safety advantage—that is, lethal overdoses are extremely uncommon. As a class, these medications have been a major advance in the medical pharmacopoeia, although they present with several major problems: they tend to be overused, they are often prescribed without an adequate monitoring plan, and they tend to be used too long. Overuse stems from the use of these medications as a quick fix for a potpourri of symptoms, such as poor sleep hygiene, excessive caffeine intake, and poor problem-solving skills. When used for anxiety and agitation, a good general plan for benzodiazepines is to use them for approximately 1 month at doses that provide relief, then reduce the dose for about 2 months, and then discontinue the medication. Longer use can result in physical dependence and tolerance. There are certainly indications for longer term use, and you need to document these in your chart notes if you prescribe longer than 3 months. The discontinuance of benzodiazepines can produce a variety of withdrawal symptoms, with seizures being the most worrisome. Additionally, when these medications are stopped, some individuals suffer, often several days later, either from rebound anxiety or rebound insomnia. In a suicidal individual, all of these phenomena can lead to increased dysphoria, agitation, and increased potential for suicidal behavior. When you are working with a patient who has been on benzodiazepines for a significant time, a good strategy is to set up a structured, gradual withdrawal program that may include the use of adjunctive medication such as clonazepam or carbamazepine. Managing withdrawal can be tricky. If you are not familiar with these procedures, you need to consult with a colleague for this necessary treatment.

Antidepressants are a class of drugs that have undergone significant refinement in the past 10 years. The newer agents, represented mainly by the selective serotonin reuptake inhibitors (SSRIs), are no more effective than the older agents for treating depression but have fewer significant side effects and are generally easier to dose. Monoamine oxidase inhibitors (MAOIs) and tricyclic antidepressants (TCAs) were both developed in the 1950s and remain in widespread use. The TCAs continue to be the most commonly used medications in this class. The side effect profile of these drugs often creates compliance problems. However, a more serious problem is the overdose potential of this drug class. Because of the cardiotoxicity of tricyclics, a 2- or even 1-week supply can be lethal. Often, because the patients cannot be seen at more frequent intervals, these medications are prescribed on a once-a-month or more basis.

There are two concerns in the use of antidepressants with the suicidal patient. First, it is important to verify the diagnosis of depression. As we have stressed repeatedly, suicidality per se is not a sufficient condition for the diagnosis of depression, and there is no firm evidence that there is any medication that is helpful with suicidality per se. A common mistake made by medical practitioners is to diagnose depression, formally or informally, with cardinal sign weight given to suicidality. When the diagnosis turns out to be incorrect, the medical treatment has little chance of working and leaves the patient expecting a positive change that will not occur. This failed expectation runs the risk of increasing the patient's suicidality. Second, if antidepressants are indicated, make sure the number of pills in the bottle makes up less than a lethal dose. This generally means 1-week prescriptions, keeping the total amount available under 1500–2000 mg. Work with pharmacies to promote this. For example, you can write four 1-week prescriptions, dated to cover a month, rather than one script for the entire period. If this is difficult, for example, when it is not easy to get to the drugstore, family members or friends can be recruited to help keep your patient supplied with a reasonable amount.

The problem with these management techniques is that although they promote safety, they also can emphasize passivity and dependence. Therefore, it is important to work to gradually increase a sense of competency and security in self-managing medication. For example, you should rehearse ways in which your patient can take the initiative in discussing with the pharmacist ways of getting smaller prescriptions more frequently. Of course, patients will always be able to hoard medication, increasing the risk that, if they do overdose, the results will be fatal. However, dealing with the total available dose as a treatment issue may well make hoarding less likely.

There is another technique that is unfortunately not readily available in the United States. This involves packaging medication in individual wrappings. Over-the-counter medications are frequently dispensed this way. Many patients who overdose do so impulsively. The person is angry or upset and often is consuming alcohol. There is very little lead time, sometimes just a matter of a few minutes, between when he or she decides to overdose and when the medication is ingested. Generally most of the pills in the bottle will be consumed, and generally the person assumes this will be a lethal act. It would be quite different if the patient had a long string of individually packaged medication. Unwrapping each pill might certainly interfere with the impulsivity of the moment and make the situation safer.

Antipsychotic medication presents a different concern. Although benzodiazepines can produce physical dependence and some antidepressants have lethal overdose potential, the concern with antipsychotics also includes the side effect profile and its relationship to suicidality. Specifically, all the currently available antipsychotics, with the exceptions of clozapine and risperidone (at certain doses), run a substantial risk of inducing neurological side effects. The most common are what are known as extrapyramidal symptoms (EPSs). One EPS is akathisia, which is best described as an overwhelming desire to stay in motion, a constant and uncomfortable restlessness, an inability to sit still. People experiencing this side effect can have a sustained and terrifying experience. Undiagnosed and untreated, akathisia has been specifically described in suicide notes as a cause of the patient's deadly behavior. This has occurred when these medications are being used to treat a psychotic illness, but it has also occurred when patients are given this class of drug for other indications (e.g., nausea and vomiting). A second EPS that can be quite uncomfortable and is related to increasing suicidality is akinesia, which is a difficulty initiating movement. As a chronic side effect, this gives many patients a blunted and unresponsive physiognomy. Facial muscles do not work too well, arms do not swing normally when walking, and the person looks stilted and odd. The overall effect can be medication-enhanced difficulties with communication and resulting social isolation. Both of these side effects can be instrumental in producing suicidality in a person if they are not diagnosed and adequately addressed.

Multimedication Regimes

With the advent of additional and more sophisticated medications in almost every drug class, a variety of augmentation strategies—coupled with a perception that each symptom can be individually targeted by a particular drug—has often led to using several medications at once in treating a patient with a psychiatric illness. The more numerous a patient's symptoms are, the more likely he or she will be taking multiple drugs. Multiple diagnoses are often approached with one or more medications for each illness. For example, a patient diagnosed as having bipolar illness and borderline personality disorder might well be taking a combination such as lithium, valproic acid, haloperidol, lorazepam, benztropine, and propranolol to cover an array of symptoms and side effects.

The judicious use of multiple medications certainly has a place in modern psychiatry, but dangers do arise. We note them here because it is not unusual to find a suicidal person taking several different drugs, especially if he or she has made several attempts and especially if he or she has several different psychiatric diagnoses. First, some patients get to a polymedication state through one of several irrational processes. Several physicians may have prescribed medication, with each not knowing of the other's involvement. One of us (J.A.C.) looked at the medications being prescribed for approximately 600 psychiatric patients by other clinics in a large county hospital and found that 22 patients were being given psychoactive medications (either anti-anxiety or antidepressant agents) by these clinic physicians. In the majority of these cases, these medications were not recorded in the psychiatry chart. The information only became available when the hospital opened up its integrated pharmacy database (if you have access to one of these, check your patients through it). Another irrational process is continuing medications after the prescribing physician quits the case. Some physicians have an unfortunate tendency to add new medications but not subtract old ones. Some pharmacies continue refills indefinitely. One of us (J.A.C.) treated a distressing case of tardive dyskinesia that emerged after a 48-year-old woman had been treated with thioridazine for 15 years. This medicine, at 50 mg per night, had originally been prescribed for insomnia. The treating physician died, and the local drugstore continued to refill for years. The woman saw other doctors during this time for treatment for depression. None of them were aware of the ongoing antipsychotic treatment. Make sure when you become involved in the care of a patient that multipharmacy has been arrived at via a rational process (more discussion on this follows).

A second problem with polymedications is side effects. The possibility of adverse side effects increases rapidly as more medications are prescribed. These side effects can be additive. For example, a patient taking several drugs with anticholinergic properties can develop insidious constipation, a condition sometimes not reported and often not asked about. Multiple medications can create side effect profiles, consisting of actions from each drug, creating many unwanted symptoms. Last, medications can interact with each other's metabolism in a variety of ways that create swings in blood levels that can in turn lead to adverse events. You must understand the pharmacokinetics and pharmacodynamics of the medications you prescribe to be in the best position to avoid or treat these interactive problems. However, all your knowledge ceases to be of much use when three or more drugs are being used at once. At this point, it can get so complex that nobody knows what is going on or what might happen.

Here are a few rules that will help to keep you out of trouble with multimedication regimens:

1. Have a good reason for adding another drug, and document it.
2. Use a medication in sufficient dose and for a sufficient length of time to determine whether it is working.
3. Stop the medication if it is not working. Do this, if possible, in a tapering fashion to avoid adverse rebound or withdrawal phenomena.
4. Keep your patient as active as possible in sizing up the effect of the new medication (i.e., get your patient's assessment into the clinical trial process).
5. Change only one drug at a time when possible. It is hard enough to gauge the effect of the addition or subtraction of one drug, let alone two (or three).

The Psychiatrist-Therapist-Patient Triangle

A number of patients see both a psychotherapist and a pharmacotherapist. At its best, this triangle of care provides a rich and well-coordinated treatment program infused with ideas from two perspectives. At its worst, one provider, willingly or unwillingly, can be set against the other. Success in a triangular relationship is accomplished by a clear definition of roles and responsibilities, and joint agreements on types of treatment that are being applied. The patient should give informed consent to the treatments involved. Various clinic policies, including fees for both providers, should be made clear. Both therapists should be explicit in how they handle emergencies and how coverage will be arranged when neither is available. The limits of protecting the patient's confidence between providers should be discussed, and a clear statement should be made that each provider will consult with the other on a regular basis. Both providers need to keep good written records. A basic rule for establishing triangular arrangements is that neither provider should commit the other to a course of treatment. A patient should never be guaranteed that he or she will be given medication or a certain form of psychotherapy. A referral should always be something such as, "This might be a good idea; let's see what my colleague thinks." Further readings about integrating pharmacotherapy and psychotherapy are presented at the end of this chapter.

One of the more volatile and potentially destructive moments in the course of treatment occurs when one provider believes the treatment implemented by the other provider is not helping the patient. This scenario takes a variety of forms with which most practitioners are personally familiar, which may involve the practitioner feeling that a therapy is groundless, wandering, or occurring so infrequently as to be hardly beneficial to the patient. The medical practitioner may begin to harbor beliefs regarding the therapist's competence to handle the difficulties imposed by the patient. At the same time, the patient may indicate a strong sense of rapport and caring for the therapist, making treatment efficacy an extremely sensitive issue to approach. Another common scenario is when the medical practitioner feels the therapist is advising the patient about how to use medications or is passively encouraging the patient to discontinue medication because he or she feels that the medications are not working. On the other hand, nonmedical therapists often experience frustration over the fact that medication regimes do not seem to be working but are nonetheless being continued by the medical practitioner. A more basic difficulty can involve suspicion about the value of medications in general in treating mental disorders. The therapist may be strongly opposed in principle to the use of any medication despite both the patient's request and data to support the drug's use. Rather than put this agenda on the table, the therapist may subtly sabotage the patient's compliance and passively undermine the medical practitioner. In another scenario, the therapist senses that the interactions between the medical practitioner and the patient are for one reason or another undercutting the treatment being delivered by the therapist. The therapist may have assumed the patient is going to the medical practitioner for medications only and feels undermined when the patient is given advice about how to deal with problems by the medical practitioner.

The solution to these troublesome situations is obvious; the two practitioners need to consult with each other regarding how the treatment is going and how the limits of professional responsibility are being met by each. Unfortunately, this can be a difficult professional interaction to undertake. As a consequence, this interaction is frequently and easily avoided. Good practitioners need to see it as their ethical responsibility to negotiate these types of troubled waters. Generally, it is the patient's welfare that is at stake, even though the practitioner's ego may be on the line. Another troublesome aspect of this type of situation is that when a confrontation between colleagues does occur, the patient may get blamed for splitting the therapist and the medical practitioner. In other words, the patient is presented as manipulative as an explanation for a basic professional boundary disagreement between the therapist and the medical provider. Remember this point: *If no split exists between the two providers, there will be no splitting.*

Substance Abuse and Suicide: The Sometimes Unclaimed Patient

All health care providers are aware of the enormity of substance abuse problems. Whether you work in a general health care setting, a trauma center, or a mental health facility, many of your patients have the added impairment of substance abuse/dependency. This area is of particular concern in psychiatric medicine, in which mentally ill, chemically affected individuals are a large part of the treated population, especially in the public setting. The combined disorders usually cause severe impairment. All areas of functioning can be adversely affected, including family and social interactions, employment, and the ability to meet the basic needs of shelter and food. Drug and alcohol use disorders vary markedly, ranging from infrequent bouts of alcohol intoxication to the daily use of a number of substances. In many cases, it is not uncommon to find someone who is using marijuana, cocaine, and alcohol on a daily basis, and who has a number of medical problems in addition to or because of substance abuse. Patients with substance use disorders are often difficult to treat, and a major component of that difficulty can be a lack of motivation for treatment and lack of compliance with treatment. There is an extensive literature on the practical issues involved in the rehabilitation and recovery from substance use disorders; several references that we have found helpful are contained at the end of this chapter. Our concern is that this is a population fraught with suicidality. The patients can be difficult to treat, and the patients can find themselves caught between agencies and finding no one to address the totality of their problems. A problem-solving approach can work with these individuals, but someone has to do it.

A major difficulty in providing effective management of the substance-abusing suicidal patient is the reluctance to assume responsibility for care that affects both mental health and chemical dependency treatment systems. This distressingly common scenario is played out in the following way: The mental health clinician or the inpatient psychiatric unit refuses to work with the patient because of the continuation of substance abuse. The message is that the patient must get his or her substance abuse cleared up before mental health treatment can proceed. On the other side, the substance-abusing patient enters the chemical dependency treatment system, either an inpatient or outpatient program, and develops suicidality. The patient is immediately discharged from that system with the message that the suicidality needs to be brought under control before chemical dependency treatment can be administered. Although some have suggested that the real answer for this dilemma is to create a third service delivery system, the dually diagnosed patient treatment system, this approach seems to obscure the fact that both mental health and chemical dependency counselors are professionally responsible for being able to diagnose and treat the array of mental and substance abuse conditions that are associated with patients who seek care in either system. A mental health counselor needs a strong and sophisticated set of skills in diagnosing and treating substance abuse. A chemical dependency worker needs a good working knowledge of how to deal with suicidal behavior. Unfortunately, both of these disciplines have put too much energy *into criticizing* one another, a practice that does little to alleviate the fact that a large number of patients travel between both systems and are not receiving comprehensive care. Remember, in any setting, it is your professional responsibility to become concerned with the diagnosis and treatment of conditions that are presented to you for care. Often, patients do not do a very good job sorting themselves out according to our ideas on how to treat them. The accommodation is our responsibility, not theirs. Practitioners in the chemical dependency, mental health, and general health care systems need to be prepared for the issue of suicidality and concurrent substance abuse.

The Substance-Abusing, Suicidal Patient

The following are some steps in treating a substance-abusing, suicidal patient. The first step is to learn how to ask about substance abuse and then ask about it. This may seem easy, but it can be a complex diagnostic task. It is not only a question of remembering to ask. It is also a question of persistence, of getting across your desire to be helpful, and of learning how not to be defeated by denial. A colleague related the following story, which demonstrates the scope of the problem. A woman appeared at a university-based affective disorders clinic for a treatment of depression and persistent suicidality. Because it was a teaching clinic, over time she was interviewed by medical students, residents, and faculty. Each time, using structured interview techniques, she was systematically asked about substance abuse. In every instance, she denied any difficulties. Over the course of a stormy year of treatment, she showed little response to medicines or psychotherapy. During this time she made several suicide attempts. At the end, she failed to keep several appointments and her relationship with the clinic stopped. About a year and a half later, one of the physicians in the clinic came across an article in a newspaper about this woman. She was being interviewed about her successful recovery from a severe cocaine addiction. In the interview, she talked about a decade-long addictive disorder and a successful treatment program she had been working in for 6 months. There was no mention in the interview of her year-long treatment for depression and suicidality!

The lesson from this story is to ask, ask again, and ask in different ways. If physical symptoms, laboratory tests, and/or reports from family and friends keep your index of suspicion high, keep inquiring. Persistence can sometimes pay off. An undiagnosed and untreated addiction problem will make treatment of any other problem, including suicidality, difficult. It is almost a prescription for treatment failure.

Also, ask about both the actual use of substances and the effects of substances. A good question, using alcohol as an example, is as follows: "How many days during the past month have you had a drink? On those days when you had a drink, how many drinks did you have?" A frequently used acronym for substance abuse is *CAGE*. This refers to four questions. *C* stands for *cut down:* "Have you ever tried to cut down on your substance use?" *A* stands for *annoyed:* "Have other people become annoyed with you about your substance use?" *G* stands for *guilty:* "Have you every felt guilty about your substance abuse?" *E* stands for *eye opener:* "Have you ever used (this drug) the first thing in the morning in order to avoid withdrawal symptoms (i.e., an eye opener)?" A positive answer to any of these can indicate a problem.

The second step is to understand substance abuse in the context of your patient's suicidality. The presence of suicidality suggests that a tandem addictive disorder may be present. People who use suicidality as a means of problem solving often engage in binge eating, binge drinking, and various forms of substance abuse. When you are working with your patient, always try to figure out the role of alcohol, cocaine, marijuana, or whatever else is being abused in the context of the patient's suicidality. Does your patient view suicidality as a solution to the chronic addiction? Does the patient use drugs or alcohol to escape the emotional pain associated with daily hassles and major stresses? When you are using problem-solving therapy, the effects of substance use can be most detrimental. Just when your patient needs to be thinking most clearly, the use of drugs can adversely affect judgment, concentration, and ability to think things through, and cause the patient to become more impuls-ive. This can be a deadly combination, as the alcohol level in many a coroner's report regarding suicide will tell you. In addition, when overdose is the method of suicide attempt, many drugs of abuse, especially alcohol, will potentiate the lethal effects of the overdosing medication, making the situation that much more deadly.

The third step is to deal with substance abuse in a crisis management plan. A common scenario is as follows: The person whom you are treating is in a problem situation, dealing with an interpersonal difficulty. The patient becomes frustrated and angry. He or she starts to drink to alleviate this emotional pain. The drinking persists, and suddenly, and usually very rapidly, the solution of suicide becomes real. At this moment, the patient will often grab a bottle of pills and take them with the intent to die. Impulsivity is increased by the alcohol and so is the potential lethality of the overdose substance. It is a bad situation. The crisis management plan needs to address this situation before it arises: *When you are thinking about suicide,* the golden rule is, *"Do not drink! If you are drinking, stop!"*

Alcohol on Breath: AOB in the Clinic

A common dilemma in working with the substance-abusing, suicidal patient occurs when your patient arrives for treatment intoxicated. Your challenge is to use this event in a way that ultimately benefits your patient and avoids a potential showdown over whether the substance abuse will continue. You must do your best to maintain a relationship with an impaired patient. Moments like this can provide a rare opportunity to access something your patient may be very reluctant to talk about: the desperation with which negative feelings are avoided. Do not cancel the session or ignore the circumstance. Rather, praise your patient for having the courage to bring such a problematic behavior directly into the treatment. When you do this, you are being philosophically consistent with the problem-solving approach to suicidal behavior, namely, that it is permissible to bring your problems into the therapeutic context without the therapy unhinging. The goal in this strategy is certainly not to reinforce drinking behavior. The goal is to get past the impairing effects of drug and alcohol consumption and to understand what your patient is experiencing during this impaired state. Alcohol disinhibits the expression of emotion and cognition. Although alcohol has a depressant quality, it is likely that much of the feeling and thinking that is expressed by your patient under the influence has a real and substantial independent life. It is your task to sort out what part of the intoxication is impulsive and temporary, and what part is giving you a look at thoughts, feelings, and reactions that are integral to your patient's world view. This requires a rapport between you and your patient, and it requires you to adopt a nonconfrontational stance concerning alcohol or drug consumption. Perhaps 50% of all suicide attempts occur in the context of alcohol or drug use, so it is quite likely that proceeding on with the session will give you some insight into the process by which your patient engages in suicidal behavior. A behavioral crisis protocol is easier to produce if you have an in-depth view of the way that this behavior develops during an episode of alcohol or drug abuse.

Occasionally, your patient may arrive at the session intoxicated *and* acutely suicidal. Here, your task is to help the patient through impulsive and potentially lethal moments until a clear head prevails. It is generally advisable to keep the patient in a safe setting or to send the patient home with a friend or family member with explicit instructions that that person should remain in the immediate vicinity until the intoxication has cleared. Always, the general philosophy is to use whatever your patient brings in a way that provides some advantage for your patient. In this respect, it is sometimes helpful to call the patient back and debrief whether the episode of alcohol or drug use seemed to work in terms of improving or worsening both mood and general life outlook. The more you can use dysfunctional problem solving and connect it with the experience of nonworkability, the more leverage you will have in getting your patient to consider alternatives.

The Inpatient Substance Abuse Unit

Staff on inpatient chemical dependency units deal with somewhat different problems from those found in an outpatient chemical dependency settings. The chief task of inpatient treatment is to assist the patient through withdrawal and into early stages of sobriety maintenance. Withdrawal can be associated with an increase in suicidality. It is often a difficult process, one that is both physical and psychological. Withdrawal can create agitation, physical discomfort, and significant mood swings. Because withdrawal symptoms can persist in some people for 2 months or more, it is sometimes difficult to ascertain what is long-term psychological dysfunction and what is short-term dysfunction due to drug withdrawal. Whereas most physical effects of addiction and withdrawal often abate within 10 days to 2 weeks, both sleep difficulties and the psychological components can continue for some time to influence the patient's behavior. Depression is often a major and complicated problem, which is both sustained by continuous substance abuse and, in many cases, existed prior to the substance abuse. Your patient may be dealing with a "double whammy": organically induced depression due to a stage of drug use (acute or chronic withdrawal, sustained use, intoxication) combined with a preexisting tendency to be depressed. Add the agitation and physical discomfort often associated with drugs, and the stage is set for potentially lethal suicidal behavior.

Many substance-abusing patients have comorbid psychiatric conditions. These include depression, anxiety, personality disorders, and schizophrenia, all of which are associated with suicidal potential. There should be a psychiatric examination, including an assessment of suicidality, of any patient who is admitted to a substance abuse unit. By all accounts, this is a population at high risk for both completed and attempted suicide, and admission to detoxification is a particularly critical phase in their disorder. Staff need to assess and manage suicidal potential, especially during intensive substance-abuse treatment. This is done with the same techniques used on a psychiatric inpatient service (see the hospital chapter), and there is no reason to believe that applications of these strategies would be any less effective in a substance-abuse treatment facility. The task is to provide as much safety and security as possible while avoiding an invasive, antitherapeutic milieu. The unit should adopt policies and procedures that systematize the way in which suicidal behavior assessments are conducted, with appropriate attention paid to documenting and treating any psychiatric conditions that may further increase the patient's suicidality.

A clinically significant difference between many substance-abusing patients and their nonabusing counterparts is the tremendous mood variability that occurs in the first 30 days of treatment following withdrawal. Suicides on detoxification units sometimes occur when the patient is reporting a positive and stabilized mood. Micro episodes of dysphoria can occur within the context of overall improvement and can occur quite rapidly. The suicidal situation may happen in a matter of seconds or minutes, when the patient experiences a sudden devastating decline in mood and resorts to lethal behavior. The detoxifying patient is not likely to experience a positive mood because a decision to commit suicide has been made but not revealed. Rather, the suicidality seems to be linked to a rapid and unpredictable change in mood often associated with alcohol or drug withdrawal. Staff need to be alert to these potential mood changes and specifically discuss the possibility with the patient at the onset of detoxification. Observation is not enough. Your patient needs to be asked frequently about mood and told repeatedly about the *necessity* of reporting any significant mood changes. Do not forget to do this as discharge back into the real, and often troubled, world approaches. Mood changes may be pronounced in this period, be missed, and be fatal.

The Special Case of Schizophrenia

Individuals with schizophrenia are prone to suicidal behavior in all its forms. Often, their illness interferes with their relationships and their ability to concentrate and think clearly. From our point of view, their tools for problem solving are impaired. Isolation is a fact of life for many individuals with schizophrenia. Many are homeless, and many of these seem likely to remain homeless. In this harsh atmosphere, they are not likely to have access to treatment, or they have trouble being compliant with treatment when it is available. These individuals often suffer from more than one illness. This tendency toward comorbidity encompasses both psychiatric and general medical disease. Substance abuse has become a rampant problem among patients with schizophrenia. All of these factors can produce a life of hassles and a sea of daily troubles far beyond that of the rest of us. With so many problems, and the deficiency in the tools needed to deal with them, it is little wonder that suicidality is a major concern with this group.

Individuals with schizophrenic illness are the core group of the chronic mentally ill. The lifetime rate of suicide in this population may be as high as 5%. One-third to one-half of schizophrenic individuals have made a suicide attempt, and suicidal ideation is so common as to be nearly ubiquitous. For decades, individuals with this illness have shown only a partial response to treatment. The good news is that hope may be on the way. With the advent of clozapine, and a group of new atypical antipsychotic medications under investigation, improvements are being seen in schizophrenic patients that would have been judged quite improbable even 5 years ago. If you are a clinician working with schizophrenic patients, part of your job from this point on is to keep them going until new and better therapies are widely available. Suicidality is one of the risk factors with which you must deal. What follows are some special techniques that should help you in this work.

First, pay meticulous attention to the assessment of suicidality. Ask about suicidality and always remember this rule: It's the answers, *not the affect,* that's important. Apathy and indifference are symptoms of schizophrenia. Answers to your questions will often be given in a flat and monosyllabic way. This is a far cry from an anxious, depressed, or despairing individual who talks about suicide and whose affect adds to the impact of what is said. Do not allow the lack of affect to subtract from the importance of what an individual with schizophrenia is saying. Lack of affect does not mean lack of risk. It is *what* is being said, not how it is being said.

Second, remember that antipsychotic medications can have a role in suicidality. As we noted earlier, the side-effect profile of these medications can produce a high level of discomfort. It is a terrible mistake to view these symptoms as an indication of increasing severity of schizophrenia and treat with even more medication. If you are not comfortable with the intricacies of medication management in schizophrenia, be sure you work with someone who is. Additionally, remember that abrupt discontinuation of antipsychotic medication can produce both a number of withdrawal difficulties and an exacerbation of psychosis. Unless you have a very good reason not to (e.g., the development of agranulocytosis), always taper when you are stopping a drug.

Third, use the problem-solving approach to suicidality in this population and be especially practical about it. Make every effort to involve supportive persons either from the family or without. Carefully understand past episodes of suicidality, particularly as they relate to phase of illness. Talk over what happened before and develop management strategies for its possible recurrence.

The Young

It is hard to know what to make of suicidality and prepubertal children. Completed suicide is extremely rare in this group, even though both thoughts of death and thoughts of suicide are reported. There seems to be something about cognitive immaturity that protects against suicide. With adolescence, and particularly middle to late adolescence, suicidality becomes a significant issue. There are many similarities between the suicidality seen in adolescence and that seen in adulthood. The model presented in this book has been successfully applied with adolescents. The sole caveat is that more attention must be paid to family based matters. Often, suicidal adolescents experience significant turmoil in their families. The turmoil starts in childhood and does not stabilize during adolescence. Indeed, adolescence produces further instability, and from all this comes suicidality.

An Adolescent Suicidal Behavior Scenario

A frequently seen adolescent suicidal behavior scenario starts with a long-term identity as a problem child. In early to middle adolescence, the usual mild to moderate troubles that arise from raising a teenager are escalated. The teenager can be the cause of family conflict and the destroyer of family harmony. Parents may block out the adolescent, pretend indifference, and view the teenager as somehow expendable. In some families, one or both parents may directly suggest that the family would be better off if the teenager was dead. This has the net effect of making family attention increasingly contingent on extreme behavior. When problems are discussed, unrealistic and immediate solutions are emphasized over more practical ones. Parents can assume that the adolescent is willfully acting bad rather than lacking the tools to change his or her behavior. In this scenario, suicide can easily take on a positive valence.

When coupled with ongoing family conflict, other forms of instability can fan the fire. This can include changes in residence, school troubles, loss of relationships (including parental divorce), and the phenomenon of *fractured romance*. Fractured romance is a situation in which a troubled adolescent has essentially put all his or her eggs in one basket. Another individual is seen as all important and imbued with unique powers to bring stability into the teenager's life. When this falls apart, as it often does, a major negative emotional event ensues. The potentially suicidal adolescent already has difficulty tolerating emotional distress, and the new distress seems overwhelmingly intense and persistent. When this is coupled with an impulsive behavioral style ("actions speak louder than words") and alcohol or drug abuse, a scenario for suicidal behavior has been produced.

Family Evaluation and Therapy

Family dynamics can play a major role in adolescent suicidal behavior. Table 11–1 lists out some of the more common features found in studies of families in which suicidal behavior has occurred. Not all families containing a suicidal adolescent are dysfunctional, but some certainly are. In any case, a family evaluation will be helpful and will guide your decision making.

In the face of family dysfunction, you can, at one end, engage the family in treatment to build cohesion and learn group problem solving, or, at the other end, help extricate the adolescent from the system. There is not much evidence one way or the other concerning the utility of family therapy per se with the suicidal adolescent. Some families strongly resist change and cannot, despite strenuous effort, be enlisted as a viable support for their teenage member. The dynamics of some families actively undermine the process of treating an adolescent using the problem-solving model. In a family environment that emphasizes action over words, models alcohol/drug abuse, and demands instant change, it is very difficult for an adoles-

Table 11–1. The suicidal behavior–prone family

A. Chronic difficulties
   1. Long-term hostility, insecurity, asocial conduct, economic distress, alcohol abuse, troubled marriages
B. Active parent-child conflict
   1. Verbal, physical, sexual abuse
   2. Families report "daily fights"
C. Social characteristics
   1. Socially isolated
   2. May be very mobile
   3. Constance life stress (sea of troubles)
D. Fixed roles—rigid style
   1. Scapegoated child, parentified child, expendable child
   2. Position maintained by intolerance for loss and separation; change not possible, only escape
E. Loss of parent
   1. Divorce, desertion, separation
   2. Physically and emotionally distant parents are very demanding during infrequent contacts
G. Communication
   1. Ineffective
   2. Language has little problem-solving value—"spare the rod, spoil the child"
   3. Parents align to shut out children, yet will bolster child's negative stance toward outside intervention
   4. "Scapegoating" to "solve" parental conflict
   5. Basic belief that people can change by force of will; they do not have to learn anything new

cent to effectively practice problem-solving skills. Much of the work done in this type of circumstance is to prepare the adolescent for an early emancipation from the system. Frequently, this preparation involves teaching your patient limit setting and conflict resolution skills as well as specific anger management strategies. Sometimes the most important steps involve lining up an alternative residence with the parent of a willing friend or supporting the adolescent's effort to move in with a relative who is more supportive. The intent is not to break up families but to acknowledge that there is a power differential in family systems and that the adolescent is typically at the low end of the totem pole. In effect, moving to the level of where the adolescent lives is a form of problem-solving behavior. This may be one of the few examples where escaping or avoiding a stressful environment is a healthy maneuver.

Our overall recommendation with teenagers is to pursue the approaches toward suicidality outlined in this book. Dysfunctional family behaviors need to be addressed. A family evaluation should always be done, and, if possible, the family should be in that part of treatment designed to put together a competent social support system. Working with suicidal adolescents can provide a maximum challenge to a provider's skills. Some parents can seem persistently contentious, uncooperative, and angry. Skill in knowing when and when not to deal with families is an essential prerequisite for working with this group.

A final point to keep in mind when treating adolescents is the tremendous importance of constantly looking for actions and thoughts that can be given a positive connotation. Negative self esteem is a significant and near universal problem for this group. An unresponsive teenager can be praised for coming and being in the session, even when the task at hand seems overwhelming. Similarly, the adolescent whose fury at parents is massive can be praised for loyalty, as in the following example: "Your loyalty to your family is quite strong. Your anger, pain, and frustration are very evident, but somehow you've been able to stick with them. You are hanging in there every day, fighting to get them to change. Where do you get the strength?" A good rule to keep in mind is that the only time you have a reason to get upset is when your patient does not show up for treatment. When you are working together, your most important job is to find the positive side of ambivalence and the hidden strengths that will improve self-esteem.

The Forgotten Many: Suicidal Behavior in the Elderly

You are old, you are sick, you are poor, and you are forgotten. Most of your life is not before you, it is behind you. Your country's media worries about an adolescent suicide epidemic, with little mention that the rate of suicide in your age group is several times higher. You live, ignored, in a sea of troubles. It is depressing, and it can lead you to thoughts of ending it all.

Although the interventions described in this book can and should be applied to the elderly, there are several factors that make working with older people somewhat clinically complicated. First and foremost is the fact that elderly patients, at least in our times, are not likely to seek out treatment from the mental health system. They are far more likely to visit their family physician, seeking relief from a chronic illness or complaining of a panoply of physical symptoms that mask their emotional distress. For this reason, elderly patients need to be regularly assessed by their primary care doctor for suicidality. In addition to not seeking treatment for suicidality, the elderly do not talk about it much nor do they make as many nonlethal suicide attempts as other age groups. Suicide in the elderly can be an insidious, silent lethality.

An additional concern in working with the elderly patient is that many of the stimuli for suicidality in this group are environmentally driven and realistically represent major challenges to the patient's quality of life. For example, an elderly, nonambulatory patient with chronic lung disease is realistically facing a marked decline in quality of existence. Although these types of difficulties can be successfully handled within the problem-solving model, it takes a clinician who is strongly committed to the inherent value of living to keep the work positive and upbeat in content. Many conventional indicators of quality of life have often been removed from the landscape of the elderly person. Success and satisfaction often revolve around finding spiritual meaning in a life that is in danger of being marked by loneliness, financial worries, and/or chronic physical illness. Elder abuse may be an increasingly common precipitant of suicidal behavior, particularly when the perpetrator is a family member who is charged to take care of the patient. This type of family turmoil is often so painful for the elderly patient to acknowledge that suicide seems to be the only way of saving face.

It is sometimes hard to know the role that psychiatric illness, particularly depression, plays in suicidal behavior in an elderly person. Demoralization can be mistaken for signs of clinical depression. Demoralization consists of separate responses to specific environmental losses. The demoralized elderly patient has been let down by society, and to a larger extent, by life. Plans for a happy retirement are suddenly demolished upon the sudden unexpected death of a spouse; dreams of financial security in retirement years give way to living on an inadequate fixed income; many friends and loved ones die, change residences, or move into nursing home facilities. These demoralizing events can dash hopes for a productive, relatively worry-free late life. The sadness and loss of interest that results from these events can precipitate suicidality, which in turn can be addressed by a problem-solving approach. Be judicious in using antidepressant medications in this age group. Pills only work when you take them as directed. They never work when you take them all at once. Pills do not necessarily cause other people to change, and they rarely cause pensions to increase. Demoralization is caused by tangible problems. Find out about problems, and develop an overall plan to deal with them.

The problem-solving approach with demoralization involves building, in a step-by-step fashion, a new set of life supports. Rather than allowing your patient to give up on connecting socially, emphasize opportunities available to meet new people. Where physical disease has eliminated some of your patient's traditional leisure time and recreational activities, make sure the search is on for alternative types of leisure and recreation that will continue to challenge your patient's sense of independence and physical capacity. In other words, rather than challenging beliefs about what types of losses have occurred, acknowledge that these losses have occurred and set up treatment so that rebuilding is possible. Finding that spark that makes life a continued challenge and joy is the crux of the therapeutic task for the suicidal elderly patient.

Development of a competent social support network is perhaps the most important single factor in treatment. Self-help groups, peer support, and an organized approach by the family's younger generation are most important. The grown children of the older suicidal person can feel overwhelmed and powerless. Work with them. In particular, help them to find the limits of what they can and cannot do, especially in the context of raising their own families. For example, an elderly woman living alone had a great fear of accident or illness and insisted that her daughter call her every day. The daughter lived in a different city and, although she wanted to help, she came to resent both the demand and the expense. The relationship deteriorated. The mother recognized the effects of her demands, but the fears persisted. Demoralization set in. The answer? An answering machine. Each day, at her expense, the mother would call and leave a message: "Hi, everybody. I'm OK." The deal was that if there was no message, the daughter would call and check. Otherwise, they talked on the phone about once a week, a level of contact that was satisfying to both of them.

Helpful Hints

♦ Know your medications and their side effects. Remember to watch for dysphoria, agitation, akathisia, and akinesia.

♦ Avoid polypharmacy when you can.

♦ Give medications a trial. If a medication is not working, stop it.

♦ Consult with your fellow practitioner when you are working with the same patient.

♦ Substance abuse and suicidality cannot be separate. Individuals who work with one must be able to work with the other.

♦ Be persistent in asking about suicidality when you suspect or know of substance abuse.

♦ Understand substance abuse in the context of suicidality.

♦ Include substance abuse in your crisis management plan.
♦ If a problem behavior occurs in a session (e.g., drunkenness), try to understand it and use the information to the patient's advantage.
♦ Substance abuse in all its forms can produce almost any psychiatric symptom, *including* suicidality.
♦ Actively inquire about mood change and suicidal thinking on detoxification units.
♦ In working with schizophrenia patients, assess suicidality, know your medications, and be very practical in your approach.
♦ Always assess a suicidal adolescent's family.
♦ The elderly are the most suicidal age group, and effective treatment must address the real world challenges associated with aging.

Selected Readings

Allebeck P, Varla A, Kristjansson E, et al: Risk factors for suicide among patients with schizophrenia. Acta Psychiatr Scand 76:414–419, 1987

Bartels SJ, Drake RE, McHugo GJ: Alcohol abuse, depression, and suicidal behavior in schizophrenia. Am J Psychiatry 149:394–395, 1992

Blazer DG, Bachar JR, Manton KG: Suicide in late life: review and commentary. J Am Geriatr Soc 34:519–525, 1986

de Wilde EF, Kienhorst I, Diekstra R, et al: The relationship between adolescent suicidal behavior and life events in childhood and adolescence. Am J Psychiatry 149:45–51, 1992

Hawton K, Fagg J: Deliberate self-poisoning and self-injury in adolescents: a study of characteristics and trends in Oxford, 1976–89. Br J Psychiatry 161:816–823, 1992

Miller ML, Chiles JA, Barnes VE: Suicide attempters within a delinquent population. J Consult Clin Psychol 50:491–498, 1982

Murphy GE, Wetzel RD: Multiple risk factors predict suicide in alcoholism. Arch Gen Psychiatry 49:459–463, 1993

Power AC, Cowen PJ: Fluoxetine and suicidal behaviour: some clinical and theoretical aspects of a controversy. Br J Psychiatry 161:735–741, 1992

Rich CL, Young D, Fowler RC: San Diego Suicide Study; I: young vs old subjects. Arch Gen Psychiatry 43:577–582, 1986

Shear M, Frances A, Weiden P: Suicide associated with akathisia and depot fluphenazine treatment. J Clin Psychopharmacol 3:325–326, 1983

Westermeyer JF, Harrow M, Marengo JT: Risk for suicide in schizophrenia and other psychotic and nonpsychotic disorders. J Nerv Ment Dis 179:259–266, 1991

Philosophies About Suicide

I. Suicide Is Wrong

1. **Suicide** does violence to the dignity of human life.
2. **Suicide** is against basic human nature.
3. **Suicide** is oversimplified response to a complex and ambivalent situation.
4. **Suicide** is a crime against the state.
5. **Suicide** is an irrevocable act that denies future learning or growth.
6. It is only for God to give and to take away human life. **Suicide** is rebellion against God.
7. **Suicide** does violence to the natural order of things.
8. **Suicide** is no different than homicide.
9. **Suicide** adversely affects the survivors.

II. Suicide Is Sometimes Permissible

1. **Suicide** is **permissible** when in the individual's view of things the alternatives are unbearable. An example is extreme and incurable physical pain.

III. Suicide Is Not a Moral or Ethical Issue

1. **Suicide** is a phenomena of life that is subject to study in the same way that any other phenomena of life should be studied.

2. **Suicide** represents neither a morally good nor a morally bad action and is an action that takes place beyond the realm of reason.
3. **Suicide** is a morally neutral act in that every man has a free will and has the right to move and act according to that will.

IV. Suicide Is a Positive Response to Certain Conditions

1. When life ceases to be enjoyable or pleasurable, one has the right to end his life.
2. A person has the innate right to make any decision, provided it is based on rationality and logical thinking. This includes the right to **suicide.**
3. There are certain times in life when death is less an evil than dishonor.
4. Some **suicides** are demanded by society as a way of dispensing justice.
5. **Suicide** is a **permissible** act when it is performed for some great purpose that transcends the value of the human life.

V. Suicide Has Intrinsic Positive Value

1. One must affirm one's self and make decisions. **Suicide** may be an affirmation of his or her soul, in which case it is fulfillment to carry through this action and it would be morally wrong for anyone to interfere with this decision.
2. **Suicide** is sometimes a way to save face, as in the case of hari-kari, after the individual has lost his or her honor.
3. **Suicide** has positive value when it provides the means by which a person can enter a meaningful afterlife that he or she desires.
4. **Suicide** is a way to embrace a personified and eroticized death.
5. **Suicide** has positive value because it is a way in which one can be immediately reunited with valued ancestors and with loved ones.

Appendix 2

Consequences of Suicidal Behavior

Sometimes people with problems attempt suicide. If, for whatever reason, you were to *attempt suicide but didn't die as a result,* please write on the lines provided below, all of the things that might happen as a result of your attempt. Then for each item you list, please indicate whether you feel the result is *mostly good* or *mostly bad* and then indicate how *important* you feel that result is. Please try to think of at least four results. However, if you can't think of that many, just leave one or more lines blank. Do your best.

Result 1: _____
O = Bad   O = Good
not at all important O 1 O 2 O 3 O 4 O 5 extremely important

Result 2: _____
O = Bad   O = Good
not at all important O 1 O 2 O 3 O 4 O 5 extremely important

Result 3: _____
O = Bad   O = Good
not at all important O 1 O 2 O 3 O 4 O 5 extremely important

Result 4: _____
O = Bad   O = Good
not at all important O 1 O 2 O 3 O 4 O 5 extremely important

If you were to *commit suicide,* that is, if you died as a result of a suicide attempt, what are all the things that would happen as a result—

To you after death:

Result 1: _____
O = Bad   O = Good
not at all important O 1 O 2 O 3 O 4 O 5 extremely important

Result 2: _____
O = Bad   O = Good
not at all important O 1 O 2 O 3 O 4 O 5 extremely important

To those left behind:

Result 1: _____
O = Bad   O = Good
not at all important O 1 O 2 O 3 O 4 O 5 extremely important

Result 2: _____
O = Bad   O = Good
not at all important O 1 O 2 O 3 O 4 O 5 extremely important

If you were to *commit suicide,* what reasons do you think you would have for doing it?

Reason 1: _____

Reason 2: _____

Reason 3: _____

Reason 4: _____

When other people *attempt suicide but do not die* as a result, why do you think they do it?

Reason 1: _____

Reason 2: _____

Reason 3: _____

Reason 4: _____

When other people *commit suicide,* why do you think they do it?

Reason 1: _____

Reason 2: _____

Reason 3: _____

Reason 4: _____

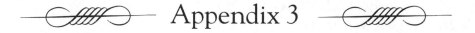

Reasons for Living Inventory Items

Survival and Coping Beliefs

1. I care enough about myself to live.
2. I believe I can find other solutions to my problems.
3. I still have many things left to do.
4. I have hope that things will improve and the future will be happier.
5. I have the courage to face life.
6. I want to experience all that life has to offer and there are many experiences I haven't had yet that I want to have.
7. I believe everything has a way of working out for the best.
8. I believe I can find a purpose in life, a reason to live.
9. I have a love of life.
10. No matter how badly I feel, I know that it will not last.
11. Life is too beautiful and precious to end it.
12. I am happy and content with my life.
13. I am curious about what will happen in the future.
14. I see no reason to hurry death along.
15. I believe I can learn to adjust or cope with my problems.
16. I believe killing myself would not really accomplish or solve anything.
17. I have a desire to live.
18. I am too stable to kill myself.
19. I have future plans I am looking forward to carrying out.

20. I do not believe that things get miserable or hopeless enough that I would rather be dead.
21. I do not want to die.
22. Life is all we have and is better than nothing.
23. I believe I have control over my life and destiny.

Responsibility to Family

24. I would hurt my family too much and I would not want them to suffer.
25. I would not want my family to feel guilty afterwards.
26. I would not want my family to think I was selfish or a coward.
27. My family depends upon me and needs me.
28. I love and enjoy my family too much and could not leave them.
29. My family might believe I did not love them.
30. I have a responsibility and commitment to my family.

Child-Related Concerns

31. The effect on my children could be harmful.
32. It would not be fair to leave the children for others to take care of.
33. I want to watch my children as they grow.

Fear of Suicide

34. I am afraid of the actual "act" of killing myself (the pain, blood, violence).
35. I am a coward and do not have the guts to do it.
36. I am so inept that my method would not work.
37. I am afraid that my method of killing myself would fail.
38. I am afraid of the unknown.
39. I am afraid of death.
40. I could not decide where, when, and how to do it.

Fear of Social Disapproval

41. Other people would think I am weak and selfish.
42. I would not want people to think I did not have control over my life.
43. I am concerned what others would think of me.

Moral Objections

44. My religious beliefs forbid it.
45. I believe only God has the right to end a life.
46. I consider it morally wrong.
47. I am afraid of going to hell.

Appendix 4

Suicidal Thinking and Behaviors Questionnaire

1. Since the first time you thought of suicide, how have your suicidal thoughts changed in intensity?

   ○ 1   ○ 2   ○ 3   ◉ 4   ○ 5
   decreased   the same   increased

2. Have you thought about killing yourself in the past 24 hours?

   ◉ No   ○ Yes

3. When you think of killing yourself, what are the most important problems you are having that cause you to have these thoughts?

4. Before coming to this office, have you ever told someone that you were thinking of committing suicide?

   ◉ No   ○ Yes

5. How many times have you attempted suicide, that is, intentionally physically injured yourself in a manner which, at the time, you or someone else considered a suicide attempt? __5__

6. Would any of your problems be solved if you killed yourself?

   ○ 1   ○ 2   ○ 3   ○ 4   ◉ 5
   Definitely no   Definitely yes

7. How many people love or care for you? __1__

8. Among the people who love or care for you, how many are capable of helping you? __1__

9. Do you personally know anyone who committed or attempted suicide?

   ○ No   ◉ Yes

References

Allebeck P, Varla A, Kristjansson E, et al: Risk factors for suicide among patients with schizophrenia. Acta Psychiatr Scand 76:414–419, 1987

American Psychiatric Association: Diagnostic and Statistical Manual of Mental Disorders, 4th Edition, Revised. Washington, DC, American Psychiatric Association, 1994

Applebaum S: The problem-solving aspect of suicide. Journal of Projective Technology 27:259, 1963

Appleby L: Suicide in psychiatric patients: risk and prevention. Br J Psychiatry 161:749–758, 1992

Apter A, Bleich A, King RA, et al: Death without warning? A clinical postmortem study of suicide in 43 Israeli adolescent males. Arch Gen Psychiatry 50:138–142, 1993

Avery D, Winokur G: Mortality in depressed patients treated with electroconvulsive therapy and antidepressants. Arch Gen Psychiatry 33:1029–1037, 1976

Bancroft J, Marsack P: The repetitiveness of self-poisoning and self-injury. Br J Psychiatry 131:394–399, 1977

Bancroft J, Skirimshire A, Casson J, et al: People who deliberately poison themselves: their problems and their contacts with helping agencies. Psychol Med 7:289–303, 1977

Barraclough B, Bunch J, Nelson B, et al: A hundred cases of suicide: clinical aspects. Br J Psychiatry 125:355–373, 1974

Bartels SJ, Drake RE, McHugo GJ: Alcohol abuse, depression, and suicidal behavior in schizophrenia. Am J Psychiatry 149:394–395, 1992

Battin MP: Ethical Isues in Suicide. Englewood Cliffs, NJ, Prentice-Hall, 1982

Beauchamp TL, Childress JF: Principles of Biomedical Ethics, 2nd Edition. New York, Oxford University Press, 1983

Beck A, Freeman A: Cognitive Therapy of Personality Disorders. New York, Guilford, 1990

Beck AT, Steer RA: Manual for the Beck Hopelessness Scale. San Antonio, TX, Psychological Corporation, 1988

Beck A, Rush J, Shaw D, et al: Cognitive Therapy for Depression: A Treatment Manual. New York, Guilford, 1979

Beck A, Schuyler D, Herman I: Development of suicidal intent scales, in The Prediction of Suicide. Edited by Beck AT, Resnik HL, Lettieri DJ. Bowie, MD, Charles Press, 1974, pp 45–56

Beck A, Steer RA, Kovacs M, et al: Hopelessness and eventual suicide: a 10 year prospective study of patients hospitalized with suicidal ideation. Am J Psychiatry 142:559–563, 1985

Beck A, Weissman A, Lester D, et al: The measurement of pessimism: The Hopelessness Scale. J Consult Clin Psychol 42:861–865, 1974

Beck AT, Brown G, Berchick RJ, et al: Relationship with psychiatric outpatients. Am J Psychiatry 147:190–195, 1990

Beck AT, Brown G, Steer RA: Prediction of eventual suicide in psychiatric inpatients by clinical ratings of hopelessness. J Consult Clin Psychol 57:309–310, 1989

Beck AT, Kovacs M, Weissman A: Assessment of suicidal intent: the scale of suicidal ideation. J Consult Clin Psychol 47:343–352, 1979

Beck AT, Kovacs M, Weissman A: Hopelessness and suicidal behavior. JAMA 234:1146–1149, 1974

Beck AT, Resnik HLP, Lettieri DJ (eds): The Prediction of Suicide. Bowie, MD, Charles Press, 1974

Beck AT, Ward CH, Mendelsohn M, et al: An inventory for measuring depression. Arch Gen Psychiatry 4:561–571, 1961

Black DW, Winokur G, Mohandoss E, et al: Does treatment influence mortality in depressives? A follow-up of 1076 patients with major affective disorders. Annals of Clinical Psychiatry 1:165–173, 1989

Black DW, Winokur G, Nasralish A: Suicide in subtypes of major affective disorder. Arch Gen Psychiatry 44:878–880, 1987

Blazer DG, Bachar JR, Manton KG: Suicide in late life: review and commentary. J Am Geriatr Soc 34:519–525, 1986

Blumenthal SJ: Suicide: a guide to risk factors, assessment, and treatment of suicidal patients. Med Clin North Am 72:937–971, 1988

Blumenthal SJ, Kupfer DJ: Suicide Over the Life Cycle: Risk Factors, Assessment, and Treatment of Suicidal Patients. Washington, DC, American Psychiatric Press, 1990

Blumenthal SJ, Kupfer DJ: Generalizable treatment strategies for suicidal behavior. Ann N Y Acad Sci 487:327–339, 1986

Black DW, Winokur G: Suicide and psychiatric diagnosis, in Suicide Over the Life Cycle: Risk Factors, Assessment, and Treatment of Suicidal Patients. Washington, DC, American Psychiatric Press, 1990, pp 135–153

Bond B, Witheridge T, Wasmer D, et al: A comparison of two crisis housing alternatives to psychiatric hospitalization. Hosp Community Psychiatry 40:177–183, 1989

Bongar B: The Suicidal Patient: Clinical and Legal Standards of Care. Washington, DC, American Psychological Association, 1991

Breier A, Astrachan CM: Characterization of schizophrenic patients who commit suicide. Am J Psychiatry 141:206–209, 1984

Brent DA, Kupfer DJ, Bromet EJ, et al: The assessment and treatment of patients at risk for suicide, in American Psychiatric Press Review of Psychiatry, Vol 7. Edited by Frances AJ, Hales RE. Washington, DC, American Psychiatric Press, 1988, pp 353–385

Brent DA, Perper JA, Aliman CJ: Alcohol, firearms, and suicide among youth: temporal trends in Allegheny County, Pennsylvania, 1960–1963. JAMA 257:3369–3372, 1987

Brook B: Crisis hostel: an alternative to psychiatric hospitalization for emergency patients. Hosp Community Psychiatry 24:621–624, 1973

Chafetz L: Issues in emergency psychiatric research, in Emergency Psychiatry at the Crossroads: New Directions for Mental Health Services. Edited by Lipton F, Goldfinger S. San Francisco, CA, Jossey-Bass, 1985, pp 79–92

Chemtob CM, Hamada RS, Bauer GB, et al: Patient suicide: frequency and impact on psychologists. Professional Psychology: Research and Practice 19:421–425, 1988

Chiles J, Strosahl K: The suicidal patient: assessment, crisis management and treatment, in Current Psychiatric Therapy. Edited by Dunner D. Toronto, Canada, WB Saunders, 1993, pp 494–498

Chiles JA, Carlin AS, Benjamin GAH, et al: A physician, a nonmedical psychotherapist, and a patient: the pharmacotherapy-psychotherapy triangle, in Integrating Pharmacotherapy and Psychotherapy. Edited by Beitman BD, Klerman GL. Washington, DC, American Psychiatric Press, 1991, pp 105–118

Chiles JA, Strosahl K, Cowden L, et al: The 24 hours before hospitalization: factors related to suicide attempting. Suicide Life Threat Behav 16:335–342, 1986

Chiles JA, Strosahl KD, McMurray L, et al: Modeling effects on suicidal behavior. J Nerv Ment Dis 173:477–481, 1985

Chiles JA, Strosahl K, Zheng YP, et al: Depression, hopelessness, and suicidal behavior in Chinese and American psychiatric patients. Am J Psychiatry 146:339–344, 1989

Churgin M: An essay on commitment and the emergency room: implications for the delivery of mental health services. Law, Medicine, and Health Care 6:297–303, 1985

Cohen-Sandler R, Berman AL, King RA: Life stress and symptomatology: determinants of suicidal behavior in children. Journal of the American Academy of Child Psychiatry 21:178–186, 1982

Corder BF, Halizlip TM: Environmental and personality similarities in case histories of suicide and self-poisoning in children under ten. Suicide Life Threat Behav 14:59–66, 1984

Coryell W, Noyes R, Clancy J: Excess mortality in panic disorder. Arch Gen Psychiatry 39:701–703, 1982

Crammer JL: The special characteristics of suicide in hospital inpatients. Br J Psychiatry 145:460–476, 1984

Crook T, Raskin A, David D: Factors associated with attempted suicide among hospitalized depressed patients. Psychol Med 5:381–388, 1975

deShazer S: Clues: Investigating Solutions in Brief Therapy. New York, WW Norton, 1988

de Wilde EF, Kienhorst I, Diekstra R, et al: The relationship between adolescent suicidal behavior and life events in childhood and adolescence. Am J Psychiatry 149:45–51, 1992

Diekstra RFW: The complex psychodynamics of suicide, in Suicide in Adolescence. Edited by Diekstra RFW, Hawton K. Boston, MA, Martinus Nijhoff, 1987, pp 30–55

Dorpat TL, Ripley HS: A study of suicides in the Seattle area. Compr Psychiatry 1:349–359, 1960

Douglas JS: The Social Meaning of Suicide. Princeton, NJ, Princeton University Press, 1967

Drye RC, Goulding RL, Goulding ME: No-suicide decision: patient monitoring of suicidal risk. Am J Psychiatry 130:171–174, 1973

Durham ML, La Fond JQ: The empirical consequences and policy implications of broadening the statutory criteria for civil commitment. Yale Law Policy Review 3:395–446, 1985

Ebert BW: Guide to conducting a psychological autopsy. Professional Psychology Research and Practice 18:52–56, 1987

Erdman HP, Greist JH, Gustafson DH, et al: Suicide risk prediction by computer interview: a prospective study. J Clin Psychiatry 48:464–467, 1987

Ettlinger R: Evaluation of suicide prevention after attempted suicide. Acta Psychiatr Scand Suppl 260:1–135, 1975

Ettlinger R: Evaluation of suicide prevention after attempted suicide. Arch Gen Psychiatry 39:701–703, 1982

Farberow NL, McKelligott J, Cohen S, et al: Suicide among cardiovascular patients, in The Psychology of Suicide. Edited by Shneidman ES, Farberow NL, Litman RE. New York, Science House, 1970, pp 369–384

Farberow NL, Shneidman ES (eds): The Cry for Help. New York, McGraw-Hill, 1961

Fawcett J, Scheftner W, Fogg L, et al: Time related predictors of suicide in Major Affective Disorder. Am J Psychiatry 147:1189–1194, 1990

Fawcett J, Scheftner W, Clark D, et al: Clinical predictors of suicide in patients with major affective disorders. Am J Psychiatry 144:35–50, 1987

Fawcett J, Scheftner W, Clark D, et al: Clinical predictors of suicide in patients with major affective disorders: a controlled prospective study. Am J Psychiatry 144:35–40, 1987

Fingerhut LA, Kleinman JC: Suicide rates for young people. JAMA 259–356, 1988

Foster DP, Frost CEB: Medicinal self-poisoning and prescription frequency. Acta Psychiatr Scand 1:567–574, 1985

Fox K, Weissman M: Suicide attempts and drugs: contradiction between method and intent. Soc Psychiatry 10:31–38, 1975

Frances R, Franklin J, Flavin D: Suicide and alcoholism. Ann N Y Acad Sci 487:316–326, 1986

Frederick C, Resnik HL: How suicidal behaviors are learned. Am J Psychother 25:37–55, 1971

Garvey MJ, Spoden F: Suicide attempts in antisocial personality disorder. Compr Psychiatry 21:146–149, 1980

Garvey MJ, Tuason VB, Hoffman N, et al: Suicide attempters, non-attempters, and neurotransmitters. Compr Psychiatry 24:332–336, 1983

Gilboy JA, Schmidt RJ: "Voluntary" hospitalization of the mentally ill. North-Western University Law Review 66:429–453, 1971

Goldstein RB, Black DW, Nasrallah A, et al: The prediction of suicide. Arch Gen Psychiatry 48:418–422, 1991

Greenberg DF: Involuntary psychiatric commitments to prevent suicide. New York University Law Review 49:227–269, 1974

Greer S, Bagley CR: Effect of psychiatric intervention in attempted suicide: a controlled study. BMJ 1:310–312, 1971

Guggenheim FG: Management of suicide risk in the psychiatric emergency room, in Manual of Psychiatric Consultation and Emergency Care. Edited by Guggenheim FG, Weiner MF. Northvale, NJ, Jason Aronson, 1984, pp 23–32

Gutheil TG: Paranoia and progress note: a guide to forensically informed psychiatric recordkeeping. Hosp Community Psychiatry 31:479–482, 1980

Gutheil TG, Bursztajn H, Brosky A: Malpractice prevention through the sharing of uncertainty: informed consent and the therapeutic alliance. N Engl J Med 311:49–51, 1984

Guze SB, Robins E: Suicide and primary affective disorders. Br J Psychiatry 117:437–438, 1970

Hawton K: Suicide and Attempted Suicide Among Children and Adolescents. Newbury Park, CA, Sage, 1986

Hawton K, Catalan J: Attempted Suicide: A Practical Guide to its Nature and Management. Oxford, UK, Oxford University Press, 1982

Hawton K, Catalan J: Attempted Suicide: A Practical Guide to its Nature and Management, 2nd Edition. New York, Oxford University Press, 1987

Hawton K, Fagg J: Deliberate self-poisoning and self-injury in adolescents: a study of characteristics and trends in Oxford, 1976–89. Br J Psychiatry 161:816–823, 1992

Hayes S: A contextual approach to therapeutic change, in Psychotherapists in Clinical Practice: Cognitive and Behavioral Perspectives. Edited by Jacobson N. New York, Guilford, 1987, pp 327–387

Hayes S: Comprehensive distancing, paradox and the treatment of emotional avoidance, in Paradoxical Procedures in Psychotherapy. Edited by Ascher M. New York, Guilford, 1989, pp 184–218

Hayes S, Strosahl K, Wilson K: Acceptance and Commitment Therapy. New York, Guilford (in press)

Holinger PC, Offer D: Prediction of adolescent suicide: a population model. Am J Psychiatry 139:302–307, 1982

Ivanoff A, Jang SJ: The role of hopelessness and social desirability in predicting suicidal behavior: a study of prison inmates. J Consult Clin Psychol 59:394–399, 1991

Jamison KR: Suicide and bipolar disorders. Ann N Y Acad Sci 487:301–315, 1986

Kessel N, McCulloch W: Repeated acts of self-poisoning and self-injury. Proceedings of the Royal Society of Medicine 59:89–92, 1966

Kovacs M, Beck AT, Weissman A: The use of suicidal motives in the psychotherapy of attempted suicides. Am J Psychother 19:363–368, 1975

Krammer JI: The special characteristics of suicide of hospital inpatients. Br J Psychiatry 145:469–463, 1984

Kreitman N (ed): Parasuicide. New York, Wiley, 1977

Kreitman N, Smith P, Tan ES: Attempted suicide in social networks. Br J Prev Soc Med 23:116–123, 1969

Kreitman N, Smith P, Tan ES: Attempted suicide as a language: an empirical study. Br J Psychiatry 116:465–473, 1970

Kresky-Wolff M, Matthews S, Kalibat F, et al: Crossing place: a residential model for crisis intervention. Hosp Community Psychiatry 35:72–74, 1984

Lester D: Biochemical Basis of Suicide. Springfield, IL, Charles C Thomas, 1988

Lettieri D: Suicidal death prediction scales, in The Prediction of Suicide. Edited by Beck A, Resnick H, Lettieri D. Bowie, MD, Charles Press, 1974, pp 163–192

Levenson M, Neuringer C: Problem solving behavior in suicidal adolescents. J Consult Clin Psychol 37:433–436, 1971

Liberman RP, Eckman T: Behavior therapy vs insight-oriented therapy for repeated suicide attempters. Arch Gen Psychiatry 38:1126–1130, 1981

Linehan M: A social-behavioral analysis of suicide and parasuicide: implications for clinical assessment and treatment, in Depression: Behavioral and Directive Intervention Strategies. Edited by Glazer H, Clarkin JF. New York, Garland, 1981, pp 229–294

Linehan M, Camper P, Chiles J, et al: Interpersonal problem-solving and parasuicide. Cognitive Therapy and Research 11:1–12, 1986

Linehan M, Goodstein J, Nielson S, et al: Reasons for staying alive when you're thinking of killing yourself: the Reasons for Living Inventory. J Consult Clin Psychol 51:276–286, 1983

Linehan M, Nielson SL: Assessment of suicide ideation and parasuicide: hopelessness and social desirability. J Consult Clin Psychol 19:773–775, 1981

Linehan MM, Armstrong HE, Suarez A, et al: Cognitive-behavioral treatment of chronically parasuicidal borderline patients. Arch Gen Psychiatry 48:1060–1064, 1991

Linnoila M, Virkkunen M, Scheinin M, et al: Low cerebrospinal fluid 5-hydroxyindoleacetic acid concentration differentiates impulsive from non-impulsive violent behavior. Life Sci 33:2609–2614, 1983

Litman RE: Hospital suicides: lawsuits and standards. Suicide Life Threat Behav 12:212–220, 1982

Litman RE: Long term treatment of chronically suicidal patients. Bull Menninger Clin 53:215–228, 1989

Litman RE: Psycholegal aspects of suicide, in Modern Legal Medicine, Psychiatry, and Forensic Science. Edited by Curran W, McGarry AL, Petty CS. Philadelphia, PA, FA Davis, 1980, pp 841–853

Litman, RE, Farberow NL: The hospital's obligation toward suicide-prone patients. Hospitals 40:64–68, 1966

Maltsberger J: Suicide Risk: The Formulation of Clinical Judgment. New York, New York University Press, 1986

Mann JJ: Psychobiologic predictors of suicide. J Clin Psychiatry 48 (suppl 12):39–43, 1987

Mann JJ, McBride PA, Brown RP, et al: Relationship between central and peripheral serotonin indexes in depressed and suicidal psychiatric inpatients. Arch Gen Psychiatry 49:442–446, 1992

Manton KG, Blazer DG, Woodbury MA: Suicide in middle age and later life: sex and race specific life table and cohort analyses. J Gerontol 42:219–227, 1987

Maris R: Pathways to Suicide: A Survey of Self-Destructive Behaviors. Baltimore, MD, Johns Hopkins University Press, 1981

Maris R, Berman A, Maltsberger J, et al (eds): Assessment and Prediction of Suicide. New York, Guilford, 1991

Martin RL, Cloninger R, Guze SB, et al: Mortality in a follow-up of 500 psychiatric outpatients. Arch Gen Psychiatry 42:58–66, 1985

Marzuk PM, Leon AC, Tardiff K, et al: The effect of access to lethal methods of injury on suicide rates. Arch Gen Psychiatry 49:451–458, 1992

Maxmen JE, Tucker GJ: No exit: the persistently suicidal patient. Compr Psychiatry 14:71–79, 1973

Meichenbaum D: Cognitive Behavior Modification: An Integrative Approach. New York, Plenum, 1977

Michel K, Valach L: Suicide prevention: spreading the gospel to general practitioners. Br J Psychiatry 160:757–760, 1992

Miles CP: Conditions predisposing to suicide: a review. J Nerv Ment Dis 164:231–246, 1977

Miller MH: If the Patient is You (or Someone You Love): Psychiatry Inside-Out. New York, Scribner, 1977

Miller ML, Chiles JA, Barnes VE: Suicide attempters within a delinquent population. J Consult Clin Psychol 50:491–498, 1982

Miller ML, Coombs DW, Leeper JD, et al: An analysis of the effects of suicide prevention facilities on suicide rates in the United States. Am J Public Health 74:340–343, 1984

Modestin J, Kopp W: Study on suicide in depressed inpatients. J Affect Disord 15:157–162, 1988

Monahan J: The Clinical Prediction of Violent Behavior. Rockville, MD, National Institute of Mental Health, 1981

Montgomery SA, Montgomery D: Pharmacological prevention of suicidal behaviour. J Affect Disord 4:291–298, 1992

Morgan HG, Barton J, Pottle S, et al: Deliberate self-harm: a follow-up study of 279 patients. Br J Psychiatry 128:361–368, 1976

Moscicki EK, Boyd J: Epidemiologic trends in firearm suicides among adolescents. Pediatrician 12:52–62, 1985

Motto J: The psychopathology of suicide: a clinical model approach. Am J Psychiatry 136:516–520, 1979

Murphy GE: On suicide prediction and prevention. Arch Gen Psychiatry 40:343–344, 1983

Murphy GE: Problems in studying suicide. Psychiatry Developments 1:339–350, 1983

Murphy GE: Suicide in Alcoholism. New York, Oxford University Press, 1992

Murphy GE: The physician's responsibility for suicide; I: an error of commission. Ann Intern Med 82:305–309, 1975

Murphy GE: The physician's responsibility for suicide; II: errors of omission. Ann Intern Med 82:305–309, 1975

Murphy GE: The physician's role in suicide prevention, in Suicide. Edited by Roy A. Baltimore, MD, Williams & Wilkins, 1986, pp 171–179

Murphy GE, Wetzel RD: Multiple risk factors predict suicide in alcoholism. Arch Gen Psychiatry 49:459–463, 1993

Murphy GE, Wetzel RK: Family history of suicidal behavior among suicide attempters. J Nerv Ment Dis 170:86–89, 1982

Murphy JA, Wetzel RD: Suicide risk by birth cohort in the United States, 1949 to 1974. Arch Gen Psychiatry 37:519–523, 1980

Narrow W, Regier D, Rare D, et al: Use of services by persons with mental health and addictive disorders. Arch Gen Psychiatry 50:95–107, 1993

Neuinger C: Dichotomous evaluations in suicidal individuals. J Consult Clin Psychol 25:445–449, 1961

Neuinger C: Rigid thinking in suicidal individuals. J Consult Clin Psychol 28:54–58, 1964

Newscom-Smith J, Hirsch S (eds): The Suicide Syndrome. London, Croom Helm, 1979

Nolan JL (ed): The Suicide Case: Investigation and Trial of Insurance Claims. Chicago, IL, American Bar Association, 1988

Paerregaard G: Suicide among attempted suicides: a 10-year follow-up. Suicide 5:140–144, 1975

Patsiokas A, Clum G, Luscomb R: Cognitive characteristics of suicide attempters. J Consult Clin Psychol 47:478–484, 1979

Paykel E, Prusoff B, Myers J: Suicide attempts and recent live events: a controlled comparison. Arch Gen Psychiatry 32:327–333, 1975

Paykel ES, Myers JK, Lindenthal JJ, et al: Suicidal feelings in the general population: a prevalence study. Br J Psychiatry 124:460–469, 1974

Perr IN: Suicide litigation and risk management: a review of 32 cases. Bull Am Acad Psychiatry Law 13:209–219, 1985

Petrie K, Chamberlain K: Hopelessness and social desirability as moderator variables in predicting suicidal behavior. J Consult Clin Psychol 51:485–487, 1983

Pfeffer CR: Suicidal behavior of children: a review with implication for research and practice. Am J Psychiatry 138:154–159, 1981

Pfeffer CR: Suicide prevention: current efficacy and future promise. Ann N Y Acad Sci 487:341–50, 1986

Phillips DP, Cartensen LL: Clustering of teenage suicides after television news stores about suicide. N Engl J Med 315:685–689, 1986

Pokorny AD, Strosahl K, Chiles J, et al: Prediction of suicide intent in hospitalized parasuicides: reasons for living, hopelessness and depression. Compr Psychiatry 33:366–373, 1992

Pokorny AD: Prediction of suicide in psychiatric patients: report of a prospective study. Arch Gen Psychiatry 40:249–257, 1983

Pokorny AD: Suicide rates in various psychiatric disorders. J Nerv Ment Dis 139:499–506, 1964

Power AC, Cowen PJ: Fluoxetine and suicidal behaviour: some clinical and theoretical aspects of a controversy. Br J Psychiatry 161:735–741, 1992

Rich CL, Young D, Fowler RC: San Diego Suicide Study; I: young vs old subjects. Arch Gen Psychiatry 43:577–582, 1986

Richman J, Charles E: Patient dissatisfaction and attempted suicide. Community Ment Health J 12:301–305, 1976

Rissmeyer D: Crisis intervention alternatives to hospitalization: why so few? Psychosocial Rehabilitation Journal 9:54–63, 1985

Robins E, Murphy GE, Wilkinson RH Jr, et al: Some clinical considerations in the prevention of suicide based on a study of 134 successful suicides. Am J Public Health 49:888–899, 1959

Roy A: Risk factors for suicide in psychiatric patients. Arch Gen Psychiatry 39:1089–1095, 1982

Roy A: Family history of suicide. Arch Gen Psychiatry 40:971–974, 1983a

Roy A: Suicide in depressives. Compr Psychiatry 5:487–491, 1983b

Scheftner WA, Young MA, Endicott J, et al: Family history and five-year suicide risk. Br J Psychiatry 153:805–809, 1988

Schotte DE, Clum G: Suicide ideation in a college population: a test of a model. J Consult Clin Psychol 50:690–696, 1982

Schotte DE, Clum GA: Problem-solving skills in suicidal psychiatric patients. J Consult Clin Psychol 55:49–54, 1987

Schotte DE, Cools J, Payvar S: Problem-solving deficits in suicidal patients: trait vulnerability or state phenomenon? J Consult Clin Psychol 58:562–564, 1990

Shear M, Frances A, Weiden P: Suicide associated with akathisia and depot fluphenazine treatment. J Clin Psychopharmacol 3:325–326, 1983

Sorenson SB, Rutter CM: Transgenerational patterns of suicide attempt. J Consult Clin Psychol 59:861–866, 1991

Stanley M, Stanley B, Traskman-Bendz L, et al: Neurochemical findings in suicide completers and suicide attempters, in Biology of Suicide. Edited by Maris R. New York, Guilford, 1986, pp 204–218

Strosahl K: Cognitive and behavioral treatment of the multi-problem patient, in Psychotherapy in Managed Health Care: The Optional Use of Time and Resources. Edited by Berman W, Austad C. Washington, DC, American Psychological Association, 1991, pp 185–201

Strosahl K: The risk prediction dilemma in therapy with the suicidal patient. Paper presented at the annual meeting of the Western Psychological Association, Seattle, WA, May 5, 1986

Strosahl K: Prevalence studies of suicidal behavior in the general population. Paper presented at the annual meeting of the Western Psychological Association, Seattle, WA, May 5, 1986

Strosahl K, Jacobson N: The training and supervision of behavior therapists, in The Clinical Supervisor 4:183–206, 1986

Strosahl K, Chiles J, Linehan M: Prediction of suicide intent in hospitalized parasuicides: reasons for living, hopelessness and depression. Compr Psychiatry 33:366–373, 1992

Strosahl K, Linehan M, Chiles J: Will the real social desirability please stand up? Hopelessness, depression, social desirability and the prediction of suicidal behavior. J Consult Clin Psychol 52:449–457, 1984

Sunqvist-Stensmann UB: Suicides in close connection with psychiatric care: an analysis of 57 cases in a Swedish county. Acta Psychiatr Scand 76:15–20, 1987

Sussman LK, Robins LN, Earl F: Treatment seeking for depression by black and white Americans. Soc Sci Med 24:187–196, 1987

van Egmond V, Diekstra RFW: The predictability of suicide behavior: the results of a meta-analysis of published studies, in Suicide and Its Prevention: The Role of Attitude and Imitation. Edited by Diekstra RFW, Maris R, Platt S, et al. New York, Brill, 1989, pp 37–61

Vinoda KS: Personality characteristics of attempted suicides. Br J Psychiatry 112:1143–1150, 1966

Von Korff M, Shapiro S, Burke S, et al: Anxiety and depression in a primary care clinic. Arch Gen Psychiatry 44:152–156, 1987

Weisman GK: Crisis-orientated residential treatment as an alternative to hospitalization. Hosp Community Psychiatry 36:1302–1305, 1985a

Weissman MM, Klerman, GL, Markovitz JS, et al: Suicidal ideation and suicide attempts in panic disorder and attacks. N Engl J Med 321:1209–1214, 1989

Wells K, Hays R, Burnam M, et al: Detection of depressive disorder for patients receiving pre-paid or fee for service care. JAMA 262:3293–3302, 1988

Westermeyer JF, Harrow M, Marengo JT: Risk for suicide in schizophrenia and other psychotic and nonpsychotic disorders. J Nerv Ment Dis 179:259–266, 1991

 # Index

Page numbers appearing in **boldface** refer to tables or figures.